Y0-CBG-820

DREAMS OF ACES

THE HAL FISCHER STORY
Korea and Vietnam

Colonel Harold E. Fischer
With
Penny Wilson

2113484

$2500

Printed by
GREAT IMPRESSIONS
Printing and Graphics
444 West Mockingbird
Dallas Texas 75247
E-mail:gibooks@aol.com Phone # (800) 879-9095

DEDICATION

For all the men with whom I flew in Korea and Vietnam,
my friends, colleagues, fellow fighter pilots, and
the crew chiefs and their men who worked day and night to keep us flying...
and to all those good souls who never made it home....

You have all been very much a part of my life.

Check six.
Hal

All Rights Reserved
Copyright © 2001 Harold E. Fischer and Penelope E Wilson

No part of this book may be reproduced or transmitted in any form or by
any means, electronic or mechanical, including photocopying, recording,
or by any information storage and retrieval system, without the prior
permission in writing from the authors.

ISBN #0-9711556-0-7

75334.2171@compuserve.com

CONTENTS

Introduction
Tribute to Hal Fischer
Harold E Fischer

INTRODUCTION

Over the years Hal has always been reluctant to publish his story and his friends had almost given up on asking him to do so. He claimed it was too much like hard work and he had more exciting things to do than fighting a computer that did inexplicable things with a penchant for swallowing and digesting his literary efforts.

However, when he got home from Korea and later Vietnam, he diligently spent 20 minutes a day pounding away on an old typewriter and recording his thoughts and memories. During our conversations and the many questions I had, he would just give a wry smile and hand over to me what he had written, and answered questions later. I was given the book of press cuttings that his mother had dutifully kept during his time in Korea and imprisonment in China, along with access to his photographs, computer, letters and documents.

His story fascinated me. This modest man with a gentle smile and twinkling eyes could not possibly have been the tiger the countrywide media, magazines, Life magazine, New York Times magazine and numerous others across the country made him out to be, with two inch headlines spread across the pages. Slowly it all slotted into place and with comments from his friends and data gleaned from the media coverage of his exploits, I started editing his writing as a surprise Christmas present for him. I felt that as much of his story should be in one file as possible, for this period of aerial warfare encompassed the first predominantly jet missions, the first jet aces, the beginnings of the Cold War, and the first Cold War political prisoners.

Word spreads fast and I started to get e-mails and phone calls asking if it was true that I was putting Hals story together and asking when it would be published. So the story that was going to be a private copy and a Christmas surpise has materialized into a published book.

And to think that when I first met Hal I had the audacity to ask him if he had ever flown a tail dragger...

Penny
December 2001
pennywilson@compuserve.com

I first met Penny Wilson when someone we both admire and respect was "shutting down" and experiencing systems failure. Penny saved his life. Marion F. Kirby is a legend in his own time, a P-38 ace and we belong to the same organization, the now 80th TFS, Audentes Fortuna Juvat (Fortune Favors the Brave). M.F. Kirby sends Morale Folders to the fighter pilots who are serving around the world and to his loyal and devoted followers. He continues to this day to do so, because of Penny.

Penn has an amazing capability to recognize a situation, touch people with her kindness and an almost legendary knowledge of aviation and individuals associated with aviation. She started editing my work as a surprise for me and it developed from there when I found out what she was doing.

In college, I took a course in management and one topic was "The Fiction of Superior Authority." It states that true authority resides at the bottom with the people who actually accomplish the work and manage to get things done at base level. Col. Robin Olds (later to become General Olds) also a legend in his own time, I found was universally respected and admired by the men he commanded in Vietnam. A typical example of true authority. He probably wrote this concept of authority being quietly powerful at base level!

And so with Penny, I put down words, she put it together, she made the decisions, and she did the work. It is her book.

Hal Fischer

December 2001

TRIBUTE TO HAL FISCHER

When it became known that Hal's story was being put together some of his friends sent the following comments to me about their old colleague and fellow fighter pilot. Here is a selection.

I attribute, in part, my success as a fighter pilot in Korea, to my association with Lt Hal Fischer, who flew as my #2 on many missions.

He was an outstanding young pilot, with a natural flying ability and an intuitive capacity for being in the right position, at the right time. A dependable, aggressive, yet cautious team member who engendered confidence in our ability to handle any combat situation. On many occassions we were outnumbered 30 plus to 4, but I had no hesitation in committing our section to combat, knowing I had the support and flying skill of Lt Fischer.

He had a quiet, confident demeanor both in the air and on the ground; an obvious desire to become an outstanding fighter pilot and eventually an "Ace" amongst Sabre pilots. Of all the young pilots of our Squadron he impressed me with his maturity, his skills, his passion to excel and his devotion to duty.

Col Douglas Lindsay (ret) RCAF

Col Douglas Lindsay

I had the privilege of flying combat in Korea with Hal Fischer. I was with him on more than one mission when he shot down a MiG.

Over the years, Hal has been a great friend and confidant and we have shared many good times together.

One of the happiest memories I have of Hal was when I ran into him at Maxwell AFB when he was being debriefed after his long years as a POW.

You are one hell of a guy, Hal. Check 6.

Archie Tucker

It was early 1951 when the 80th Fighter Bomber Sq. received replacement pilots for the F-80C's in use at that time. In particular, the 'FNG's for 'B' Flight were Freddie Poston, William Lesueur, Dusty Hayes and Hal Fischer. Since I was about halfway through my 100 missions I had these chaps as either wingmen or element leads for a period of time.

Oh what fun we had! As hard as I tried to shake him off, Hal always had a way of finding the flight and re-joining. It was Hal who was with me on a TWO ship flight to dive-bomb downtown Pyongyang.

During these times I taught him that "He who breaks the same way twice in a row coming off a target, may not be able to break any way the third time".

When complimenting Hal for a good mission, he would give you that little Iowa farm boy foot shuffle and say, "Ah shucks".

Hal was smooth in the air and I consider him among the 12 best flyers in the world along with Bob Hoover, "Bones" Marshall, James Harold Doolittle and myself. I will let the other seven chaps argue amongst themselves for ranking.

Hal is a guy that once you know him, it is hard as hell to forget him.

Archie Caldwell

Hal Fischer is my friend. As I've discovered over the years, depending on the individual, that term can vary widely in meaning, all the way from "casual acquaintance" to the extreme of loyalty and dedication which describes my devotion to this permanently youthful and slightly insane Iowan.

We met back in the seventies, at the monthly gathering of the Washington DC "River Rats" (Red River Fighter Pilots Assn.). We hit it off immediately, both taking great delight in embarassing and shocking our stuffier comrades. Without going into detail, we had an immediate mutual affection and respect for one another — Hal the MiG-killer in North Korea, I the SAM-dodger in North Vietnam. The only "war stories" we have ever shared directly are those absurd instances wherein luck, not skill, saved our respective butts.

Today I know that whenever the phone rings at some ungodly hour, it will be Hal, proposing yet another wild excursion into the unknown, e.g. flying a Russian Antonov biplane ("Annie") to Guatemala. Always a welcome relief from the relative boredom of life as a retired fighter jock.

Hal Fischer is my friend. If that means risking my life, my reputation, or my fortune — Hal, you got it, mate.
Cheers,
Sam Cottrell

I felt, as probably many others have, that Hal was one of the many people we share life with that has a positive affect upon us. I came away from the association feeling he was a very good friend. With Hal, what you see is what you get. He certainly is not out to try to impress anyone. Hal is one heck of a guy. It would be nice to clone him and put him back into the USAF.
Milt Uzelac

Hal was in B flight as a Lieutenant. I was a flight commander of D flight, and later operations officer. He was a sharp pilot and a real asset on any mission.

He flew with me on numerous occasions. As fighter bombers, we were seldom without plenty of activity and stimulating experiences. Hal was one that you did not worry about. He knew what had to be done and he was always right in the thick of the action. No sneaking around and hiding behind a tree.

He was not talkative but listened well. Kind of a quiet sort of young pilot. His return to combat in F86's certainly speaks well for his "tiger" streak and dedication to his roll in the USAF. If we had more like him, we could have shortened the war.
Bill Yoakley

Hal, a person gifted with expert flying skill…the expertise to eliminate the enemy…and above all, abundant compassion for his fellow man. I admire you deeply, Hal.
M.F. Kirby

I met Hal Fischer when we were assigned to the 80th Squadron, 8th F.B.G., Itazuke, Japan, in Jan. 1951. We flew our missions in the F80C, from Itazuke, followed by Kimpo (K14), then Suan (K-13).

Hal, Dusty Hayes, and I spent many evenings at the Aryan (Officers) Club in downtown Itazuke. It was our misssion there to educate the young Army nurses in the finer points of aerial warfare.

After his tour in F-80's, Hal had a stint at 5th AF HQ in Tokyo where he wangled a job back at Suwon making history in the F-86.

Hal and I later flew combat from different bases in Vietnam. It was a real pleasure to meet him there at Bien Hoa in the summer of 1970. We had a happy time exchanging old and new war stories.

Hal has been a great and loyal friend all these years.

<u>Billy V. Dixon</u>

HAROLD E. FISCHER

Hal began his military career as a Navy cadet, was commissioned into the Army, and transferred to the Air Force where he became the United States 25th jet ace. Born on 8th May 1925, in Lone Rock, Iowa, he grew up as a farm boy in Swea City.

In 1944, Fischer became a Navy cadet, but was released from training at the end of World War II. In 1949, after two years at Iowa State University, he persuaded the Army to give him a direct commission. On assignment to Korea, he set his sights on becoming a pilot and through some creative paper handling, wangled a transfer to the Air Force. He eventually earned his wings in December 1950 and was soon sent to the Far East. Initially flying from Itazuke AB, Japan, he tasted his first combat with the 80th Fighter-Bomber Squadron. As a young pilot in a squadron of "old heads," he was fated to fly over Korea in one of the oldest Lockheed F-80 Shooting Stars, which he named "Kismet." He completed 105 missions, but "Kismet" did not!

Next, he flew a battle-worn Aeronca observation plane as pilot for a British general. After a staff tour in Far East Air Force Headquarters in Japan, he again managed to organise another tour of duty in Korea to fly North American F-86 Sabres in the 39th Fighter Interceptor Squadron. As a First Lieutenant flight commander, he shot down his first enemy aircraft on 26 November 1952; he chalked up his fifth aerial victory on 24 January 1953 to become an ace in only 47 missions. On 7 April, with 10 confirmed victories to his credit, he jumped three MiGs. The Iowa farm boy downed one and hit another, then fate intervened and he ended up a victory for a MiG-15 pilot.

Hal became a prisoner-of-war and was held in China until 1955. Released, he returned to Iowa State to pursue a Masters Degree in Industrial Administration. He remained at the university teaching in the Reserve Officer Training Program, and then served as an intelligence officer, first at Offutt Air Force Base, Nebraska and then at Ramstein Air Base, Germany. He then worked in the human factors field, before becoming research associate in 1978 at the Massachusetts Institute of Technology. During the war in Southeast Asia, he served as Chief of the Air Force Advisory Team Three at Bien Hoa Air Base where he also flew South Vietnamese helicopters, and propeller and jet fighters.

In February 1973, Fischer took command of the Air Force Human Resources Laboratory at Brooks Air Force Base, San Antonio,Texas. His final assignment was to the United States Department of State in the Arms Control and Disarmament Agency. He retired as a colonel in May 1978.

Since then he has been involved in managing and consulting for The Fischer Trust and Unique Operations Ltd, predominantly with aviation related projects. He has been involved with POW research and assistance.

In April 1994, he traveled to Kiev, Ukraine, to meet former Soviet pilots who flew in Korea. There he met one of his adversaries from the dogfight of 7 April 1953.

In November 1997 he met General Han Decai, who invited him back to China, to discuss a Chinese American Foundation meeting in Nanjing 27 June to 30 June 1998. This coincided with Presidents Clinton's visit. General Han Decai has official credit for shooting him down 7 April 1953.

Awards: Distinguished Service Cross, Silver Star, Distinguished Flying Crosses, Air Medals, Legion of Merit, Joint Staff Commendation, Meritorious Service Medal and numerous medals from the Republic of Korea and Vietnam.

CHAPTER 1

YOUTH

Imagination is more important than knowledge.
Knowledge is limited.
Imagination encircles the world.
Albert Einstein

My earliest memory was of wanting to be a cowboy followed by a fire engine driver. Soon a fascination with cars set in. Our first car was a Model T Coupe and later a 1936 Chevrolet. I could identify every car and the Pierce Arrow was my ultimate idea of excellence in the transportation field, but they were scarce as hen's teeth on the dirt and gravel roads of our Iowa farming community.

Somewhere in that time frame I developed an interest in the airplane and the wonders of the Wright Brothers and their invention.

At that time oranges were individually wrapped in tissue paper and I used this along with tooth picks and twenty four hour glue to construct a replica of the first flying machine. I was immensely proud of this rather crude model and my original idea of constructing it from the only materials available to me. It took at least three days to complete since the glue took forever to dry.

We made a twice-weekly pilgrimage to our small town of Swea City for groceries, and on one of these trips I spied in the drugstore window, model airplanes that once assembled would actually fly. With endless hours of enjoyment in building and flying these model airplanes, the price of ten cents each seemed fair and I started a

About 8 years old and first mode of transport.

collection. The first one that I built was a Boeing F4B4 and this remains one of my favourite airplanes as it epitomized the best of flight and the romance of it, with an open cockpit, the pilot wearing a helmet and a long white silk scarf wrapped around his neck.

It enchanted me that with bits of balsa wood and tissue paper, famous airplanes could be constructed and launched into the air. The Boeing was eventually put into retirement after hours of fun and hundreds of logged flight hours. On its final flight I had wound up the rubber band, held it aloft and with a gentle push to attain its flying speed, released the propellor. It pitched up briefly then dived at a 45degree angle to the earth, splintering the landing gear. It was duly retired. The Boeing was a naval aircraft and it was the Navy that sparked my initial interest and afforded me the first opportunity to begin my flying career

Many models followed the Boeing; the SE-5, Waco N, Albatross, Bellanca, Gloster Gladiator and Bristol Fighter. A few of these aircraft were solid models but most flew, though being heavier were not as successful as the first Boeing F4B4. However the Bristol Fighter was an excellent glider.

From Swea City Herald in 1932.

GRANT BOY BUILDS AIRPLANES
In the Grant community there is a boy working for the future. Each night after school Harold Fischer Jn comes home and begins work on his airplanes. His work is very good. He gets the material and assembles the planes. To date he has made nearly every type. He can tell you all about the parts and the names of each. His ambition is to be a pilot. As it looks now he probably will be one. It is worth anyone's time to see some of his planes.

I also developed an avid interest in reading, fostered by pulp magazines such as "Flying Aces." Authors such as Arch Whitehouse, a WW I flyer, made the aces of that time come to life in stories told over and over again with a similar theme. The main story line usually ran along the lines of some new secret method of waging war that would ensure victory for the Germans. The hero of the story would emerge with some skillful feat of flying and destroy the enemy just as they were about to win the war. Another story line was the German spy who had infiltrated the front lines and stupidly blown his cover while drinking beer just before an offensive. He would steal an airplane and be shot down by the squadron hero in a magnificent battle. In the case of an American spy in a German unit, he would always manage to escape by stealing a new airplane and when intercepted by the German squadron hero, would manage to shoot him down and claim a heroic victory. These stories told over and over captivated this young farm kid and I flew in my dreams with the aces of that war. Names like Mannock, Rhys-Davis, Luke, Rickenbacker, Voss, Von Richtofen, Brown and Guynemer were all familiar to me and became a young boys hero's.

From the interest in WW 1, I built models of that era; the SE-5, Bristol Fighter, Albatross and Pfalz. The Pfalz was the first expensive model that cost me all of 75 cents. At that time it was a sophisticated model with movable controls in the cockpit, connected to the elevators, rudder and ailerons by thread. I decided that its fate was to be launched from the windmill, aflame on its last gallant flight, finally to crash with imaginary victorious Spads, Neiuports, Camels and SE-5s circling the flaming wreckage.

From a press report published in the De Moines Register when Hal was a POW in China from April 1953 to June 1955.

Few people outside the immediate family knew that as a boy of 6 he took up tap dancing to overcome lameness caused by polio.
That became known shortly after he was taken prisoner when his mother told a reporter about her son's childhood.
As a boy Fischer use to make model airplanes and painfully climb his way up a windmill on his weakened legs to launch the planes.

Much to the chagrin of my father, I was able to draw a Spad or Fokker in great detail but the talent for drawing cars or farm machinery was not quite so acute. He often muttered that I thought more of airplanes than I did of the farm chores. He was amazed at the endless patience I exhibited working on small balsa parts and my total lack of patience when doing farm work. To the end of his days he commented on this fact.

An instructor, Dwight Dinsmore, who eventually joined the Air Force, formally fostered my interest in aviation. At that time, he was fresh out of college and on his first teaching assignment at the small consolidated school that all the farm children in the area attended. He went into partnership with two others and bought a Taylorcraft airplane that he kept on a local farm. It was in this 55hp Taylorcraft that I received my first instruction with a good friend of mine, Roger Holmes. We felt that we could fly an airplane purely from our extensive reading and avid interest in flying!

Dwight Dinsmore also took me to see the aviation epic of the time "Men with Wings" and through his encouragement my interest grew. A dedicated and serious educator can have a tremendous influence over a pupil and he certainly had a great affect on my life. It is unfortunate that even today, teachers earn a pittance compared to other professions, yet they can have such an influence in molding a young mind.

During these years, I requested literature from all the airplane manufacturers and diligently studied it. Perhaps they should have screened their mailing lists more thoroughly as I am sure it took no little sum to send all that literature to north Iowa. Beech aircraft did in fact once request that a letter be sent on company stationery before information would be sent on a Beech Staggerwing. The aircraft cost over $5,000 and I couldn't raise the paltry sum of 50cents. During this period, a new Piper Cub sold for $999 and I raised the money to buy a raffle ticket for a drawing on one. There was no doubt in my mind that I would win it and waited in vain for the day I would be told to collect it. The odds were against me and my dreams were shattered when I realized that I would not be the proud owner of a new Cub.

The state fair was a big event and a vacation for the community. It was here that my family was treated to an airplane ride. We took off from the municipal airport in a Waco cabin aircraft. It was smooth and a wonder to me to look down and see the buildings, cars, haystacks and miniature houses. All too soon the ride came to an end as the pilot cut the engine and glided down to a landing. Taxiing to the hangar, we saw a pilot working on a biplane of ancient vintage and our pilot said that he was Captain Frakes who was going to crash the aircraft into a building at the fair grounds on 'thrill day,' a day set aside for unusual stunts to attract the crowds. We took our seats on the grandstand to watch Captain Frakes, who was late, due to the Civil Aviation Authority refusing to give him permission to fly his airplane, as they considered it not airworthy. He therefore hid the airplane on a field near Des Moines and flew it from there to do his crash stunt.

8 years old after a first flight in a Waco

The old biplane appeared low over the horizon, circled the track once and headed for the building. When the wheels were about two inches off the ground, he cut the power and hit the side of the building. The fuselage emerged out of the other side with bits of wreckage hanging from it and after what seemed to me an eternity, Captain Frakes was helped from the wreckage. The crash was a success.

This stunt was similar to the one Dick Grace was famous for and performed many times on movie sets. It was the first crash that I had seen and I was pleased that the pilot was not injured.

Many interests that one has growing up are fleeting and soon pass, only to be replaced by some new idea. But for me, airplanes and flying did not pass with the weeks or years. It remained with me throughout grade and high school. Many other interests came and went, but nothing ever replaced my fascination with airplanes and flight.

At one time, I sent for the plans to build a glider, a clumsy affair as I recall it. Moving the weight distribution of the pilot changed the attitude of the glider. The wood, linen and hardware came to about $125, which was a significant sum in those days, so the project was abandoned. This was also the time of the Baby Bowlus, a glider in kit form costing about $325. It was one of the first aircraft in kit form that I remembered reading about.

But these were all dreams of youth and not reality, as the war clouds loomed and events were taking place in the world that I could not understand.

CHAPTER 2

MANHOOD

You don't just stumble into the future
You create your own future.

On December 8th, 1941, all classes at our school were dismissed and the students gathered in the assembly hall to listen to Franklin Delano Roosevelt's radio announcement that a state of war had been declared with Japan due to their attack on Pearl Harbor the previous day.

I will never forget his calm voice, solemnly exuding confidence as he spoke to the nation. Although my parents did not agree with his policies, he was, in my opinion the true leader of the American people and the epitome of what a president should be. The communists use the psychology that their subjects look up to the leader of their country as a father figure and it acts as a welding force for the nation. A man who has ruled for much of his life takes on the role of a father figure particularly to the youth and those who desire change. Lenin, Stalin, Mao-tze-Tung were leaders who all had extended reigns at the helm of their respective governments. Roosevelt by his unprecedented third term, had a similar affect on the minds of the American youth of that time as the undisputed leader of his country, although perhaps no other president has caused as much controversy during his life, or indeed subsequently.

It was with trepidation that I listened to his words that day and I expected immediate and drastic changes in our lifestyle. But changes came gradually.

In my senior year, I noticed a poster in the school library stating, "Win Your Navy Wings of Gold," with an address in Minneapolis to write for further information. There was much emphasis placed on finishing high school before enlisting in the service. It stated that a student could enlist at 17, finish high school and then be called into active duty at the completion of his schooling. This seemed like a very good opportunity for me to fly, go to sea, get a commission and above all to serve my country in its time of need. I requested further information on this good deal, and almost by return of mail received a directive to appear in Minneapolis for further testing and an interview.

My father drove me to Minneapolis and his parting remark was, "Now you have no life of your own son." I passed the physical and mental examination without a hitch and was accepted as a cadet, given a gold pin and placed in the V-5 program. There was no one in the world prouder than I was and no badge worn with more pride, than that small gold pin signifying that I had been accepted into the Navy flying program.

The concept of what we were fighting for was brought home to me when I discovered some literature in the mailbox that initially I did not fully understand. It pertained to racial supremacy and the dangers of expanding Jewish power to the world. It was rabidly anti-semetic and defended the German policy of the day. A member of the local German Lutheran church, which at that time was the center of a pro-German minority and might have been connected to these radical pamphlets, had visited us the previous day. The visit was ostensibly to purchase some Brown Swiss cattle. Receiving this propaganda was a cause of concern to me. With our German name of Fischer perhaps it was thought that our sympathies would lie with Germany.

I mentioned this literature to one of my school instructors and he asked to see it. After reading it he told me to say nothing about it and I promptly forgot about it. It was a revelation to me that information of this type could exist in our country when we were at war with Germany supposedly to eradicate these radical notions.

After graduation, I expected that it would be a matter days before the papers arrived ordering me to active duty. Every day I waited impatiently for the mail and day after day disappointment awaited me. I was convinced that a mistake had been made and that my serial number had been lost due to the bureaucracy of the naval service. It was not until fall that the orders came for me to report to Minneapolis and my career in the U.S. Navy.

There was a touch of sadness when I said goodbye to my parents and perhaps a lack of understanding on their part as to why I was going. They felt that there was no real need for me to go, as a deferment would be possible since we were farming so much land. Remaining at home at that time would have been unthinkable to me.

Instead of reporting to flight training, our entire contingent was sent to Texas, where the cadets were set to work on the flight line until vacancies arose in flight school. This was another blow to the plans that I had of quickly gaining my wings and going off to fight for my country.

After almost a year in the service, going to school and biding time, we were finally selected for flight training. We were sent to Wooster, Ohio, for indoctrination and training as naval cadets and the time honored traditional Navy way of doing things. There was the right way, the wrong way, and the Navy way. The reason for doing things the 'Navy way' was simply because it had always been done that way!

There was an old Meyers OTW training airplane parked out in front of the college dormitory, as a reminder to the cadets of what lay ahead. I used to look longingly at that old fabric covered bi-plane and wish fervently that I could take it up and fly.

Completing the training at Wooster, Ohio, we were then sent to Kalamazoo, Michigan. It was here that I first saw the Waco UPF-7, the airplane that I would solo in. It had originally been designed to compete for an Army contract as a basic training airplane. The Army rejected the Waco and instead selected the Stearman as their trainer because the Waco had a nasty tendency of ground looping at the slightest provocation if the student pilot failed to keep alert during a landing.

The Waco was a biplane, in the best WW1 tradition, with a seven cylinder uncowled radial engine. The fuselage was blue and the wings yellow. The front cockpit was wide enough for two passengers when the control stick was removed. The back cockpit had a headrest that blended smoothly into the horizontal stabilizer. It was the biggest and best airplane that we had ever seen and an exceptional challenge to every one of us. Our class was the first one in which naval students got their initial flying training in the larger 220 horsepower aircraft. In the past, flying cadets had received their initial instruction in the small Piper Cub aircraft propelled by a 65 horsepower engine. Civilian contractees gave flight instruction with a Naval flying officer in charge of the program.

After extensive ground instruction, we were ready to fly, and a man named Chapman was assigned to teach me. The instructor took the front seat with the student in the rear. My first solo flight is a little hazy, probably due to my excitement at being responsible for what seemed like such a huge piece of machinery. I do recall that the three required landings for the first solo absolutely terrified me. The third and final landing was especially traumatic, as a gust of wind raised the left wing and I sat powerless, unable to take any corrective action. Standard procedure would have been to apply power, opposite rudder and if need be to go around and try again. As it was, I was so pleased to be back on the ground, that there was no desire to jeopardize my position even at the expense of dragging a wing tip. It was not until my first solo flight in the local practice area that the thrill and realization that I was truly master of the aircraft came over me. It was a bright spring day and the air was smooth and perfect. Looking down, I could see for miles and in the distance, I could see one of the Great Lakes. The airplane climbed as if it was inspired and soon I was higher than I had ever been before with the instructor. To dissipate altitude, I practiced accidental spins. The airplane was held in a turn and the turn tightened until the airplane stalled. As it stalled, the aircraft would roll to the outside of the turn, spin rapidly and then go into a normal spin. However, from the excitement and the acrobatics, my tummy rebelled.

After our solo flight, we were indoctrinated into the more precise maneuvers required of naval pilots. There were slips to a circle, a maneuver where the aircraft was slipped to within a few feet of the ground and just before touching down, was rolled out to a fully stalled position and landed. It was no wonder that just before I left, the Waco's were being sold because they had broken main spars in the wings where the lower wing attached to the fuselage. The aircraft were being sold for around $600 apiece.

After accumulating around 56 hours in the Waco, there was a cutback in the training program of naval pilots, resulting in the class being chopped by 50%. Those below the median of the class were forced to drop out. The pilots in the upper 50% of the class, had the choice of completing the program and gaining their wings. I was given the opportunity to continue if I so desired.

With the apparent need for my assistance at home and the navy not requiring more cadets at this late stage of the war, I chose with great reluctance to return to the farm. I was sent to the Great Lakes Naval Training Station in Chicago for final processing, where I was interviewed for over an hour by a Lieutenant trying to persuade me to remain in the program. My German ancestry with its dogmatism prevailed. I had made my decision and was sticking to it, so was duly discharged.

CHAPTER 3

DECISIONS

*Only those who risk going too far can
possibly find out how far one can go.*
T.S.Elliot

The desire to fly remained dormant for a number of years as I spent two years in college before returning to the farm. I was an only child, and for a time I seriously contemplated joining my father and making farming my life's work. But lurking at the back of my mind was always a niggling feeling of restlessness at the thought of spending the rest of my life as a farmer. As I drove the tractor I would gaze up at airplanes passing overhead and wonder if perhaps I had what it took to be up there in the pilot's seat and if I would be able to make the grade as a pilot.

Eventually the yearning to fly again became so strong that I decided to blow my life savings on my very own airplane, an Aeronca Champion, which I discovered was for sale in Fort Dodge in Iowa. One afternoon I hitch hiked into Fort Dodge and as soon as I laid my eyes on it, it seemed that the answer to a lifelong dream sat before me on the grass. It was the standard yellow and orange and was in excellent condition. The price of $1350 was almost exactly the amount in my savings account.

With apprehension and excitement, I handed over my personal check but the airport operator required a certified check. I was duly checked out by one of the pilots ensuring that I was competent to fly the airplane and it was agreed that I would return with a certified check and become the new owner of the Champ.

I mentioned the proposed purchase of my dream to my parents and their reaction was decidedly unfavorable.They considered that buying an airplane was a completely foolhardy and irrational undertaking and wanted nothing to do with the whole project. I had envisaged using and keeping the airplane on the farm, as many farmers were doing at the time but my father frowned upon this plan. For some reason he had a deep-seated fear of the dangers associated with flying or even having an aircraft on the premises. He forbade me from keeping it on the farm and since the only alternative was to put it seven miles away at Algona airport, the whole plan fizzled out. Faced with such strong opposition, I never went back to Fort Dodge and the purchase fell through. However, this episode marked a turning point in my life.

Many people have asked me whether I enjoy flying small slow airplanes as much as larger, faster, more powerful ones. I always reply that both are a thrill and that flying is flying, be it in an airplane of 65 horsepower or 6500 horsepower. As long as I am airborne, the basic urge of flight is satisfied. Mastering the B-25 gave me as much satisfaction as checking out for the first time in the F-86. This urge to fly, which I had set my heart on when very young, continued to torment me during the months after my abortive attempt to buy my own airplane and made me very dissatisfied with my life on the farm. It was a frustrating situation. I felt tense, restless and uncertain about my future and finally realized that I had to make a break from the farm. I knew that it would be a final, hard, maybe even brutal severance, but I also knew that I had to follow my dream of flying.

It was 1949 and there was a need for servicemen and also for trained pilots. The least expensive way to get involved with flying was to join one of the services, so I applied for flying training with the Air Force. My request was postponed, but an opportunity arose to join the Army as a platoon leader. There were vacancies in the infantry for those who had two years of college, previous military experience and the desire to serve. Having attended Iowa State College after the war, I met the basic educational criteria. The Army captain who sent me to be interviewed by the Selection Board told me that if asked why I wanted to join the Infantry, to simply say that it appealed to me. The interview for a commission and waiting for the decision was one of the most trying periods I can recall, but the Captain's advice must have been good, because I was selected to attend a special training course at Fort Benning, Georgia.

The group I was to train with was not a very homogeneous one. There were men with varying degrees of experience from all the services, which qualified them for the course. All had received a commission which they would retain only if they successfully completed the course. The school aggressively attempted to make leaders of all the men who reported to camp for the course and we were thus subjected to physical and psychiatric testing upon arrival. We were all interviewed by an army psychiatrist. This took only a few minutes and I was diagnosed as "normal" perhaps because the doctor and I shared the same name of Fischer!

The man in front of me was not so fortunate. After a short interview he was diagnosed as a potential manic-depressive. It made me marvel at the science of psychiatry; that such a supposedly accurate diagnosis could be made from so brief a consultation.

The classes were taught by instructors from various segments of the Army and almost all of them ended with a pitch promoting their particular area and suggesting that perhaps it might not be a bad idea to transfer from the infantry. During the three month course all the students were given a chance to fill leadership positions, and opportunities to fire all the weapons of an infantry battalion. It was good training and just enough for me to realize, while on a ten-mile hike with a full pack, that perhaps this was not what I had in mind when I stated that I liked the Infantry.

It was here that I bought my first airplane. A sergeant was selling an L-2 Taylorcraft for $200. Being an innocent in the ways of business, I jumped at the opportunity and was tendered a "Bill of Sale" which was nothing more than a piece of paper stating that he relinquished all claim to the aircraft. The airplane flew and I became a proud owner. It was very satisfying to fly my airplane to an adjacent field, land, look around and dream of how this airplane could be used to set up a business. It was also here that I learned one of the hard facts concerning aircraft ownership, namely the cost of maintaining them!

Faced with some necessary and expensive engine and fabric work, I made an agreement with an ex-student to fly the airplane to the west coast, where he assured me that he could sell it at a profit. I turned it over to him and eagerly awaited the money that he would send me as soon as he reached the west coast. For weeks I heard nothing from him. Finally a letter arrived saying that an accident had befallen the airplane in Arizona and that he had left it at an airport and it had been sold pending the clearance of the title. It was a lesson that cost me $200 and one that I have never forgotten. A year and a half later, I came across the airplane at an airport near Phoenix. The title was still under litigation.

Nearing the completion of the school, the long-expected papers arrived, notifying me that I had been accepted as an aviation cadet in the Air Force. I had tried to transfer to the aviation branch of the Army but there was a one year waiting period after the completion of the course before I would be able to fly. At graduation from infantry school, orders were read assigning me to the Far East, with duty station in Japan after the completion of airborne paratroop training.

I was now faced with a decision, either accept the orders and go to Japan as a platoon leader or see if there was a way to change my status, transfer to the Air Force and take flying training immediately. I was at a loss as to how to begin the transfer request until a recruiting sergeant for the Air Force suggested that something might be possible through the Pentagon. He also gave me the name of an Air Force captain who might be able to help me there. I secured leave by indicating a personal emergency in the Washington area and boarded an airplane from Maxwell AFB in Alabama.

I regard Washington D.C. as the greatest rat race in the world and where bureaucracy has achieved its finest form. Nevertheless, this bureaucracy can sometimes be used to one's advantage and it proved to be so in my case. In that administrative maze no one could be found who was willing to make a firm decision on my case. More importantly, no valid reason seemed to exist to justify denying my transfer from Army to Air Force. I hiked from office to office, telling the Air Force that the Army would release me if the Air Force accepted me, and telling the Army that the Air Force would accept me if the Army released me.

The transfer was finally granted. One lesson I learned that day, which has stood me in good stead on many occasions since, is that one should always treat the office secretaries with the greatest consideration and courtesy. With them on your side, your case will be presented in the most favorable light to the officer making the decision. Indeed, in some cases, the secretary may well make the decision if the officer is new to the job.

Now there was one final step that was necessary before leaving the Pentagon. I had to go and formally accept the flying assignment that I had been allotted as a cadet. When I returned to the Air Force office to do so, the officer in charge began asking questions and discovered the truth of inveigling myself into the flight program. He was furious at what I had done and when I broached the subject of a flying class, he vetoed the entire idea. However, I was now a bona fide member of the Air Force and he had to give me an assignment of some kind. I was summarily dispatched to Lackland AFB as a training officer and finally things were starting to work out well and slot into place.

Before taking up my new assignment, I had to return to Fort Benning for a short time, where I found myself in the ambiguous position of being an Air Force officer assigned to the Army. Although I was in the Air Force, I was without authorization since the paper work had not arrived and no one knew what to do with me. As a result, I was made mail orderly, office clerk and errand boy, all of which kept me busy and taught me a little more about the Army. My former classmates did not know what to make of me as they were going through a very demanding jump-training course at the time, while I appeared to be doing nothing constructive. I must confess that it made me feel uncomfortable as I was due to have been training with them, yet here they were going through all Hell while I was about to realize my long held dream of joining the Air Force, and very happy with the prospect.

Finally, the papers arrived, detailing me to Lackland AFB. The reporting date was in August 1949 and so began my time in Texas, where almost every serviceman will spend time during his career, regardless of his service affiliation.

CHAPTER 4

FLYING TRAINING

There shall be wings.
Leonardo Da Vinci 1452-1519

Reporting into Lackland AFB, I was assigned to the Training Analysis and Development Division and began my work with the school curriculum. It was our duty to sit in and listen to the various instructors and evaluate them. The difference in the teaching ability of the instructors was amazing. Since they were a select group, theoretically there should have been little difference between them, but there were a few who were exceptional and stood out from the rest. These were the men who enjoyed teaching, and it showed.

Having arrived at my new duty station, as soon as diplomatically feasible, I again applied for pilot training and eagerly awaited news of my request. Specific forms were required for the application, and these were in short supply. Sam Darby, a mobilization assignee, also wanted to apply for pilot training, so together we went to Brooks AFB, where the reserve affairs were handled, and filled out the necessary forms.

I kept in close touch with the T/Sgt. who worked at wing headquarters, and regularly appealed to him for any information that might get me assigned to a flight class without a lengthy wait. It was here that I learned an important fact of life, that in many cases the T/Sgts and M/Sgts are capable of rendering more assistance than their officers. They usually have long service, are in responsible positions, intelligent, and know the ropes and loop holes. If there was ever something to be done, and the answer was not in the book of red tape regulations, then I looked for the ranking M/Sgt, since they were usually familiar with the methods of getting things done quickly and all the handy loopholes.

Finally my orders arrived and I read them with great enthusiasm and delight. The Air Force had saved itself a great deal of money and at least assigned me to the logical base in the Texas area, where I was presently based. The orders read: "To report to Randolph AFB, San Antonio, Texas." It was known as the West Point of the Air and it justly deserved its fine reputation. The architecture of the base had a Spanish influence so prevalent in the San Antonio area. The administration building encompassing the water tower is a familiar site to millions of Americans who have served in the Army Air Corp and Air Force.

I hoped that perhaps my training would lead to something important in my life and reporting into Randolph AFB I felt that at least one of my goals in life was about to take shape. I never dreamed that an opportunity to be assigned to the base that I had read so much about would ever actually happen.

Too much time was taken up by red tape processing and the student officers had a great deal of free time. We saw what the cadets were enduring and I was thankful that I was going through the program with all the privileges of an officer, and not a cadet. Besides, the difference in pay was several thousand dollars. Several times I was detailed the duty of student duty officer and ate with the cadets where the difference was truly apparent, as the cadets ate the unappetizing "square" meal in their mess hall, a step down from the relatively good food the officers had. I once witnessed a cadet break down and be carried from the mess hall; the strain was too much for him and he cried like a baby.

Flight training began a month after our arrival, in the North American T-6, the Texan, so aptly named since the majority of the training bases at that time were located in Texas. The engine developed 550 horsepower, which was more than sufficient I thought to indoctrinate us into the world of the aviator, and double that of the first airplane that I had soloed, the venerable Waco UPF-7. My instructor was a young First Lieutenant, who had come back on active duty. To me, he exemplified the essence of what I thought a fighter pilot to be. However, he disliked instructing and did everything in his power to get out of it. He finally secured his release and reported to a unit in Korea to fly fighters.

Flying the T-6 presented no particular problems to me, one reason being that I spent so much time in the cockpit of the airplane memorizing the procedures, that flying it was not complicated by trying to recall procedures as I knew them by heart. Soloing the airplane was no more than a psychological problem. With a touch of pride, felt by most soloing student pilots, I was sent up from an auxiliary field to make the required three landings and take-offs.

It was particularly gratifying to fly the airplane solo and during the flights every minute was spent perfecting my flying techniques with, I must admit, a degree of time devoted to a few techniques and maneuvers that were not strictly speaking approved of. It was expressly forbidden to fly formation with other aircraft, but students often made plans to rendezvous over a certain point, at a particular altitude. The aircraft would cautiously approach each other with an element of trepidation, for fear that an instructor might also be in the airplane and take note of the number. Being caught flying formation was grounds for board action, including the possible elimination from the program.

One day, the mobilization assignees that I had applied for flight training with, decided to rendezvous in the air. Over the pre-agreed area, I began to join up with another aircraft and saw that there were two men on board, more than likely an instructor. Breaking off, much shaken, I climbed back up and saw another T-6 approaching me. I took all the evasive action that I could and the other aircraft finally gave up. I breathed a sigh of relief since I was sure that it was an instructor pilot trying to get the number of my aircraft. On the ground, my flying partner asked me what the hell I had been trying to do, since he exceeded the red-line airspeed on his aircraft three times trying to catch up with me.

Another day while dog fighting, with neither of us wanting to be the first to break it off, our aircraft drifted out of the local area designated for solo flying and we got lost. I stuck close to Sam, in the hopes that his navigational skills would lead us back to base, and at least presumed that he knew where he was. When it became apparent that he was as lost as I was, I decided that it would be best to find my own way back alone. Turning on the radio set, I made a radio range orientation, determined where we were and managed to land just at the end of the training period. These experiences rather dampened my desire for doing the forbidden and the flying program progressed without incident.

Graduating from the basic T-6 phase of flying school the pilots were assigned to either single or multi-engine school depending on their desires, abilities, recommendations of the instructors, and the needs of the service. I felt that the reciprocating or the piston, propeller driven airplanes were the ones that I had mastered, and that if I continued with this type, I could become an excellent pilot rather than just a good one.

Multi-engine aircraft had never really interested me, for in my opinion they were devoid of any romance of flying and further, only the students of lesser ability in flying school seemed to be sent to multi-engine training. So I decided to put in for single engine or fighter aircraft and had an opportunity to apply for F-51 training. With my instructor's recommendation, my request seemed assured. The P-51 was one of the great fighters of WW II. On the day of graduation, the orders were read and I was sent not to Las Vegas, Nevada for F-51 training as I had set my heart on, but to Williams AFB in Arizona for single engine jet training. The F-51 training program had been canceled and there was no alternative, as all advanced training was now to be in jets. This was not what I had planned for and a disappointment.

August of 1950 in Arizona was the hottest place that I had ever known. The heat seemed to roll over me in waves. July in Texas was hot, but August in Arizona was unbearable. I now began flying the T-33, the two-place version of the F-80 that we would ultimately progress to when allowed to solo. Prior to our jet indoctrination, we got more time in the familiar T-6, largely to give us more instrument training and increase our proficiency. This involved flying without visual reference to the horizon and had begun while we were in basic training. Learning to trust the instruments rather that the physical senses, was something not easily transitioned to. Even experienced pilots have had accidents caused by trusting physical senses rather than the mechanical indications of the instruments. I spent many hours in the link trainer getting to master the mechanics of blind flying. Having checked out and got more time in the T-6 again, the long process of transitioning to jet training began.

After extensive training in the T-33, where an oxygen mask was always worn, the machine burned fuel at the phenomenal rate of hundreds of gallons per hour, and an emergency was declared with 80 gallons of fuel on board, I was finally ready to solo. I had always felt confident that I was the master of any airplane that I flew; but this was certainly not the case with the F-80. The crew chief literally had to hold the ladder to keep my knees from knocking together and vibrating it away from the airplane. I felt like a man climbing voluntarily into his instrumented casket. I cannot remember the flight, but the fear of getting into the cockpit I recall most vividly. I kept thinking that this was not what I had in mind when I volunteered for fighter aircraft; the F-80 was vastly different from the F-51 that I wanted to fly.

Flying has its fair share of accidents and the first one that I witnessed, was when I was working on the flight line during my training with the Navy. I was watching an Army aircraft come in on the wrong runway, when it suddenly turned to the right and went into a spin at a low altitude. After completing two and a half turns, the twin-engine Lockheed Ventura crashed and a moment later I observed a sight that I was later to become familiar with, a big black cloud of smoke coming from the burning wreckage.

During my training, I again witnessed an accident when four of us, three students and the instructor, were taking off on a training flight. The four aircraft lined up on the runway; the leader and number two released their brakes a few seconds before the second two aircraft released theirs. I was leading the second element of two aircraft. As we climbed out and commenced a turn to join up with the lead aircraft, number four called and said that he had smoke in the cockpit. Routine instructions were given to him as to what to do. Shortly thereafter, he cried in a voice fraught with panic, that it was getting hot and that the airplane was on fire. The leader told him to bail out. These particular aircraft were not fitted with armed ejection seats as was normal with this type of aircraft. They had been disarmed because armed seats were apparently dangerous around inexperienced pilots. The only way for a pilot to get out was to climb over the side. If the airspeed was above 300 mph, the pilot would go above the horizontal stabilizer and if it was substantially below, he would go under it on bail out. At an airspeed close to 300 mph, the pilot would strike the horizontal stabilizer causing serious injury or even death.

The F-80 began a shallow dive that steepened and the pilot still did not bail out. I found myself shouting into my facemask to "GET OUT". Suddenly at a very low altitude and in a 45-degree dive, a figure departed from the doomed craft and we saw the welcome sight of the billowing canopy. With a sigh of relief, I climbed my aircraft up to altitude to burn out the fuel then came in to land.

By this time, the helicopter had located the pilot and radioed back that he was injured. We learned later that he had hit the horizontal stabilizer and because of this, his leg had to be amputated. He was only a few weeks away from graduation and there was an effort made to secure a commission for him so that he could retire and draw officers' pay. This endeavor was not successful, although the feeling among the instructors and the cadets was that it would be excellent for motivation and a well-deserved reward for a well-liked, popular cadet. During graduation, it was customary for the newly commissioned officers to pay a dollar to the first enlisted man who saluted him to ensure, as superstition claimed, a successful military career. It was thus arranged that the newly commissioned officers filed past in front of the recuperating cadet, who saluted them. His wife stood beside him. When all had marched out of the building, I looked back and he was covered with dollar bills and wiping tears from his eyes.

Any small incident that happened to a student while flying, would put him under surveillance and very often would require that he take a check ride, particularly if he dropped the tip tanks on the airplane, which was a fairly common occurrence. On a take-off, during a hot early morning flight, the tip tanks dropped off my airplane just as it became airborne. The first I realized that they were gone, was when the instructor called from the lead airplane and asked if I had the tanks on when I took off. It was standard operating procedure to arm the tanks on take-off so punching a button on the stick in case of an emergency would drop them. After a few minutes, the instructor called and ordered me to burn out my fuel, land as soon as possible and find out what happened. On landing, I explained the situation to the line chief and as strongly as possible suggested that there must have been a malfunction in the switch. In fact, I felt so strongly about this that I bet him a case of beer that there was indeed a malfunction. Then I had to explain the situation to the Major in charge of flying operations. As I was talking to him, a call came from the maintenance shack saying that a short had been found in the hand grip in the stick, which caused the tanks to drop. That case of beer was the best investment I ever made and no one found out about it until the night of the graduation party, after I had received my silver wings.

There was one other close call and that was probably not of great importance except to me. I was on a cross country to the Grand Canyon and nearing Phoenix on my return flight, I glanced down and looked at the map in the cockpit; when I looked up there were four airplanes coming directly at me from the right. I altered my course a little to the right and down and flew right through the formation. The leader and the number two man did not see me but the pilot in the third airplane reported my airplane to the leader as I went down and slightly under him. It made we aware of the terrific closure speed and the great importance of always watching and looking around. The old adage so often repeated about keeping one's head out of the cockpit was never more indelibly imprinted in my mind than that day. The rate of closure and the tricks that the eyes can play at high altitude were severely impressed upon me. The sky could appear completely clear one minute, and occupied by aircraft the next.

Graduation was in two phases, the commissioning on one day, and the awarding of the wings on the next. The graduation parties were the most fabulous that I had ever attended, and in a little less than two years a whole new life had presented itself to me. There were carved ice statues and so much food that one spoonful of each dish would make any man fit to burst even one with a large healthy farmer's appetite.

The next day, our wings were awarded, and the acrojets performed. The skill with which they presented their program amazed both the trained pilots and equally impressed their families and guests who had no understanding of the complexities of their maneuvers. They flew their F-80s with breathtaking skill. The only time that I saw them waver was when their flight path took them within a few hundred feet of a C-47 that was flying near the base

After graduation, orders were again received, and I found myself once again ordered to the Far East. The Korean War had been going on for six months and by this time, had my course in the military not changed, I could possibly have been a platoon leader being forced back to the Pusan perimeter instead of a jet pilot about to fly above the same area.

I was to report to Nellis AFB, Nevada for gunnery school and thence to the Far East. Nellis gave us complete flying freedom, the intention being that if a pilot could not hack it here, it would be better to find out now, rather than send him overseas and let him fail there with possible fatalities involved. The sky was filled with F-51s, F-80s and other combat type aircraft. At peak traffic, there was one airplane landing and taking off every 30 seconds. This was truly the final testing ground for flying talent and natural ability. As soon as I reported in I was told that my airplane was waiting for me out on the ramp and to take an immediate orientation ride and solo in the F-80. I had thought that there would be some type of orientation ride again with an instructor, since I had not flown the airplane for about thirty days, but this was not the case. With a degree of trepidation, I again approached the faithful F-80 and made a very thorough pre-flight inspection, as I do when I am a little apprehensive about flying an airplane. In a way this is a means of getting acquainted and settling into the correct mind set. The flight was uneventful and gave me renewed confidence in my ability to handle a jet.

There was a story doing the rounds at that time of a F-51 pilot who had been recalled to duty. On his return to Nellis from his first flight he radioed the tower requesting that the crash trucks be called out. The control tower asked the pilot what type of emergency he was experiencing, so that they could clear out the landing traffic. He replied that this was his first landing in five years in the F-51, and thus it was an emergency to him and to all others in the vicinity.

At Nellis the students were taught to get the maximum performance out of the airplane as well as themselves. Naturally, under these circumstances, there were many casualties, as every flight demanded the utmost from pilot and airplane. Our instructor was a bachelor, very popular with the students, and we could not have wished for a better man. He demanded the utmost from each one of us; Lieutenant Paul Woods, Lieutenant Delbert (Dusty) Hays and myself. It was absolutely impossible to scare him and I am sure that luck alone prevented us from crashing into him and ourselves while on our training flights. We were soon trying formation acrobatics. Initially I found it almost impossible to remain in tight formation at the top of a loop, where precise control was lost as the airspeed reduced. Tight formation was when there was less than a foot between aircraft. Our flight usually made passes over the field in diamond formation. It was always a pleasure to feel the exhaust from the lead ship vibrate the rudder pedals, massaging the balls of my feet and peering up the tailpipe, seeing the flame at the top of it, knowing that I was in position as slot man directly behind the leader.

Dogfights were not expressly forbidden as in our previous training programs, but now actively encouraged. There was much rivalry between instructors, and woe betide the student who did not see the formation being attacked and call out the attackers. This would end up in the inevitable Lufberry circle, where each flight attempted to get on the tail of the other.

I enjoyed going up solo and waiting for a flight to pass below and then jump them. The F-51s bore the brunt of our attacks and there was much rivalry between the 51s and the F-80 squadrons. If the rule that the F-51 should not be turned with was ever violated, the hapless F-80 pilot would be looking back at the propeller spinner of the Mustang pilot pulling lead. The most successful tactic used against the Mustang was to dive, make one pass and use the excess speed to zoom up for another pass.

One day Paul Woods and I were sent up together for a practice flight. After flying around in a two-ship formation, we separated, and keeping Paul in sight, I climbed and made a pass on him. I had loaded guns and pulling the circuit breaker so the guns would not fire, I took pictures of him with the gun camera. When the film was developed, I showed him the pictures and he was highly indignant and got very agitated that I had pulled the trigger of my guns in order to take a picture of him. Paul was a quiet Texan, short in stature and he always landed in a crab so that he could see over of the nose. He was kidded about his method of landing but he always touched down with the longitudinal axis of the aircraft pointing a few degrees off the landing runway.

There were a few close calls during the six weeks at gunnery school that encompassed formation, rocketry, strafing and air-to-air gunnery. One of the criteria for successful graduation from the course was a low altitude navigation flight and return with minimum fuel. It required a climb to an altitude of around 11,000 feet to clear Mount Charleston, the highest peak in the vicinity, and then a letdown to within a few feet of the ground. The weather was marginal when we took off and we were able to clear Mount Charleston and commence our planned mission up the valley to the north. Buzzing has always been a favorite pastime, but frowned upon by the Air Force. Here we had a training mission giving us a legal license to buzz the desert. Enthralled with the mission and the speed, neither of us noticed that the weather was deteriorating. When we noticed that we were getting low on fuel we decided to climb and look around for a hole in the ceiling and to climb above it. There were no holes and there was nowhere to go except up to conserve fuel and clear Mount Charleston. Neither of us had our radio compass tuned in to our home base station, so we decided that one of us would fly straight and level while the other tuned in his radio compass. When we went into the overcast, I had been on Paul's wing and when I checked the artificial horizon in the cockpit, it was indicating a 90-degree turn to the left. Paul was unsuccesfully trying to tune his compass so we decided that I should fly straight and level with him on my wing while he tuned in. This did not work either and he lost me. We called the emergency channel, requesting an emergency steer to the base. We were both lost with 80 gallons of fuel on board, in the clouds, with a high mountain in the vicinity. It was the closest that I have ever been to bailing out on a training mission. The calm voice of the ground controller acted as a steadying influence and we both broke out over the base with 40 gallons of fuel on board. I kissed the ground on our return.

Striking the ground on low-level missions was a danger that we were constantly aware of. On a low-level formation mission, I was stacking high on the leader and going over him on turns, rather than under him as is the case in formation at high altitude. Watching the leader on one of these low level flights, I did not notice the rising desert floor of the valley we were flying in, and I pulled up at the last possible second. The same thing occurred at the last second on the high angle strafing range. Wanting to be sure to hit the target, I delayed the pull out a second too long; the desert floor slid by beneath the airplane, with what must have been inches to spare. In both these instances, the floor of the desert seemed to reveal itself in every detail and I could almost distinguish the individual rocks.

The last of my narrow escapes involved another aircraft. We were flying an air-to-air mission and for this it was essential to keep all the airplanes in the gunnery pattern in sight for we were using live ammunition. Two airplanes made the same firing pass on the same target. I was one of them. I simply had not seen the other airplane when going in for the firing pass. It was all in knowing were to look, and after this narrow escape, I learned rapidly and improved my own performance in the gunnery pattern.

The stint in Las Vegas was not without its fatalities. Two of my classmates from Williams were the unfortunate victims of the rigid training program. On our first actual strafing exercise, we strafed a mock convoy of trucks, a group of wrecked cars. Our flight pulled off the target and another reported in. The number two man of the second flight became so intent on the target that he delayed his pull out and struck the desert floor in a level flight position, at around 350mph. I was later told that it had been reported that it was my airplane that had crashed. The rescue helicopter pilot was a friend of mine and was reluctant to come out and pick up 'my' remains. The other class mate, delayed his pullout from a high angle strafing run, just as I had done, but he had delayed it a fraction of a second longer, and he too hit the ground flat. In both cases the aircraft immediately disintegrated and the pilots were killed instantly.

Before graduation from Nellis, a long cross-country flight was required of us. The plans were for four of us to fly from Las Vegas to New York, Miami and then back to Nellis AFB. Due to some technical trouble our take off was delayed till late in the afternoon. Consequently, it was dark as we flew over Illinois scheduled to land at Detroit, Michigan. Just as we broke out of the overcast on the initial approach to the airfield, my oxygen regulator became defective and the oxygen pressure rushed into my mask and caused difficulty in both talking and breathing. We landed in drizzle and were again delayed due to the faulty regulator. It was a little disconcerting to think what might have happened had the regulator failed at high altitude and caused us to descend to a lower altitude, with no immediate available fields to land and not enough fuel to fly to Detroit.

We continued the flight to New York where one of the pilots had a close childhood friend. He was a womanizer who usually managed to have his way rather easily with any women of his choosing including many married women making advances toward him. He remembered this particular girl in New York as one who had resisted his advances in the past and consequently she presented a challenge to him. While in New York, he was successful in gratifying his physical desires but the affair must have had a disturbing effect on him and hindered his mental attitude, for the following morning he committed one of the cardinal sins of flying in not doing a stringent pre-flight check on his airplane. He did not remove his airspeed cover or pitot cover and he had to abort his take off half way down the runway. His airplane came to an inglorious halt in the mud at the end of the runway. The rest of the flight burned out fuel on a low level mission over the New York and Long Island area, then came back and landed. A very sheepish and embarrassed pilot buddy greeted us, as his airplane was being pulled from the mud. The delays that were encountered by faulty oxygen regulators and pitot covers resulted in the cancellation of our extended cross country flight and we flew back to Nellis AFB without any further problems.

There was no formal graduation as such, just a wish of good luck from our instructor. He was an excellent man who happened to be exceptional at his job, loved to fly and a truly great fighter pilot. It has always been a source of great disappointment to me, when the ability of pilots is not recognized by the Air Force. Years later, I heard from a mutual Air Force friend that he was still instructing and that he was still a Captain. The criticism that had been levied against him was the fact that all he could do was fly. There were individuals in the Air Force, who have no other desire but to fly, but in this case, he had ability, personality and surely he must have stepped on the wrong toes at the wrong time.

The last I saw of Las Vegas for many years was the strip fading away in the night as the C-45 that I had boarded as a passenger winged its way to San Francisco. The last sight of it was the famous Wilbur Clarks Desert Inn, our reporting point to ground control on approaches to Nellis AFB.

San Francisco, the port of embarkation for millions of American personnel during WW II was still functioning in the same way as thousands of Americans still passed through on their way to the Far East. Paul and Dusty met me and we went through the shot line together to bring our inoculations up to date so we would not hold up the war through being stricken with some dreadful foreign malady. It was a lonely, sad place and a rather poor send-off to a foreign shore where I am sure everyone wondered at one time or another, whether he would ever return to these shores. Finally the information came that we were to report at 3:00am and from Travis AFB we would board a C-54 transport airplane for the Far East. There were numerous men on board who had celebrated a little excessively the night before and they soon slid into the arms of a sweet hangover sleep.

CHAPTER 5

FAR EAST

In the mold of this new profession,
A new breed of men has been cast.
Antoine De Saint -Exupery

We were delayed for an engine change in Hawaii and it gave us an opportunity to look over the island. It was an excellent place to have engine trouble. Air Force units were stationed here and I thought a tour of duty in Hawaii would make a nice break. We immediately made plans to spend a few days in this garden spot on our return to the ZI or zone of interior as it is called.

Finally, the DC-4 or C-54 as it is known in its military form, lifted from the islands and took up a course for Japan, where a mere six years before the country had been our enemy. It made me wonder if we were living in a sane society.

Aboard the aircraft were replacement crews for the police action in Korea. All would be assigned to Korea unless they had special skills that were needed in Japan. The majority were rated officers on flying status. Three of us were just out of flying school and from the same flight at Nellis gunnery school. We had learned to use our jet aircraft as gunnery platforms and as bomb and rocket launching devices. We felt that we had received the best training in the world and that we were a special breed of "tiger." Lt Paul Woods, Lt Delbert Hays and myself. Our plans were to go immediately to Korea and get in the same flight together. We felt that the war would soon be over and that our training should be put into action to shorten the war. Such were the sentiments of young fighter pilots!

The aircraft touched down on Japanese soil, which still bore the scars of the last war. The date was March 14th, 1951. A popular song at the time was "Wheel of Fortune" and it expressed my feelings about flying and fighting, in this far corner of the world.

Our luggage, consisting of one B-4 bag apiece and whatever we could carry, was loaded on lorries. We exchanged our dollars for Japanese yen and military script then hopped on a bus which took us to the processing squadron where we received our assignment orders to a flying and fighting unit.

The journey from Haneda to Camp Fuchu was a revelation and a shock to us. The Japanese way of life is entirely different from what we were accustomed to and it is easy to regard anything new with a degree of suspicion. The streets were narrow and bicycles, three-wheeled motorcycles, buses, army lorries, passenger cars as well as small charcoal burning Nippon vehicles used as taxis, mingled together. Small children toddled to the side of the road, restrained by a child not much older than itself. "Mamasons" attired in Kimono's with babies tied to their backs, clipped along on their "getas" held on with two thongs. The houses were unpainted and many were thatched.

On the way to Fuchu we passed a park, where the driver informed us that the first American raiders on Tokyo were beheaded. However none of the residents of the town would admit to knowing anything about it.

Souvenir stores catering to military personnel dotted the street as well as the notorious cabarets of the Orient. The stench was horrible and we had our first encounter with the "honey-bucket", carriers of human excrement used to fertilize the rice paddies and vegetable plots of the farmers. Slow oxen or horses pulled the carts carrying the "honey-buckets". Horses were occasionally used, but Japanese were never seen riding them. This custom supposedly dated back to the time when the Emperor rode his famous white horses and issued a decree stating that riding a horse was strictly for those of royal blood.

The bus turned into Area B at Camp Fuchu after passing several laundries, oriental gift shops and cabaret joints just outside the gates. Several Japanese girls, "ojosons," loitered close to the armed sentry. The cabaret signs proclaimed their wares of beer and girls. Food was not advertised much as all armed services personnel were warned not to eat any native cooked or grown food for fear of contamination, as human excrement was used as fertilizer.

We unloaded our baggage, checked in with the Sergeant at the main administration building and were assigned to a large dormitory. The first rush was to the shower after our long flight from the states. As we waited in line for the showers, a Captain quipped, "Far East on Good Friday, first combat mission on Saturday and shot down on Easter Sunday." Not many laughed.

An officer sitting next to me on the bus to Fuchu had a brief case on his lap which I presumed was stuffed with orders and official papers. In fact it was filled to overflowing with an assortment of pill bottles. Every two hours he would pop a pill, presumably to inoculate himself from the many and varied diseases that the Orient is noted for.

There was nothing for us to do until the next morning and many of the officers took advantage of this opportunity to go to Tokyo on the Air Force bus, which ran to the central railroad station serving Tokyo. They came back with mixed reactions and reports. One of the officers, who was assigned later to Korea, had been to one of the"geisha" houses and reported the treatment he had received of being served breakfast while sitting on the floor with his feet stuck down in a recess where a charcoal fire burned. A blanket covered his knees and kept the heat in as it was still cold in late March. He had also purchased an ornate pool cue, which struck me as being a little ludicrous for there were no pool tables where we were going. But there is no accounting for an American with money in his pocket when he sees a "bargain".

Paper work, the lifeblood of the Air Force, occupied us for the next few days and then we awaited our assignments. Paul, Dusty and I were sure we were going to Korea and we were ready, eager and willing to get there. Without us, we felt an indispensable cog in the war machine was missing. We thought we would be assigned to the same unit. There was a good spirit of camaraderie that had developed between the three of us, having been in the same flight together at gunnery school. Our instructor had been a real educator and leader and had forced us to fly to the very best of our ability at all times and initiated us into the intricacies of team aerobatics. He was a very brave man!

We eagerly jostled each other to see the assignments as they were tacked on the bulletin board. Our eyes traveled down the alphabetical list. My name was first, assigned to the 8th Fighter-Bomber Wing, APO 929, Fukuoka, Japan, along with Dusty Hays. Paul's read to the 49th Fighter-Bomber Wing, APO 970, Taegu, Korea.

It was a shock, first to be separated and then to be sent to what we considered a base where missions were slow. All of us were there to get our missions in as fast as possible, get home and on with our careers. There were pilots who had been in the Far East for 100 days and had completed their 100 missions, which at that time was considered a combat tour. We wanted to get out missions over and done with. Paul had the best chance and we envied him.

Dusty and I were to take the train down to Fukuoka and Paul had to catch a flight out of the nearby air base of Tachikawa. We had some spare time before we were scheduled to leave, so we took the bus to Tokyo.

At the central railway station we were besieged by rickshaw drivers pulling their high-wheeled carriages. The more fortunate ones had pedal powered rickshaws. Young shoeshine boys and taxi cab drivers all offered their services. The taxis were nondescript vehicles with charcoal burning apparatus on the rear, as fuel was not readily available. It was also my first encounter with "denki gedoshas", an electric car. I thought they would be silent but they sounded like Model A Fords..

Passing by General MacArthurs's headquarters we saw a crowd of Japanese waiting for MacArthur's departure. It was about five o'clock when he made his exit to the waiting Cadillac. It seemed as if MacArthur had, to a certain extent, taken the place of the Emperor following the defeat of Japan. This perhaps was the reason for the adulation he received. Japanese policemen as well as the honor guard were on duty to control the onlookers.

The taxi took us to the Ginza, the tourist street of Japan. Street vendors crowded the sidewalk selling their wares. Jackets embroidered with dragons, imitation Ronson and Zippo lighters, fans, curios, whatnots and pipes were offered. The prices were always too high and the vendors rejoiced when there was no bargaining because a huge profit was made. Bargaining, arguing, shouting could drastically cut the asking price. The exchange rate being 360 yen for US$1, many service people became hypnotized by the enormous amount of the yen they had. There were bargains on fly rods, small alarm clocks and almost every pilot bought a small replica of a Samurai sword to carry in his flying suit to deflate the "Mae West" life preserver and life raft should it accidentally inflated during flight. There isn't much room in the cockpit of a fighter aircraft if one of those blew up.

Japanese transportation facilities had not recovered from the war. The railway platforms at the station were always bustling with crowds and when a train pulled in and the doors opened there was a rush for the door, with no regard for the elderly, children or pregnant women. It was done silently, pushing and shoving as a matter of course. It was akin to a group of animal's back on my father's farm, going up a loading chute in a rush. An elderly Japanese man suffered a heart attack and was obviously very sick yet no one paid any attention to him. Eventually some railway workers carried him to an office. No compassion was evident, just indifference. It is a sad thing to see people who have so little regard for their fellow human beings.

It was a two-day train trip down to our base at Fukuoka on the island of Kyushu. We were assigned to sleepers with a group of Marines and naval personnel who were going to Sasebo, the Naval base in southern Japan. They spent a noisy night in merry revelry but it was certainly very quiet the next day.

The scenery was monotonous, low hills dotted with shrubbery, small rice paddies, farmers with oxen, and children and bicycles everywhere. How could a nation like this, with aircraft factories under trees in the hills, a nation somewhat akin to Illinois, have held the United States and her allies at bay for four years?

The train passed from the island of Honshu to Kyushu via an underwater tunnel. We arrived in Fukuoka late at night, and struggling with our B-4 bags we arranged for transportation to the main base. Twice we were propositioned at the station and it was a new experience for us being openly propositioned on the streets by prostitutes.

The train of thought regarding oriental women usually occurred something like this. At first there was a definite aversion, with puzzlement as to how anyone could be attracted to any of the locals or their environment. Their racial characteristics are such that they could not possibly be compared to white women. White women, or round eyes, were usually preferred but they were not available except the few who were associated with the Red Cross. After about six months the complexion seemed to go unnoticed and the men who were going to fraternize with the local girls would usually do so around the six-month period.

There was a definite point in favor of the "ojosons", for they treated a man like he was the only man in the world. They poured his sake, teas, and attended to his every wish. Many officers and enlisted men had their "cobitas" or sweethearts, who they kept during their tour overseas. They would feed, clothe and entertain them for services rendered. They set up house keeping, Japanese style, sleeping on straw mats, eating rice and fish with chopsticks. Their women were adorned with western clothing bought from Sears Roebuck and Montgomery Ward catalogues. At five o'clock there would be an exodus of men from the base carrying sacks filled with post exchange snacks. When a duty tour ended, the "foreign wife" was often turned over to a best friend. A few marriages arose out of these liaisons.

The "House of Mirrors" was the officer's 'entertainment' establishment in town, and off-limits to enlisted men. It was in a district of Fukuoka where the better houses of ill repute were located. On entering, the madam of the establishment, greeted her clients, charged 3,600 yen, or the equivalent of ten dollars, shoes were removed and the girls brought out. The officer selected the girl of his choice and retired to a room. If he picked the star of the house, he would be given the room with floor to ceiling mirrors. Japanese food was available and also black market American cigarettes at double the normal price.

A technical representative from Lockheed reserved the "belle" of the house every weekend and bedecked her with western clothes. Eventually he purchased her release and set up a house with her. Later, he went back to the states, divorced his wife with two children, and came back and married her.

Though outlawed in Japan at that time, the practice still exisited of fathers selling their daughters to restaurants, geisha houses or the house with the "red" light. In the past, when a daughter was sold it was for the life of the child. In the early fifties they were theoretically under a contract for a certain number of years. Some could save up enough money to buy out their contracts but most of the establishments saw to it that their girls were never paid enough and they became even more indebted to their employers and the contract continued indefinitely.

Dusty and I hired a taxi to take us to the main base, an old Japanese air strip where the runways had been lengthened to take jet aircraft. We reported into wing HQ and were summarily assigned to the 80th Fighter-Bomber Squadron, known as "The Headhunters."

Billy Dixon, Hal, Dusty Hayes R&R in Japan Sept 1951

CHAPTER 6

COMBAT

*If I could not be a leader, then I would be
the best damned wingman the Air Force could produce!*
HF

The first tent in the row before us bore the famous yellow and black painted emblem of the 80th Fighter-bomber Squadron, a Headhunter's head. We were told to check in with base housing to be assigned quarters and the general attitude of "the war can wait" prevailed. Six of us moved into a winterized tent with no windows and two smoky oil stoves.

The operations officer welcomed us, took our flying records and told us to sign up for the replacement training unit, the RTU. This shocked us. Here we were, in our minds probably the highest trained fighter pilots around, having just completed gunnery school at Nellis and we were being assigned to a RTU. Probably at no other time in our careers would we be so finely trained, so expertly honed as right now and here we were, about to be retrained. Our respect for the Air Force dwindled as our indoctrination with the red tape of this huge organization began.

Hal outside The 80th / Headhunter Operations

The RTU was located in a winterized tent, where a number of pilots were sitting around dejectedly and rather impatiently waiting to be checked out. Aircraft were only available to the RTU when not being used on missions, hence some pilots had been waiting for weeks to complete their training. Weather conditions, as always, also hindered the training progress.

One of the RTU pilots, Captain Brown, was an old F-51 pilot, who had been shot down and bailed out over friendly lines as they were falling back. He broke his ankle and had to be carried back ahead of the advancing hordes of North Koreans and Chinese. Another pilot going through the RTU had a lot of F-51 time and was thus transferred to a F-51 unit, the 18thFBW, before he finished training. I saw him shortly after his transfer and he said that he had been flying one and sometimes two missions per day. Since 100 missions was the magic number to complete before rotation, he could easily have completed his duty tour in the record time of three months. Some pilots actually achieved this remarkably quick turnaround and after only four months overseas, returned to the ZI with a combat tour on their record. I had not seen this pilot for a while, and enquired about him from some of his squadron mates. He had volunteered to fly over his hundred missions and was killed on his 102nd.

One of our tent mates was a Lieutenant Briggs who had been flying fighters in the ZI and had recently arrived and became a flight leader. Around 3am one morning he was called for a predawn take-off mission. Something went wrong with the airplane on take-off, causing a power failure and in the dark he had tried to turn back to the field. A huge pyre of flame at the end of the runway marked his unsuccessful recovery effort and the fires lit the path for the remaining pilots. A primary rule of flying had been violated, that of never attempting to turn back to the field but to try and land straight ahead. He had attempted to turn back with good reason, in fact he had little option, as the runway being used was encircled at the end by Japanese houses and a few short miles from the end of the runway was Fukuoka Bay. A water landing at night, with a full bomb load was almost impossible. He had little choice but to attempt a turn back. For some reason, perhaps the fear of killing innocent Japanese, he did not drop his bombs or tip tanks. It was my first experience with death during combat operations. Up to now it had been merely an academic thing, we were at war and people got killed. But this was someone I knew and shared a tent with. It all became very real; we lost a good man and a good friend.

Around this time, a Major assigned to the 80th FB Squadron was killed at Taegu, Korea. The pilots all spoke of him as being infallible. Assuming that he had been killed in combat, I asked for the details. Apparently he and a fellow pilot had taken off from Taegu for an instrument practice flight in actual instrument conditions and hit one of the mountains in the area. This seemed an unfitting end to so illustrious a career.

Finally I was told that I was ready for my first blooding. At that time, newly graduated RTU pilots were sent on a mission as soon as possible. The details of the mission are hazy, probably because of the fear that was in me. First, the long over water flights of about 100 miles each way from Japan to Korea and back, and the bad weather that was invariably encountered on these long missions. I did not look forward to my first mission since formation flying in bad weather was dreaded by novice pilots. Shooting at real live targets, and being shot at by strangers whom I could not hate as individuals, suddenly became a reality. To say that I was reluctant was certainly an understatement, and the first mission was viewed with mixed emotions. I reckoned the most logical approach would be to stick like glue to the flight leader and not let him out of my sight. The number two spot is always allotted to the newest pilot and that is where I was put, with two pairs of eyes watching me from number three and four position.

It was a ground support mission along the front line, and the strike was against the village of Sinuiju. A briefing preceded each mission two hours before take-off time and covered general intelligence information, details of the target, the location of friendly and enemy troops as well as specific information, including the location of known anti-aircraft batteries. In addition our armament loads were discussed, the expected weather enroute and our ETA back at base. Emotions after ones first mission are akin to those after ones first aerial victory and kill as a great deal of time is spent reliving every detail of the event over and over in ones mind.

Communal living did not exactly appeal to any of us and none of us were particularly tidy. The sage words of a Colonel from training day's back at Williams AFB echoed in my mind as he claimed that no matter where one is stationed, too many comforts of life do not have to be sacrificed if a little work is done to improve the living environment. With this sound advice in mind, Dusty and I approached the housing office and became friendly with the Japanese in charge of the barracks and the maids. I did not smoke but always drew my ration of cigarettes and always had a carton for bartering. We were thus able to wangle an entire tent for ourselves including the luxury of reading lamps, desks and a personal maid for the tent. We also got to know the Sergeant responsible for the film shows and usually viewed them from the projection booth for an almost private showing.

A degree of tension is generated in a pilot flying combat missions, and to remain rational and functional for the fighting unit it had to be released in some manner. This was done in socially acceptable ways by some and not entirely acceptable ways by others. Some would get loaded at the bar and give vent to their feelings through demon "rum" and with drinks at only 25 cents, they rationalized that they could not afford not to drink. Some men frequented a house of ill repute, a "cat house" and relieved their tension there along with drinks and a hot community bath. Some took up with a local lady, bought food from the PX and set up 'oriental style' housekeeping. Buying food from the local market was forbidden.

My form of relaxation was riding through the nearby countryside on a used Japanese scooter. I found what I thought was the real Japan, not the Japan of the souvenir shops, the beer and sake parlors. Every chance available, I wandered through the Japanese markets and food stores. It was interesting to turn down a side street barely large enough for the scooter and find the local markets seldom seen by foreigners. The fish markets were astonishing to a Westerner, particularly the small live fish that the locals ordered, much as we bought gold fish in the dime stores. Octopus was another novelty to me. If servicemen were seen in these places it was usually an indication that they had 'gone native' and had a "cobita" or Japanese mistress.

Air Force personnel and those on Relaxation and Recreation, or R & R, frequented the Fifth Air Force Officers club located in down town Fukuoka. The food was excellent and cheap and the bar was popular and lively. The head cashier was a Japanese girl who had been educated at the Junior college in San Bernardino. Her English was probably more grammatically correct than that of the average American. After the war her father had sent her to the USA for her formal education and she had returned to her native land.

While waiting for the missions, especially when the weather was bad over the front line, the pilots sat around in the operations room playing cards, bitchin', drinking coffee and sometimes writing letters home. The sociological interaction in this small group made up of reserve officers, regular officers and Air National Guard officers, was interesting. They represented a range of backgrounds and ages. On a rainy day, one would find the older Captains clustered together, around them would be the senior grade first Lieutenants and then the newly graduated second Lieutenants. Entirely aloof from the group were the field grade officers. It was a well-defined, almost distinct caste system, and was virtually impossible to move up or across these cliques. The regular officers were the most closely knit group dedicated to the furtherance and preservation of their own careers. Friendship seemed of little importance to them, with a tendency to regard all other officers as necessary to the war, but to be relegated to a minor position as soon as it ended. I doubt that one could find a more cold, calculating, friendless group anywhere except in their own small clique.

The friendliest group were the older Captains with many years in the USAF or Air National Guard. Captain Bill Bowman had been one of the first to check out in the P-80 when it became operational near the end of WW11. He had more F-80 time than anyone else in the squadron. There was also a Captain from the Florida ANG whom I admired both as a pilot and as an officer. He had flown with the ANG aerobatic team in F-51s. If he had flown the F-86s, he would surely have been an ace. It was a shock to hear that he had been killed after the war while taking off on a night mission. On the join up he became disorientated before he could transition to instruments, and crashed into the Arizona desert.

On my first few missions the F-80's were loaded with a huge load of fuel, over 930 gallons of JP-4, or low grade kerosene, about 1,800 rounds of ammunition for their six .50 caliber machine guns, and either 500 or 1,000 lb bombs, rockets or napalm. They flew 200 to 250 miles, with only 10 to 15 minutes in the target area before returning. The climb out to Korea took about 125 miles and the maximum ceiling that we achieved with the heavy bomb load and fuel was around 23,000 to 24,000 feet. On our return we could ease up to 30,000 to 34,000 feet. I concentrated on being the best possible wingman and attempted to fly formation closer and better than anyone else. My motto was that if I could not be a leader, then I would be the best damned wingman the Air Force could produce!

Every fourth day we had standing alert duty on the strip from dawn to dusk, whereupon the night fighters would take over. The night fighter was an abortion of two 51s joined into something termed the F-82. The pilot sat in one fuselage and the radar observer in the other. The ground crews said that they were a nightmare to maintain. When on alert, we holed up in the alert shack at the end of the runway, close to our airplanes. When the buzzer sounded, we raced out to the airplanes; the mechanics started the auxiliary power unit, or APU, while we scrambled into our parachute. The common reason for a scramble would be for a C-119 coming back from Korea with its IFF (identification, friend or foe) not set. We would fly to the wayward aircraft usually around 7,000 feet, identify it and report its number.

The night before our flights alert duty was usually reserved for normal squadron revelry, and many mornings when the flight was scrambled, pilots regretted the evening's revelry with vows of never 'partying' again. It was one such morning that I came close to having an accident. The standard cure for a sick fighter pilot is usually a blast of 100% oxygen, but on this day it did little to relieve my 'morning after' grief. After take-off we were vectored to intercept a friendly cargo plane that had forgotten to turn on his IFF. On occasions we were vectored out over the water to intercept and identify fishing vessels that had been picked up on radar. We had been known to occasionally buzz the fishing vessels until the Japanese government protested and an altitude restriction was placed on the alert aircraft. After intercepting the C-46 aircraft on this particular day, we circled and climbed to altitude, flying a square pattern over an island out in the sea between Japan and Korea, waiting for targets of opportunity to give us practice. On our return I followed the leader into the traffic pattern at Itazuke AFB. There was a strong headwind straight down the runway and as was normal, no brakes were used, until I turned the airplane onto the taxiway. Taxiing at about 15 mph, the aircraft veered to the right slightly and I attempted to correct the aircraft with the left brake. Suddenly the left rudder pedal offered no resistance, which indicated a complete brake failure. At that speed the rudder offered no help in steering the airplane and there was little that I could do as the airplane slowly moved to the right side of the taxiway, toward a three-foot deep drainage ditch. A feeling of utter helplessness came over me as I watched the ditch come closer. It was barely moving when at the last minute, I hit the good right brake causing the airplane to go into the ditch at a 90-degree angle. It came to rest with the tail in the air at an angle of 40 degrees. I rather sheepishly slid back the canopy, cut the switches and pondered on the horrible day it had turned out to be.

The flight surgeon was normally the first man to check a pilot who had been involved in any form of mishap and I did not feel in any condition to be inspected by a doctor. I visually checked the brakes, attempting to determine what might have happened. Walking back down the taxiway picking up remnants of the F-80 brake pucks, the squadron commander and operations officer drove up in a jeep. The commander had passed judgment on me before hearing my explanation, so to back up my story I held out the shattered brake pucks. My explanation and the fact that there was no apparent damage to the F-80 got me off the hook and I did not have to face the flight surgeon. This taught me to forever be in the best possible physical shape when flying. I still have a photo of the gallant old F-80 with its tail in the air, and nose in the ditch like a giant iron beast kneeling down to drink.

Later I found out that there were a number of instances where the brake pucks had failed in other aircraft due to defective pucks having arrived in a supply. There

F-80 after it lost the brake pucks and ended up in the ditch 5-10-51

was no way to determine if they were defective before installation. By the law of averages a brake failure should not have happened to me again, but lightning can strike twice. On some of the missions deep into enemy territory, there was not enough fuel to return to our home base in Japan and in these cases we landed at a base in Korea called Taegu, about 60 miles inland. During this stage of the war the runway at the base was of pierced steel planking and the engineers were constantly at work repairing the damage done by landing aircraft. The 5,000ft runway was barely long enough for safe operations and the psp was extremely rough on landing. Akin, I presumed, to landing on a roller coaster. It was here that the second brake puck incident happened to me. I was flying number four in a four ship flight returning from a close support mission which had expended our fuel, and thus required a landing at K-2 or Taegu. We flew up the valley on our initial entry to the airfield, broke and began smooth turns to the final approach. The leader landed on the inside of the runway to the left and the number two on the right side. I lined up and touched down about 800ft behind the leader. As it was a short runway and the braking action on the psp was poor, I applied the brakes as soon as the airspeed

The Hal Fischer Story

diminished so they would be effective. The mushy feeling in the brake indicated that there was either a ruptured brake line or the pucks had again failed, and this time on a runway traveling at a relatively high speed. Having rehearsed the previous emergency, I immediately stop cocked the throttle, opened the canopy, and called flight ahead of me to clear the runway, as I had no brakes. Using the rudder to guide the aircraft until the speed dropped below 40mph, I aimed at the only clear space in view, as there were airplanes lined up on either side of the runway. The clear space was off the end and I left the runway still going at a fair clip and with an utterly helpless feeling watching an open ditch about 15inches across and 2 ft deep coming up to me, and a vision of a sheered nose gear about to happen. However, the aircraft having expended all but about 30 gallons of fuel, all of the ammo and ordinance on board, skipped lightly over the ditch and slid to a somewhat muddy and inelegant halt in the sticky Korean clay. This time I knew what had happened and left the job of retrieving the aircraft to the ground crew and went to a debriefing and a talk with intelligence officers regarding the mission.

Actually, a combat mission and delivering the ordinance was not what we expected it to be like. It was not worth being afraid of and not as frightening as we had anticipated. Courage is only the ability to overcome fear, and if one was courageous, combat could be termed fear inspiring. When the ground gunners of the Communists began to fire the 20mm and 40mm cannon and the projectiles started to float toward the aircraft and suddenly start to converge at tremendous speed, it increased the adrenalin flow of the most courageous of men. The cannon shells were termed 'golf balls' and the appearance of a luminescent golf ball which grew in size to that of tennis ball as it passed the aircraft, caused an almost hypnotic fascination, that was most exhilarating when they missed!

The approach to flying that I adopted was to be the best wingman possible, and when flying number two on a leader that I could trust, I would go on a strafing pass and actually be hitting a target underneath the lead airplane as he was pulling up and over the same target. Positioning myself on the inside of the lead and knowing which way he was going to turn, I commenced firing as he finished firing and pulled over the target. This worked well when it was the same target or very close together. Some leaders complained since it was distracting to pull over a target and see it come alive with light from the tracer bullets and armour piercing ricochets, although it was safe. In order to keep the lead in view, it was necessary to keep him in sight at all times and only concentrate on the target when on the actual firing run.

In regard to dropping our ordnance, napalm was the most interesting, followed by skip bombing then rocketry and finally dive bombing. To drop napalm, the pilot had to get down as low as possible, usually less than 50ft and when the target disappeared under the nose of the aircraft, the napalm was released; both tanks at once, or singly for greater coverage. It was almost impossible to miss the target and according to POWs it was the most feared weapon of the Air Force.

Skip bombing was similar to dropping napalm and with delayed fuses in the bombs, it allowed the bombs to bounce up in the air once, hit the target and explode. Again it was difficult to miss the target. It was used effectively on railroad tunnels and I recall one instance when a bomb of mine exploded on the other side of the tunnel from which the run was made. On analysis we determined that the bomb had skipped all the way through the tunnel and exploded harmlessly on the tracks.

Rocketry was more difficult and in order to be effective it was necessary to get a direct hit on the target. Since the launching technique was from about 3000ft away from the target and at an angle of 30-45deg, there were many more factors to using this successfully. The gunsights had settings for rocketry but most pilots estimated the correct range and altitude and the attacks were about as successful as throwing rocks at the enemy. Dive bombing targets was similar to rocketry but the angle of dive was steeper and the altitude for dropping the bombs was higher. The accuracy and devastation from these bombs was increased by using proximity fuses, which exploded about 100ft above the ground and rained death and destruction on all those below. Another technique used later in the war was that of glide bombing and it was a hit or miss affair.

The two most effective weapons used against the communists by fighter aircraft were napalm and the fifty-caliber machine gun. One of the greatest tragedies of the Korean War was that there was no way to determine if a village contained peaceful Koreans or was a billet for enemy troops. Pilots discussed this question and it was unofficially decided that if we had not been briefed on a village containing troops then it would not be hit. However there was a minority of pilots who thought any village near the front was fair game, since if it was not being used at the time, it could be used in the future and therefore should be destroyed. I felt that the villagers near the front were not responsible for the war they found themselves in and should not be attacked except for military reasons, and the majority of pilots felt the same way. There was one pilot who was notorious for hitting anything that had smoke coming out of it and the other pilots mocked him about hitting old men and pregnant women.

Our unit flew continuously during the Chinese communist offensive in the spring of 1951. Upon landing from a mission our aircraft were immediately refueled, rearmed and ready for take off on another mission. Pilots were briefed for the next mission before the ongoing one had returned to base and the line crews worked around the clock to keep the aircraft in good shape. Not enough credit can be given to the crew chiefs and their dedication. My crew chief was a southerner, totally devoted to his job and I made a habit of informing him of the next mission and reporting on it upon our return. All the pilots did not do this but it should have been mandatory since the crew chiefs were responsible for the safety of the aircraft, and thus the safety and lives of the pilots, and without the crew chiefs, flying operations could not run smoothly.

Being one of the lowest ranking First Lieutenants, in the unit, I was given the oldest airplane in the squadron. It took a while to decide what to call the airplane and since survival seemed to be in the hands of fate, I finally settled on "Kismet". The name, along with the crew chief and mine were duly painted on it and I was most proud of her. "Kismet" was a good and reliable airplane other than for one bad habit of throwing a turbine blade in the accessory turbine, commonly called "buckets". The aft turbine turned at about 10,000 rpm, so the loss of a "bucket" weighing a few pounds set up a mighty vibration in the engine section. Flown in this state for an extended period of time, caused a severe vibration, enough to warrant an engine shut down. However, this reliable aircraft, on losing a "bucket" would continue running until I reached home base.

My crew chief took delight in taking bets on which aircraft would make the best landing on return from a mission. I prided myself on my landings, and often helped him win, much to both our delight. The crew chiefs were always on hand to watch the landings since some of the airplanes did not always return. These dedicated men were attached to their airplanes and very often to the pilots who flew them. Their first question after landing and the engine shut down was if it was in good shape. It always gave me great pleasure to answer in the affirmative and compliment the "chief" on the condition of his airplane. There was no single group who put in longer hours, or who did a finer job, than the men who worked on the line and they got so little credit for it.

It was during this period that many engines quit soon after getting airborne and too late to abort the take off. There is nothing more morale shattering than not being able to trust one's airplane on take-off. The airfield at Fukuoka was bounded by the city on one end and rice paddies on the other, so fatalities almost always occurred in these instances of engine failure. In order to increase the thrust of the F-80s on take-off so that they could carry a greater load, a mixture of water and alcohol was used and thrust increased by up to 15%. This lasted long enough to get the airplane airborne, gear and flaps up and establish an angle of climb if used properly. After a number of accidents it was suspected that a foreign substance might be in the water/alcohol mixture, which caused an explosion and flameout. It was rumored to be a case of sabotage and led to the demise of a pilot who crashed and the airplane exploded on a pre-dawn take-off.

The F-84 was introduced into the theater during this period when an entire Air National Guard unit from Texas was assigned to Itazuke AFB. It was rumored that some political strings had been pulled to bring the Guard over as a single fighting unit. Normally, when a Guard unit was assigned to active duty, it was broken up almost immediately.

The F-84 was a newer airplane and considered more advanced. I was astounded that it carried half the load of the F-80 yet still had to use JATO to get airborne. It also had a strange landing profile, as it was pointed at the ground and allowed to fly into the ground, or so it appeared. If the same technique had been used by the

F-80s, after a week there would have been no airplanes left to fly a normal four-plane mission. On take-off with a lighter load, they even used up more runway than the F-80s and due to the summer heat some missions were cancelled because they simply could not get airborne with the available runway length.

It was a constant wonder to me why a newer, less effective airplane was ever put into production. However, it had a greater range and was well suited for escort work on the B-29s. The F-84s were viewed with contempt and many sarcastic remarks were made about them as they had a propensity for either blowing up or burning up. I recall one morning, as I crossed the runway on my scooter to take my place on alert, hearing an explosion at the take-off runway from one of the two F-84s doing a pre take-off engine check. I saw the pilot open his canopy, leap onto the wing and start running as smoke began to pour out of the tail and the intake section. The fire trucks, using all their fire fighting techniques, and prodigious amounts of foam, were unable to control the fire and the ammunition in the nose compartment began to "cook of." The fuselage settled to the ground like a melting wax effigy and only a portion of the wings and tail remained.

Many of the pilots had a Japanese mistress who they lived with and supported. Some of these liaisons were brief, but some developed into lasting relationships. One pilot completed a combat tour, returned to the States and promptly requested an assignment back to the Far East. He had been living with a very beautiful Japanese school teacher, who upon his departure had taken a new lover. However on his return they took up together again and were eventually married.

My good friend and combat pilot prowled the area of clubs and cabarets that flourished in Fukuoka where beer and dance partners were cheap. One attractive cabaret club hostess was more willowy than the usual Japanese hostess and without the typical, rather comical gait so prevalent to the local girls, especially when wearing high heels. She had taken an American name since it was almost impossible to pronounce her Japanese name. She initially resisted all his advances but they soon became attached to each other and he moved in with her.

As a small girl she and her father had been living in Manchuria and a Japanese soldier had shot her. Thus she was receiving a small pension from the Japanese government. After an evening in town, I would take him over on my motor scooter and deposit him on her doorstep. In the morning, if anything urgent came up, I would have time to dash off and collect him.

Once an early mission was called and all available pilots were needed. I requested the operations jeep on pretence of collecting my friend from the tent we occupied and tore along to get him. An Air Policeman pulled up and stopped us as it was forbidden to drive government vehicles on village side streets. Fortunately the Air Policeman was also involved with a girl in the area, so he ignored our little indiscretion.

The street girls lined up at the gates to the base after dark to offer their charms with the usual greeting of, "Where you going boysan?" These were the lowest class of prostitutes, perhaps forced into their profession by economic necessity. The hierarchy of the prostitutes could be broken down into a streetwalker, an inmate of a house of ill repute, a cabaret girl and finally the 'kept woman', who was the highest on the ladder of success. The girls at the gate quoted a price for a 'short time' or 'all night,' as they phrased it. Some of the street girls had rooms of their own and some required that the client provide the place.

The "fall" of many a true family man occurred through loneliness and cheap liquor available at the Air Force bars. One such pilot was a real character, older than most of us and an excellent cartoonist. He had trained in the F-51 and transitioned to jets. On a tow mission for air-to-air gunnery, he was forced to do an emergency landing right after take-off and ignored the rule, either by design or accident, of landing with a full fuselage tank. On the final turn, the Mustang snapped and spun into the ground. Fortunately he survived, and after a lengthy stay in hospital, was assigned to the 80th squadron. During the course of an evening's drinking at the 5th Air Force officers club in downtown Fukuoka, he started back to the base in the unit's vehicle. He was "plowed" to say the least and the closer he got to the base, the slower he drove past the good time girls waiting beside the road. Finally the urge got too much for him and he made arrangements with a girl to go to a nearby hotel. Realizing what he had done he dashed out of the hotel and in trying to turn the vehicle in the narrow Japanese street, backed into the gutter where it became hopelessly stuck. Coming to his senses, he called the Air Police who filed a report with the squadron commander listing the complaint as 'unauthorized use of a military vehicle and being off limits'.

Rumors were rife that the unit was going to be re-stationed in Korea; the thought of which did not please anyone. Determined to fly as many missions as possible, I stood by in a spare aircraft, having briefed for the mission and hoping that an aircraft would be found mechanically defective and that I could step in as a replacement pilot. It often happened that the standby pilot was used and at one time the spare aircraft even taxied out to the end of the runway with the flight, in the event of mechanical trouble immediately before take off. Always being available for a flight and sitting in on briefings, I rapidly built up my roster of missions. In one thirty day period, I managed to log 30 missions. As soon as this was discovered, I was forced to slow down in order to remain with the rest of the pilots who I had come over with. At that time it was my intention to get all my missions completed and get back to the States.

To relieve the tension brought on by steady combat flying, I frequented different places to eat my evening meal. The Army had an officer's mess down town and I often ate there, with rather staid Army officers. Then there was the ever-popular 5th Air Force officer's club down town, the officers club on base one, as well as the mess that we used on the strip. Along with these places there was also the Japanese market, which we had all been warned against, but those of us who had been in the Far East for some time, enjoyed the local food. Besides, it was cheaper and a good steak cost 200 to 250 yen, about 75 to 90 cents.

In war or in a situation fraught with danger, experienced individuals do not always act rationally. My flight leader at the time was about 33 years of age and was considered an old man. He wore his hat well back on his head and always had a cigarette dangling from his lips. He acted as if he had been around the world three times, had seen everything, knew everything and his word was gospel. His career had been mediocre and as far as we knew he had no reason to act the 'hot shot'.

Our flight was on a mission near the front lines, in close support of the ground troops. On a pass over an area where there was little visible ground fire, the flight leader called and said that he thought his airplane had been hit. Number three in the flight moved up to check his aircraft and he reported that he could see an opening under the engine which appeared to have been caused by either a small explosion in the engine or possibly a hit by a small caliber weapon. The engine evidently functioned fine, allowing the airplane to be flown to a higher altitude with no apparent problem in getting back to the airfield at K-2, the only suitable airfield in the vicinity that could be reached once the flight had climbed to altitude.

The flight leader called and said that he was gradually losing power and his airplane fell back. We remained with him, over the overcast, since the loss of power also meant that he would probably lose all electrical equipment as soon as the battery lost its charge since the generator ceased working when the engine rpm dropped below a certain point. Since it was difficult to locate the field over the broken overcast, the aircraft were slowed down so the flight leader could follow us to K-2 and then either bail out or make a forced landing. The element leader, Archie Caldwell, was having some type of generator trouble so it remained for the other wingman and myself to stay with the leader until he made his big decision. Over K-2, the field could be seen through the broken ceiling and the flight leader elected to make a landing on the field.

He set up a pattern and since he had no radio, he depended upon me to call the airfield requesting that all the traffic be cleared. I couldn't get the runway control officer who was directing traffic in a radio jeep until we were just about 150 feet above the ground. The flight leader had set up a pattern for a north landing and it looked like he was in a very good position for the landing. I coasted around close to him keeping out of his way and just when it looked like he had it made, he turned away from the field. I could not believe my eyes when I saw the F-80 as it began its last long glide in the opposite direction to the landing traffic. Although there was not much wind, he was still going to make a crash landing going downwind which placed him at a disadvantage when he needed every advantage he could get. The area he was headed for was full of rice paddies and the retaining walls were as hard as concrete. The largest field was less than an acre in size. The F-80 slowly settled toward the earth and came to rest against a dike. The point of touch down to the sudden stop was not more than 50 feet. I expected to see the familiar pall of black smoke but there was none. At the last moment before impact, the landing gear was still down.

Landing as soon as possible, Archie and I commandeered a jeep and raced to the wreck. The "meat wagon" was just taking the flight commander out of the cockpit. He was still conscious although in obvious pain. Walking beside the stretcher as he was carried to the ambulance, I looked down at a man who had made all the mistakes in the book. The man who said to bail out rather than make a forced landing if the situation was doubtful, and then under ideal conditions he made a forced landing. He "goofed" it up so badly that he almost killed himself. Fortune was smiling favorably on him to be carried away with a trace of life left in him. Yet he did not seem to be suffering from anything more than shock. It turned out later that his back had been severely hurt and he spent some time in the hospital. But for him, his combat days were over. Later, I found out that he felt a little more favorably toward me when I elected to remain in the flight when given a chance to get out because of the personality conflict.

An example of the personality conflict occurred on returning from a combat mission when the flight commander relinquished the flight lead to the element leader, without prior briefing. I took up a different position than he wanted me to. He became enraged and said over the air, "Dammit get in position." This was the day that I lost the brake pucks and when I got to the briefing after extracting myself from the mud, he said, "So you landed hot", before I could explain. It was a good thing that he did not let me fly his wing, with only two ships in the air or I swear, I was mad enough to shoot him down. Tales of platoon leaders, who were unpopular with the men under them and who were killed from bullets in the back, facing the enemy were too familiar to me and this was the first time that I thought that I could do it to someone else. But these were only passing thoughts and the flight commander put himself out of the way just as readily as if someone else had done it for him.

On May 1st of 1951, the United Nations forces decided to make a show of force on this traditional Communist holiday. It was decided that the officer's training school just outside of Sinuiju would be hit with all the fighter airplanes in the Far East. This show of force was to be within sight of the Chinese mainland. All of the airplanes of the 8th were flown to K-2 and then armed and fueled and the pilots briefed. The airplanes of the 8th were lined up on the west side of the runway and the 51st on the east side of the runway for a north take-off. It was a hot, dry, dusty day and the plans were for the 51st to take-off to the north first and the 8th to the south after all the 51st airplanes were airborne. Sitting at the far end of the runway, I watched the 51st F-80s take the runway and after the airplanes reached about 100 mph, their jato units were cut in. The first few airplanes were successful with the take-off but the thick smoke from the jato lay on the runway and the following airplanes had to fly through it. One could hear the roar of the engines and then the airplanes appeared at the far end either a few feet above the psp or about to become airborne. A few of the pilots thinking they were not going to make the take-off, punched the panic button and dropped all the ordnance and their tip tanks. Bombs and rockets fell at the end of the runway, then the F-80's leaped into the air. One pilot aborted in the smoke and slowed his airplane up, the following airplane not hearing the radio call struck the aborting aircraft, causing major damage to both aircraft. Another pilot inadvertently fired his jato as he was about to line up for take-off and the jato force pushed the airplane until it hit the ground controlled approach shack, in spite of brakes and a stop-cocked throttle.

We watched this fiasco with a degree of trepidation as we were due to take off in the opposite direction. Our armament load was restricted to rockets and since they were lighter, jato units were not used. Our flight was the second flight to take the runway, and I was flying as the number two man to Captain Sam Hoffman. The two aircraft before us had jettisoned their loads and then we roared down the psp together. The runway became smaller and I inadvertently moved my left hand from the throttle to the red button on the instrument panel, which would jettison the tip tanks and rockets. At the last moment as the wheels passed off the end of the runway, the F-80 became airborne. At this time, the throttle had been 100% and there was no attempt to remain in position on the leader and as we passed over the end of the runway, our two airplanes were line abreast. The leader delayed his gear and since we were observing radio silence while in the air, I delayed mine. Finally his gear came up but it was too late to take our planned place in the squadron formation. Later, after the mission, Sam said that he was so worried about making the take-off and so surprised that he did, that he completely forgot about the gear. The target was successfully hit and it did not seem worth all the ordnance and aircraft expended upon it. The few buildings in the complex were thoroughly destroyed. There were B-26s, F-84s, F-80s, F-51s and F-9fs all in a coordinated effort to destroy the school. Every fighter aircraft we had was aloft on a political mission and heavy fighter activity was expected from the Communists. As it turned out, the only losses we had were on take-off and landing.

Returning to K-2 all the aircraft had to be landed within a short period of time. The landing was as difficult as the take-off but fortunately no airplanes or pilots were lost.

In the hills around K-2, there were reports of guerilla activity and aircraft had been fired on while taking-off and landing. In addition, the Korean people had learned to exist off the Japanese under their some 40 years of rule so they were accomplished scavengers and nothing was safe if left anywhere that there was a chance for it to be picked up. The Korean people viewed stealing in a different light to what we do. During one RON (remaining over night) at K-2, where we were charged one dollar per night for a cot and two blankets in a winterized tent without a stove, a squadron commander from the 36th squadron had laid his clothing beside his bed. He was bald, pudgy and an all around good trooper. Awakening the next morning, everything was gone except the long winter underwear he had on and his government issue shoes. He flew back to Itazuke in long winter underwear, shoes, and nothing else.

Driving off the base on occasions, I saw the places where the Korean people lived and the dilapidation and filth that they lived in was unbelievable. It was somewhat akin to badly kept hog houses that we had back on the farms in Iowa. I was told that some of the men at the base were keeping Korean girl friends and living with them in those conditions. It was inconceivable to me how they could do so. They were actually supposed to be restricted to the base. I found out later that the armed guards around the base were not only to keep the Koreans away form the base, but to keep the Americans on it as well.

The Japanese were different in respect to stealing, in that one could leave belongings about and take normal precautions such as one would in the United States. Their feeling about stealing and thieves were akin to ours. The Japanese police had a reputation for being brutal to their own people, and this was one of the things that MacArthur had changed when he was the supreme military commander. The Koreans must have suffered greatly under the Japanese occupation.

While in Japan, I endeavored to learn as much about the Japanese people as I could and the housemaid who took care of our quarters, helped us to understand the Japanese people, their thoughts and customs. She used to eat her lunch in our tent along with the other housemaids, and speaking broken English, she tried to answer the questions we asked. Her father was a minister of the Japanese faith, which was not the militaristic religion of the Japanese Shinto belief, but of the accepted religion of the Japanese, as permitted by MacArthur

The music was also difficult for the foreign ear to understand as it always sounded so sad and as if the singers were wailing with grief. I was once invited to a local school where the Japanese instrument, the "shamuzen" was taught, and listened to the pupil's play and sing. What interested me was the pageantry that accompanied their music. The instrument was plucked something like a zither and each of the students sat opposite each other when playing the instrument.

Too soon, the time came for the unit to leave the island of Honshu and it was with much reluctance that those who were unattached left, but it was more difficult for those with wives and girl friends. Some of the pilots had their wives living at base one.

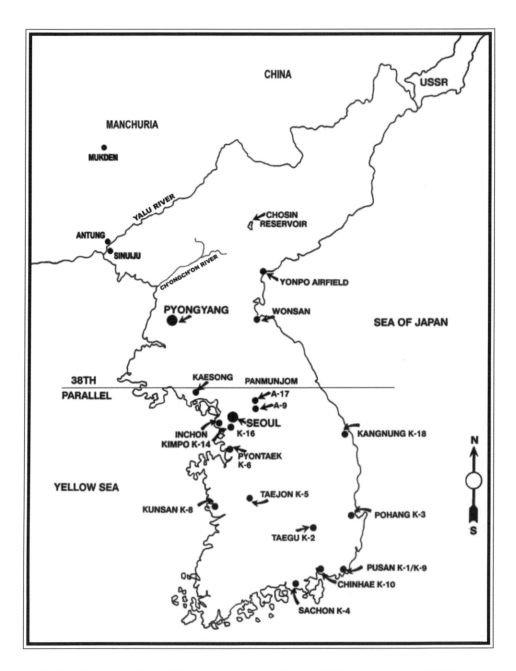

Airbase's During the Korean War

CHAPTER 7

KOREA

I learned that danger is relative,
and that inexperience can be a magnifying glass.
Charles A. Lindbergh

Some wives had been with their husbands in the Philippines when the war started, and subsequently came to Japan after the outbreak of the war, to be with their husbands. They drove their husbands to work, which in this case was flying combat, and then picked them up after the mission. It was a very unreal situation, where a pilot could have breakfast with his wife, fly a combat mission and return home safe and sound to the arms of his wife for the evening meal. It was all part of an unreal war.

Finally, one morning I climbed aboard my gallant old airplane, 659, flew over the city of Fukuoka bidding it adieu, and set course for K-14, Kimpo. Bob Given was the flight leader and he had left his wife back at base one. This was their first separation since arriving in the Far East.

The first American airplane in the Korean conflict was lost at Kimpo. A C-54 was waiting to take a group of evacuees to Japan when a Yak-9 came over and strafed the airfield. It hit the C-54 and it burned up. Later the men in my squadron were responsible for shooting down of a number of Yak-9s, one pilot accounting for two.

The one permanent structure was the remains of the administration building that was built by Pan American before the Korean War. The concrete structure was unusable, surrounded by bomb craters and riddled with machine gun bullets and scars. The permanent runway was constantly under repair and it was almost as rough as the PSP at Taegu. Tents, quonset huts and some small frame buildings, were home to the 8th air force unit. The heat during June of 1951 was oppressive and it lay like a blanket over the dusty fields and rice paddies. The airplanes were hot to touch and rain was welcomed to cool everything down.

The airplanes stationed at Kimpo were the F-82s, (which flew at night and attempted to shoot down "Bedcheck Charlie") the British Meteors, a few T-6s, RF-80s, a couple of C-47s and our own F-80s. It was hot, dusty, dry and the missions which were to have been coming faster now that we were as close to the combat area as possible, slowed down and there was very little to do.

Bedcheck Charlie's were usually the Russian wood and fabric PO-2 biplanes first manufactured in 1927 as a trainer and later used as reconnaissance bombers, and sometime crop duster and glider tug. The British in WW 11 first coined the name when the Germans bombed allied fields under cover of darkness. The PO-2s were also flown on the front by Russian women in WW 11 for the purpose of bombing German airfields at night and were called "Night Witches/Nacht Hexen" by the Germans.

In Korea, "Bedcheck Charlie's" were an irritation and a cause of harassment as the grenades and old mortar shells they dropped, inflicted on the whole, insignificant damage, but we were supposed to take cover when the sirens sounded. Jet interceptors were too fast to shoot them down and radar had difficulty detecting them because of their wood and fabric construction. With a top speed of 96mph they were able to fly at tree top height down narrow valleys and remain undetected. The most successful aircraft used against the Charlie's were the Navy F4U Corsairs and a navy Lt. Guy Bordelon eventually shot down five Charlie's to become the first ever "Charlie Ace".

Prior to coming to K-14 I was given the job of the armament officer. This was an interesting and rewarding position. I am afraid that I knew very little about armaments, and if it were not for the Technical and Master Sergeants who were assigned to the job, I would have been a hopeless flop. One of the Technical Sergeants had been an armorer with the Flying Tigers in China. He used to regale me with the tales of the days of the American Volunteer Group, the AVG, and how they tried to fit all types of armament including Japanese, Swedish and American to the P-40. He told of the fines levied on the pilots for landing long in the P-40 and how this saved many precious airplanes. I spent many interesting hours listening to his stories of this famous group that I so deeply admired.

It was while I was the armament officer that I first ran into the political aspect and red tape of the service. The incident affected me greatly and thus my relationship with the service that I had chosen. The ground crews had been working a 25-hour day servicing and arming the airplanes. There was little rest for them, because they were understaffed. One of the lads in the armament section, while charging the guns on a F-80, accidentally discharged a round, which went harmlessly into the hills around Itazuke. The guns pointed toward the hills since accidents like this were anticipated. The shot from the 50 calibers sounded like a cannon and airmen and officers immediately surrounded the poor ground crewman and there was no chance to cover up for him. A report had to be filed which went through channels up to the wing and base commander. It was a stereotype policy that anyone responsible for discharging a round would be automatically court martialed and the way the bureaucracy worked, this also involved a demotion in rank.

After talking to the airman, who openly and honestly admitted his mistake, I decided to stick up for the man. I believed that a mistake could easily happen with the difficult circumstances under which these men were working, and that it would be good for their morale if the officer in charge took a firm stand on their behalf. However it was unusual for anyone to try and buck the system.

After the preliminary investigation, I made some recommendations that were forwarded to the squadron commander. Shortly thereafter an informal meeting was held with the squadron commander and the operations officer who had read my recommendations but diplomatically requested that I change them. At first, I stuck by my convictions, but eventually under pressure I agreed to change them. I have often wondered what the outcome would have been had I stood firm on what I believed was right and just. This young airman was sacrificed for the squadron commanders' belief that this was what his superior officer wanted him to do. My conscience hurt and I wished the charge could have been dropped. I was being indoctrinated into the political aspects of this career. It was difficult to go back and tell the airman that he was now going to be court martialed. He was resigned to the fact, and much wiser than his officer in some respects, in that he knew he must be punished according to the crime and that it was not tailored to the individual or the circumstances.

Our assigned barracks were quonset huts and the sun beat down on the tin roofs making them unbearably hot and oven-like during the day. The mess hall was barely functional and the officers lined up to get overboiled, tasteless food that was a far cry from what Japanese girls served us back at Itazuke. We ate it only because it staved off the hunger pangs. The officers club adjoined the mess hall and on occasions it served beer which was flown in from Japan in a special pod carried under an F-80. The booze supply run back from Japan was as important to some of the officers as the missions they were slowly accumulating in order to reach the one hundred mark. I had developed a liking for a drink called a King Alphonse, which required crème de cacao and cream, so one of the necessary items I took to Korea with me was crème de cacao. An after dinner drink helped keep me in touch with more civilized places.

The Squadron ops was in a tent, and much time was spent there waiting for missions and watching the airplanes take-off and land. To take a shower required a vehicle ride to the north side of the base, then line up with the other troops, Army, Navy, and British, and await our turn to stand under water that smelled as if it had been pumped directly from a slough. A guard was stationed near the water supply close to the shower, because it was rumored that an attempt would be made to poison the bases' water supply. From the smell of it, I was convinced that it had already been poisoned.

There were provisions for four planes to be stationed at the south end of the runway on joint operations center alert. If a target came up which required a strike force immediately, the four F-80s were available. Sometimes two airplanes were scrambled to give the ground control interception operators practice in vectoring us. Since we were usually vectored north, we took off to the northwest. If the turn was delayed for a few minutes, our airplanes would be flown over the front lines and we were given credit for a combat mission since any airplane that crossed over the front lines met the minimum requirements to log as a mission. With missions so hard to come by, on a few occasions the ground control instructions were not complied with since the radio "developed unexplainable trouble", which miraculously corrected itself as soon as the front line was reached. Since the pilots did not know when they were scrambled if the mission was a practice run or an actual mission, they wasted very little time in getting airborne. Sometimes we were released from a practice mission to seek targets of opportunity in the vicinity of the front lines.

On one of the two ship missions that I was leading, we went up the valley of Chorwon, one of the most heavily fortified of the area. It fairly sprouted ground fire, both small caliber and 20 and 40 mm. On reconnaissance up the valley, there was a lot of fire from the ground. Looking around for the number two man, Dale Smiley, I requested his position. He replied that he was above the broken overcast about 1,000 feet above me. Back on the ground, he said that he was with me as I began the pass up the valley and when he saw all the aerial garbage being thrown at my airplane he decided to clear out of the area to an elevated position of safety. Every time I saw Dale after this, we had a good laugh about this mission. He was not afraid of being shot at, but since the Chinese and North Korean gunners invariably fired behind the jets, he was more concerned about being hit by the ground fire that was aimed at me.

During another mission at dusk, I was leading an element near the Iron Triangle, when a 40 mm gun emplacement began firing at the element. Since this was a lucrative target, I pulled the F-80 up into a modified chandelle and came back and strafed where I thought the gun position was. All was quiet as I strafed the position and I was sure that the gun crew had been knocked out, but as I pulled off the target, the unit began firing at my airplane. I came back again, determined to end this duel once and for all. With each pass completed, I was sure that there would be no return fire, but they again lofted the flaming golf balls at me. I fired all my ammunition and with the fuel supply dwindling, returned to base. As I turned away the 40 mm was still active, so I presumed the encounter ended in a draw.

During this time, emphasis was being placed on putting the available airfields in North Korea out of action so the Communists could not bring in their airplanes at night or in inclement weather to launch an air attack against our poorly camouflaged front line troops. We always knew when we were over the United Nations lines because of the many types of vehicles and troops moving on the roads. It was common knowledge that a large air force was kept and maintained in China, safe across the Yalu river, and could be brought down at any time if it was tactically and strategically advantageous. The number of aircraft that could be brought to bear against our forces was overwhelming, but I felt that it would be welcomed if they did. Most pilots envisioned a "turkey" shoot and were anxious to have done with this front line support and engage in air-to-air fighting, which is what all the pilots desired. In fact, the situation could be compared to the fighter-bomber pilots as being truck drivers, and the fighter-interceptor pilots as the sports car drivers. There was nothing glamorous about dropping bombs or strafing the enemy troops and in many cases not even seeing the actual enemy. But there was excitement about seeing another airplane disintegrate after a fair battle in the air.

On a mission to "Post Hole," the airport north of Pyongyang, which was heavily defended with anti-aircraft guns, the airplane that preceded me in the dive was hit and crashed on the runway. The flack was heavy by Korean standards but nothing compared to WW II in Europe. The communists were using 88mm's. We could tell when a burst was close, since we could see the red flame in the black ball when it burst. I was number four in the flight and our run was to come from the west and turn left on our dive bomb run. Another flight was to come over the target at the same time from the east with a right turn to the dive bomb run. In this way our forces were to be over the target at the same time. We began our turn for the run on the target with the two flights staggered. First their leader, then our leader began his run. I followed their number four with my thousand pound bomb, and noticed a pall of black smoke off the side of the runway. At that time, it did not make an impression, but when I got back to the squadron, I learned that one of the airplanes had been lost and no one had seen him crash or knew what had happened. He went in on the target and just never pulled off. It happened that his plane had preceded me on the dive run and I had evidently seen him crash, which accounted for the black pall of smoke. In the heat of battle, pilots often remember little, although there are exceptions to this.

It was during this time that twins were assigned to the squadron. They were identical in every respect and they were aptly named Bill and Will. Silent and reserved they seemed to find more enjoyment in each others company and did not socialize much. Both were regulars and they seemed to exist happily in a world of their own. The only difference between them was that one was married. James Stewart was their flight leader and he was a tremendous individual who had been a navigator and had then taken pilot training. His flight was ordered on a mission into North Korea and when he arrived over the target, the clouds had closed in beneath them. Searching for a hole to let down in, the flight began to descend. The Communists had done what had been successful before and aimed all their anti-aircraft guns at the one break in the clouds. The lead plane alerted them as it came into their view, and as the second plane descended through the break they were ready to fire. They opened up with everything they had on the third airplane. The airplane was evidently hit either in or near the cockpit for it fell lazily off on one wing and descended to the ground. The airplane did not burn nor was there any sign of life as the flight left the area when they got short on fuel. One wingman took it very badly and his immediate reaction was to retreat to his quarters in the hot quonset hut and turn his face to the wall. He remained this way for a day and a half and resisted all sympathetic attempts to talk to him and refused food. The twin who was killed was the married one and his brother was immediately flown out of the combat area. The last report was that he had married his brother's wife.

The runway accounted for the demise of a number of airplanes and pilots as it had at K-2. One of the Air National Guard pilots assigned to the unit took off from this bad runway and was just able to get the airplane airborne. I witnessed this particular take-off. The pilot maintained a few feet above the rice paddies and at this altitude he began a turn toward a prominent hill in the area that supported a radar site. The pilot burned out his fuel and came back and landed, aborting the combat mission. In talking with him afterwards, he said that he hit a high speed stall seven times and each time he was ready to jettison his load, he recovered from it. This incident caused him to be grounded and he had difficulty getting back on flying status.

One of my classmates attempted to take-off and aborted too late to prevent his airplane from hitting a Korean house and burning. He had a new issue flying suit that was extremely porous and comfortable and many pilots wanted to get one. This particular suit caught fire, welded itself to the pilots' skin and seriously burned him. As a result of this accident the flying suits were given an unusable report and they rapidly disappeared from the Air Force inventory only to appear on surplus sales counters.

The truce talks were beginning and the war was supposed to be over in thirty days so the missions dropped to practically nil. There was a great deal of waiting, reading and listening to the truce meetings at Kaeson. While we were waiting, the work went on at K-16 repairing the base and particularly the runway. I recall once being on runway control, and seeing literally hundreds of Korean men, women and children working beside the runway loading two trucks. A few of the Koreans worked at loading the trucks with shovels while the others just sat around. I asked the officer responsible for hiring the Koreans why so many were hired and why they were not working, and he said that this was one way that our government could aid the Koreans without giving them an outright grant of charity which is psychologically destructive. So this ridiculous pretence of work got them a salary.

Since I had taken the stand that I had on the lad who had accidentally fired the round, I was replaced as the armament officer by a non-rated First Lieutenant and assigned the duty of gunnery officer. This duty was simply looking over the film from the gun cameras and to maintain rolls of film for the individual pilots. I spent a lot of time splicing film and got a complete roll of my own film from strafing missions.

It was while I was at Kimpo that I became blooded or had my aircraft hit. While on a strafing mission against a village, I was on a pass and firing and just as I pulled up, the aircraft shuddered and I heard a dull thump. Sometimes the airplanes acted similarly to this on a pull out from a dive at high gravity or g forces, so I thought little of it. After landing, I left the airplane and went to debriefing. When I returned I was informed that the airplane had been hit in the left leading edge of the wing and the projectile had come out of the tank filler cap for the main wing fuel cell group. The airplane was termed a class 26 from this one round, since it had damaged the main spar. Class 26 refers to the fact that the aircraft was uneconomical to repair. Evidently the 50 caliber round had been fired directly at my airplane from the front, yet I had been totally unaware of any ground fire. It made me wonder about the airplanes that I later fired on without apparent damage and perhaps they did crash or end up as class 26's. It so happened that this was one of the older aircraft in the squadron, 578, which had more time on it than any of the others except my own 659 and it was like loosing an old friend. She retired nobly and without apparent damage except for the hole in the leading edge and near the fuel cap. Her parts were used to keep other airplanes in the air, and so in a sense, she flew on.

During these days when we were not flying and the missions were few and far between, we used to see the F-51s climbing up in squadron formation to gain altitude and then take up a course for the front lines. At that time there was a dearth of F-51 pilots and the idea struck me that this was an opportunity to grasp and be checked out in them. I decided to put in for the 51st squadron citing the lack of missions in the F-80 and the apparent need for pilots to fly the F-51. However, I did not submit the application and waited for a more appropriate time.

There were Korean families living within the confines of the base and I watched them as they went about their daily living. One evening, I watched them thresh grain by using a hand flail. Here in the 20th century, I was watching a scene literally centuries old. Another sight that amazed me was the oxen drawing wooden plows through the muddy water of the rice paddies. The paddies were small and one ox or bullock usually drew the plow.

Once while returning to the barracks on the motor scooter that I bought in Japan and had airlifted to Korea along with the engine parts, I saw a little old man dressed in western attire, surrounded by many Koreans and soldiers. There were two Air Force officers with him as he climbed out of a 1936 green Chevrolet, which had obviously survived two wars. This unimpressive elderly man, Sygman Rhee, was inspecting the air base. He was opposed to the truce talks because he wanted to unify Korea and there were daily demonstrations north of the field, which, so it was said, were made up of the people who were opposed to the end of hostilities. Literally thousands of people in white, carrying banners, could be seen from the perimeters of the base. Looking at Sygman Rhee, I wondered what we were supporting in Korea and why we were fighting. It was certainly not for the people because our being in Korea did not benefit the majority of them and in many instances it appeared to me that we were only adding to their misery. In the final essence, I thought that we would end up being hated equally by the North and the South Koreans and it seemed ridiculous for our forces to be here. I could not see, in my position, that I was helping the Korean people in any way.

One of the duties levied against the squadron was that of forward air controller and a certain number of the pilots were selected to have this honor of spending around 60 days away from their fighting unit and serving with the Army. Their job was to direct air strikes against specific targets that the Army chose. They would have two airmen assigned to them and a radio jeep. My name came up for this job and it destroyed my hopes of finishing my tour in a hurry and returning to the United States to get on with a career of my own choosing or to further my own Air Force career.

I could not get out of this duty and with my infantry experience, it was anticipated with only slight trepidation. So I signed out on orders and caught a jeep ride down to Pyontaek, about 60miles south of Kimpo along the national South Korean highway.

Taken in 1951: Bill Bowman, Hal and Edward Sanet of the 51ˢᵗ wing.

CHAPTER 8

SECRET MISSION

What sort of man would live where there is no daring?
Is life itself so dear that we should blame one for dying in adventure?
Charles Lindbergh

It was a long dusty trip by jeep down to Pyongtaek along a road lined with trees. Main roads in Korea were invariably lined with evenly spaced trees. There were groups of Koreans dotted along the roadside supposedly doing repairs. It always appeared to me that the same piles of gravel were merely moved from one side of the road to the other.

The driver stopped at a guard post at our destination and we were motioned through towards the runway, with revetments that once housed Japanese aircraft. They were dome shaped concrete constructions now used for storage and beside them were some of the best looking airplanes that I had ever seen. The aluminum sparkled in the sun and the insignia of the Republic of Korea Air Force stood out against the bright background. It was rumored that a former Korean who flew with the Japanese Air Force as an ace had commanded their flying unit. He met his end when he tried to split "s" a P-51 from 4,000 feet as he used to do with the more nimble Zero.

I was assigned to a tent with six others. It was unbearably hot and the sides of the tent were rolled up to allow air circulation but made no difference at all. Retiring on the first night, I laid my trousers across the end of the bed and fell into a sound asleep. The next morning my trousers had disappeared and it was inconceivable how they could have vanished without a trace. The next night I put all my clothes under the blanket, tied my remaining belongings in a barracks bag and placed it under the bed. My billfold was safely tucked into the lining of my shorts.

The week long course was mainly devoted to learning how to operate the jeep radio and a general bit of what was expected of us on forward air control duty.

With a lull in the flying activity, I decided that the time was right to apply for the F-51 program and eventually achieve a long held dream of flying that glorious machine. In due course, I applied to be transferred to the 18th Fighter Bomber Wing as a pilot and held my breath as to the outcome of the request.

As usual, there was a great deal of spare time available to the students and much of it was spent in a small building that had been turned into a library. One day as I was going across to the library, I noticed a great commotion on the hill where our tent was located. An old Korean gentleman was digging a hole at the top of the knoll. A Korean interpreter told me that this old man had been one of the refugees fleeing before the Communists push southwards. With the hardships encountered during this long trek, his wife had died and having little time to bury her, placed her where the grave could easily be located again after the Communists had been pushed back, so he could give her a more fitting burial. I will never forget his anguished expression as he gently moved each shovel of dirt, paused and tried to explain to the Americans watching him what he was trying to do. Those who say that the Orientals are unemotional and unfeeling should have seen his reactions at this most intimate moment of grief. Even with the language barrier, his emotional pain was evident.

Since the Koreans bury their dead sitting up and facing west, burial mounds dotted the west side of the hills. Close to the base, there were many grass covered mounds sticking up from the side of the hills like small thumbs sticking out of the ground.

Truce talks had been in progress for about 15 days with very little headway toward a settlement and our school was coming to a close. My assignment came in with orders to report to a Republic of Korea (ROK) division near the central front. A number of pilots and radio operators had been lost with the Korean forces since the North Korean and Chinese divisions attacked them first as they did not hold their areas as well as the other United Nations forces. In fact, during one of the spring offensives, the Koreans broke and a flight from our squadron was given the job of strafing trucks and equipment left behind by the ROK's to prevent them from falling into enemy hands.

During the same withdrawal an area was attacked by two flights of airplanes from our squadron. During a strafing run under the control of a FAC, the controller came on the air virtually screaming to pull off the target. After landing it was verified that our airplanes had strafed our own troops and a complete report was forwarded to our HQ. The final result was that the blame was placed on the forward controller and the pilot absolved from blame for strafing our own troops. I had heard of incidents of this nature during the big "hassle" but this was the only one that I was aware of during the Korean War. However, there might have been others.

One of the requirements for graduation from the FAC school was the completion of a flight in the T-6 aircraft that were used for forward observation and spotting. On the day of my scheduled flight, I went out to an old T-6 riddled with bullet holes from enemy small arms ground fire. The holes were patched with pieces of tin. While attending the school, I saw a T-6 land and the ambulance rush out to take the pilot from the cockpit. On his first mission over the lines, with another pilot in the rear seat, he had been hit in the temple by a 30-caliber bullet and killed instantly. The pilot in the rear had flown him back to the base, not knowing how badly he was hurt. With this in mind, I viewed the venerable old T-6 that was to carry me over some of the roughest terrain imaginable and within a few hundred feet of enemy positions. The life of the T-6 pilot was certainly not to be envied.

The sea along the east coast of the Korean peninsula bound the sector that we were assigned to. It was a beautiful day with puffy warm weather cumulus clouds giving some brief relief to the ground troops. We had been briefed on a planned air strike so descending over the front lines, the pilot began taking evasive action to confuse the gunners on the ground. It was hot and the evasive action by the pilot in the front began to have its effect on my breakfast. I have always had difficulty controlling the gyrations in my stomach when being flown by another pilot. But with the exception of my first solo in the Navy, when I performed the most drastic gyrations and spins and made myself ill, I never had any difficulty whatsoever when I had the controls in my own hands. The pilot began to circle a small valley over the front line and reported what appeared to be one soldier sitting beneath a tree down in the valley. I could not see anyone down below.

A flight of four 51's arrived following the request of a T-6 pilot. The target was a small peaceful looking village on an inlet, which reportedly was harboring enemy troops. It was difficult to believe that soon airplanes would attack it and attempt to wipe it off the face of the earth and the villagers were totally unaware of what was about to happen to them. The T-6 pilot dove his aircraft over the village to positively identify it, thus preventing any mistake. This procedure was implemented after the unfortunate strafing of our own troops. He dropped a small flare, which was attached to the under wing and it spiraled down spewing red smoke, and landed near the center of the fishing village. The 51s set up a rectangular pattern similar to the gunnery pattern we practiced at Nellis, fired their rockets first, then dropped their bombs and ended by firing their machine guns. The T-6 meanwhile had moved to the south and gave instructions to the pilots as to where they should drop their ordnance, much like a coach on the sidelines calling plays to his team on the field. The Mustangs carried an amazing amount of ordnance and they methodically went about their business of destruction. After expending all their ammunition, they pulled up into formation for the return to base, when one of the pilots reported an rpm drop and his intention of going into a small rather rough emergency field just south of the front lines. He landed the 51 and miraculously managed to stop it just short of the end of the runway. We landed behind him to render assistance but none was needed. This was also part of the FAC duty.

On our return to base, we flew about 50ft over the top of a hill and below us saw the fuselage and wing of a T-6. In his let down during marginal weather on the return to base he had obviously clipped this hilltop obscured by clouds. The wreckage was spotted about a month later and a crew was able to retrieve the bodies but nothing else was brought back as it was a fairly inaccessible place. I am sure that in other areas of the theatre there are airplanes with crew remains in them that have never been found.

Just before I was due to leave for the ROK forces, a request came for volunteers to go to Japan in preparation for a secret mission. It involved parachute jumps and training. I reckoned that I had missed out on something by not completing paratroop training at Fort Benning, so jumped at the chance to go on this high priority mission. Apparently it had something to do with the truce talks and the end of the 30-day period that had initially been allotted for an agreement between the two enemy factions. It was July 1951 and feelings ran high that hostilities would commence in earnest if the truce talks came to naught.

A few hours after being accepted for the volunteer mission, I was on my way to Japan in a C-46 with two other pilots. Landing at Ashiya AFB, just north of Fukuoka we were met by an Army Captain, who escorted us to Beppu, the "Riviera" of Japan where the 187th Regimental Combat team was based. Situated on a bay of clear blue water, surrounded by hills, it was renowned for its baths and resorts and was one of the most picturesque Japanese cities.

On reaching the Army camp, we were immediately briefed on what we had volunteered for. An operation of some type involving air borne troops was being planned in the event of the imminent complete breakdown of the truce talks. The troops were ready to embark by rail to Ashiya AFB, where they would be picked up by C-119s and air dropped behind the lines. The equipment needed for the operation was ready for loading on a rail siding at Ashiya. The operation could be put into effect and troops loaded onto airplanes within a matter of hours. Word was expected to come authorizing the mission at any time. We would jump with the battalion commanders so that we could radio the Air Force or United Nations aircraft to render air support if needed. The Air Force had promised their full support and the Army had been assured of more backup than they could conceivably use. It was a high priority operation and all the supplies, troops, material, had been organized to ensure the success of the mission. This would be our first voluntary parachute jump, with a full pack and radio gear for the purpose of directing air support if so required.

The tension was at fever pitch; all leave had been postponed and attending this school meant extra hazard pay, which enticed the trainees. I now had the chance to fulfill my desire of completing jump school, which I had missed when I transferred my commission from the Army to the Air Force.

This course lasted for two weeks compared to the same month long course at Fort Benning in Georgia. Both emphasized physical conditioning and calisthenics were the order of the day, all day and double timing from dawn to reaching the barracks at the end of the day. Surprisingly there was also no differentiation between officers and enlisted men on this course. Lieutenants were subjected to the same discipline and harassment as the basic Army man. When we walked through the front gate, we were nothing more than students in one of the toughest physical conditioning schools in the Far East for United Nations personnel. It was reminiscent of the Naval cadet training, where quitting occurred only when it was physically impossible to continue or when one collapsed. For a violation of a rule the instructors imposed penalties of a multitude of push-ups. All of the pilots, including myself, were horribly out of condition as physical exercise to us had become climbing up the ladder to the cockpit. And so began one of the most punishing weeks of my life, fraught with mental and physical hardship.

The mornings began with a half-mile run to role call. The base, which overlooked the bay, was small with about 20 officers and men and a number of civilian chute packers. We did calisthenics in the hot sun until we nearly dropped. We were not timed in minutes, but quarter and half hour sessions. Breaks were devoted to relaxing, but lying exhausted on the ground trying to recoup all expended energy was not acceptable to the drill instructors. We were taught parachute landing falls; the proper stance when leaping from the airplane and the correct body posture when the parachute opened. We spent a lot of time in a mockup airplane being preached to on bail out procedures. The words, "stand up, hook up, and check equipment," are to me, still some of the most chilling words in the English language, followed closely by "stand in the door". We were taught to yell as we left the safety of the airplane and our throats were parched and dry with fear when emitting the yell.

A torture device frequently used was a high tower in one of the buildings, where we were conditioned to the opening shock of the parachute. Parachute harnesses were donned before climbing the 25ft high tower where the rookie troopers were lined up at the door and hooked up to a slack wire slanting down to an anchored post. A 12 ft long cord was fastened to the parachute and by a ring to the slanting wire. The trainee jumper fell about 12 feet before being jerked to a stop and then sliding down the wire to the ground. The tower did not appear to be too high and daunting from ground level, but as we climbed the steps, the height seemed to increase dramatically. The students were told to look out and not down as they jumped but these instructions were hard to follow and I pictured the spot on the ground where my body would be unceremoniously picked up. However, I hooked up, stood in the door and somehow managed to make an exit and fall the distance before suddenly being jerked to a complete stop, bounced and then slid down the wire. I can recall the fear of falling and the pain experienced as the cord became taut, since the straps are around the groin, ones sensitive private parts. One of the instructors at the school was from my hometown and he said that I looked ashen as I walked up to the door. Maybe I was, for I had never experienced anything quite as frightening as this.

Only once had I ever thought of bailing out of an airplane and that was when I had got lost on a flight out of Nellis, and I was sure that only the choice between life and death could ever make me voluntarily leave the safety of the cockpit, but here I was practicing for something which I was going to have to do voluntarily, and pride alone was making me do it. I had always been afraid of heights. There was no correlation between flying an airplane thousands of feet above the ground, and being in high places without an airplane strapped to ones body. One is enjoyable and exciting; the other scenario of hanging in a harness with only a silk canopy above one is intensely horrifying.

The last class of the day was held on the beach and started out with the normal calisthenics, the object being to continue till the last man fell with exhaustion.

Since the instructors routinely did this form of exercise they could outlast all but the most avid physical fitness fanatic. They were dedicated to the premise of it being impossible for the body to quit if the mind did not will it. Push-ups were the final exercise of the day and designed to sap the last ounce of energy from us. These continued until either the instructor signaled a halt or the student collapsed. Being stubborn, I refused to quit although the tempo of the exercise slowed dramatically. Finally we would double time back to our quarters. All of this physical punishment was given to us with little or no prior physical conditioning so our muscles rebelled, our bodies ached and resented every movement we made.

Back at our quarters, we fell exhausted onto our bunks to rest our weary bodies and bruised muscles. There was a Japanese masseur who for 150 yen, the equivalent of about 50 cents, would loosen our knotted and aching muscles with a fine rub down. The cooling waters of the swimming pool, along with a cold beer, also helped us to forget the trials of what we had gone through during the day.

It was interesting to listen to the stories the "old hands" told us about parachuting. A few of them had been with the original group that had initiated the airborne troops during the early days of WW 11. One of the men had over 100 jumps to his credit and wore the paratrooper insignia of a master jumper. He talked to us of his recent jumps and the many close calls that he had encountered. On one jump, his main parachute did not open and the auxiliary opened just a few feet above the ground. He had finally had about enough to do with parachutes and airplanes. It was interesting to note that many of the Army men were actually afraid of flying in an airplane, but not of jumping; the exact opposite of how we pilots felt about it.

One of the requirements for graduation from the school was to pack a parachute and jump with it. We were all shown how to pack and fold a parachute properly. The Army packers wrote their names on each chute they packed, and it was a standing rule that they would jump with any chute, randomly selected, that they packed. I took extreme care in packing my chute for the following day it was to carry me safely down to earth.

For our first jump we were taken by truck to Brady AFB, across the bay from the Army camp. The day before we had picked up the chutes packed and tagged with our names, and also issued an auxiliary chute, helmet liner and helmet. The feelings that I had as I climbed the ladder of our C-46 jump plane, were akin to the feelings that I experienced when going up the tower for practice jumps during our training; one of fear and uneasiness.

The pilots started the engines and from the open cargo door, we watched the runway pass beneath us. The C-46 gradually gathered speed and lifted into the air. It climbed for a few hundred feet before the pilot throttled back, began a turn and continued the climb until the aircraft leveled off at our jump altitude. The jump area was close to the runway and the golf course. The instructors jumped first to determine the wind and to act as ground counselors to the descending novices and also to call the ambulance if someone got hurt. Tension increased as the C-46 aircraft began its second approach to the drop area and as it leveled off, the dreaded words came from the jump master; "Stand up, hook up" and finally, "Stand in the door." We stood up in unison, and checked the back of each other's equipment. At hook up, we snapped our static line to the wire running the length of the cargo area. These static lines were fastened to our backpack chutes and were in turn fastened to our chutes by a small line that would break as the chute unfurled. The static line remained attached to the wire in the airplane and these dangled from the cargo door and flapped in the slipstream. The command, "Stand in the door," increased the tension for all.

At any time during the training, a candidate could simply refuse to jump and he would be released from the school without prejudice. This refusal to jump also applied to veteran paratroopers. No one was ever forced to jump during a training operation, but immediately after the jump plane landed, he would be transferred out of the unit so that it would not affect the morale of his colleagues. On a combat operation however, he would have to jump regardless and if he did not, he would be thrown out. The successful jumpmasters were the ones who applied a sturdy kick in the seat of the pants of those who suddenly lost their courage in the doorway. Had there been an easy or honorable way to not jump, I would have willingly taken it, but my conscience would not let me.

There was no turning back so I shuffled to the door behind another officer since we jumped by rank, with the highest rank leading the exodus from the C-46. Peering out the door, I saw the horizontal stabilizer looking like a knife poised to slice me in half, but we had been reassured that at this airspeed, of about 120 mph, there was no danger of hitting it. I heard the word "GO" and in an entirely numbed state stepped out into space.

I felt as if I was suspended and not moving and turning so that I was parallel to the ground looking skyward, I suddenly felt a tremendous shock and the canopy appeared above me. I mumbled, "Thank God, it opened." In the jump posture both hands are held over the emergency chest pack, so if a malfunction of the main chute occurred, the emergency chute could be pulled with ease. It was a wonderful feeling of relief as the chute opened and it was peaceful, quiet and enjoyable drifting down toward the golf course. The noise of the airplane drifted away and I heard the instructors giving orders to the jumpers in the air. A few of the golfers interrupted their play to watch us drift down. I was drifting off to one side of the selected fairway, so I pulled down on the parachute shrouds and slipped back to the intended landing place. Assuming the much-practiced parachute landing fall, I looked out toward the horizon and waited for the impact that came when I slammed into the ground with a bone shattering jar. The hard ground contact dispelled all peaceful feelings of the descent. We had been told that the landing fall was comparable to jumping from a second story window or stepping off the running board of a car doing about 30 mph, but nothing could have prepared me for the reality of it. We had been told to get up fast and either gather up the chute or collapse it to prevent the wind from dragging us along the ground. It was a relief to finally have the first jump over. We tossed our equipment in the truck, went back to camp and jumped into the pool where we relaxed and celebrated with beer and scotch.

Near the school were docks where American prisoners of war had once been held and worked at unloading ships. One of the airmen stationed at Fukuoka, had been a prisoner there, and in order to come to Japan again he had to sign a statement that he bore no animosity toward the Japanese people. He had no hatred for the people and was in fact living with a Japanese girl. However he did speak of one large Japanese guard who had given them a rough time, and he kept looking for him among the local crowds. He claimed that if he ever found him, no matter where he was, he would physically assault him.

The next day two jumps were scheduled, with no other physical activity to add more bruises and damage to our already punished bodies. This was to be the sole activity for the day, which was a relief to those of us who had bruises and strains. Looking at my body in the shower, I was covered with bruises particularly where the parachute harness fitted. The largest was on my chest, where the quick release mechanism touched my diaphragm.

The following morning the C-46 was waiting for us and we climbed aboard without delay. On this jump we were to exit out of both sides of the aircraft, using the same procedure and hearing the same dreaded words; "Stand up, hook up, stand in the door." It was a little easier to move to the door, step out and feel the wind stream carry me backwards, but the opening shock was greater and hurt more, probably because of the fresh bruises on my body from the previous days jump. Some of the experienced jumpers attempted to land on their feet without rolling. To do this they pulled on the risers, and just before ground contact, released them. If this were done correctly it would momentarily decrease the descent rate. If it was not done correctly it increased the downward momentum of the parachute, so it was not recommended for students.

The second jump of the day was a group jump, made in gusty wind conditions. When the "stick" of men were over the drop zone and given the signal to jump, there was no pausing in the doorway, each man stepped up and directly out into space. I paused imperceptibly at the door and the jumpmaster touched my left leg, which activated the mental process that sent me hurtling out of the door. The opening shock and descent were normal, but as I descended, I saw the jumpers slipping their parachutes into the wind to stay over the landing area. I braced myself for the landing but hit a concealed rut under the turf. A jeep or truck had driven over the area when it was wet and the deep track had dried to the firmness of concrete. My right hip, with my full 170lbs behind it, hit the rut and a shudder of pain surged through me. I was too shocked to move and the chute billowed out. A group came over, collapsed the chute and helped me to an ambulance, which took me to the dispensary at the air base. After a doctor had examined me and taken an x-ray, the diagnosis was nothing more than very severe bruising and advice not to jump for a few days.

I accepted the advice with mixed feelings. The thought of not jumping for a few days was gladly received, but the idea of not completing the course and getting my paratrooper wings upset me. The next day a jump was scheduled in the morning near Brady AFB and the qualifying jump made at Oita during the afternoon.

Oita was a former Japanese fighter base and it still bore the scars of strafing from WW 11. One of the pilots who was jumping with me, had been in the Navy during the latter days of the "great" war and had been a party to the initial landing after the peace treaty was signed. His duty was to move in to the air bases in southern Japan and burn all the airplanes that the Japanese had at these bases. It seemed a pointless destruction of property. So instead of jumping at Oita the next day, I took a jeep ride to the Army base.

When my hip returned to a form of normality there were no mass jumps scheduled, so we waited for the orders that would put us in the C-119's for the big jump that we had trained for. I roomed with an Army Lieutenant, who had his convertible in Japan and also a sailing boat. Our days were spent sailing on the bay and enjoying the summer. I got one of the worst cases of sunburn I ever had by lying out on the bow of the sailboat waiting for the wind to carry us to shore. Finally, I gave up all hope of getting ashore, dived in and swam back but not before my skin had turned the color of the proverbial boiled lobster.

All of the officers and men were under strain and it showed in different ways. After an exceptionally good meal at the officers mess one evening, the Army officer in charge of the Air Force forward controllers broke down and wept when one of the men sat down at the piano and played "The Old Rugged Cross." Tension showed with the various activities pursued in town and breaking restrictions that were placed upon us.

One evening I went out with the provost marshal as he made his rounds. One of the first stops was at a fashionable house of ill repute. A guard was stationed there and his sole duty was to turn away all military personnel from the door.

The rounds that evening included a visit to the detention house in the heart of the city, where the police were quartered. The sounds of fists hitting the unruly soldiers filtered from behind the doors. Even soldiers on restriction were seen jumping over the walls topped with broken glass that surrounded the Army camp. It was a revelation to see another side of life that existed within the normal garrison duty of the average soldier.

We watched the 187th Regimental Combat team make a combat jump while we were in Oita and it was very impressive. First the pathfinders marked the drop zone for the main body of the troops and set up a small radio transmitting station that the C-119s homed into. The C-119s came across in waves of three, disgorging their loads. The day was not without its casualties. One paratrooper had inadvertently failed to hook up to the static line, or perhaps had a defective lanyard, for his main chute failed to open normally and he pulled his reserve too late to prevent a very hard and disastrous landing. He broke his leg and was soon joined by another trooper who had landed on a pile of rocks. It was a paradox that on this mission, the chaplain who had jumped with them, was also hurt.

The following day the commander of the 187th and an Air Force General jumped. One hurt his back and the other his ankle. In one airplane there was a hundred per cent casualty rate to general officers. It was viewed as problematical that in any airborne operation, the 'heavy thinking' should probably be done far removed from the battlefield, and the brass moved forward by convoy once their troops were in place. The casualties of the general officers on that last jump may well have been the reason for the operation finally being cancelled.

With the operation indefinitely postponed, others who would be available for a longer period replaced the Air Force officers. We were sent back to Pyontaek and returned to our units.

CHAPTER 9

FORWARD AIR CONTROL

*Flying has torn apart the relationship of space and time;
It uses our old clock but with new yardsticks.*
Charles A. Lindbergh

When we returned to Pyontaek, our plans were to return to our units since the secret mission that we had volunteered for had not materialized. However this did not happen, since we had about thirty days left on the original FAC commitment and some pilots who had been kept on forward air control duty longer than usual needed to be relieved.

On returning to Pyontaek, I checked to see if my request to fly the F-51 had been granted. The paper work was given to me and I eagerly scanned the contents for the directive that would send me to the 18th FB Wing. It was a great disappointment to read words to the effect that jet experience was too valuable for me to be assigned back to the reciprocating engine aircraft.

The personnel officer for the Tactical Reconnaissance Squadron assigned me to the Commonwealth forces in Korea. This pleased me because an old friend who had preceded me to FAC duty, was now stationed with the Canadians. I was initially assigned to the British unit HQ of the Commonwealth forces

It was a pleasure and indeed quite a revelation to me, to eat in their mess and read the London Times. The breaks for tea were also a novelty to me and occasions I enjoyed. The batman would bring us tea with milk and sugar, bread, butter and jam. Each of the officers had a full time servant, as was the custom in the British Army. He was there explicitly to serve his assigned officer and cater to his every need. They were called a batman and I never did find out the reason for the name. I recall with a smile the first meal that I had in the mess. Green lamb curry was on the menu; a dish the English are accustomed to, due to their ties with India. It was very spicy, and hot with chili, and I kept the batman dashing back and forth bringing me water to quell the flames that raged in the lower part of my abdomen.

The British battalion had recently been pulled back in reserve so there was not much activity. One day, having time to spare, I drove the jeep over to see my old friend Dusty Hays, who was assigned to the Canadian unit. As we rounded a bend in the road I saw an old Aeronca Champion with a radio antenna protruding just aft of the cockpit that was having its propeller pulled through to start it. As we drove up, Dusty ran from his tent and hailed me as I jumped out of the jeep, asking me to join him in the Champion. There was an air of excitement in the camp. Dusty jumped in the airplane and without a moment's hesitation I hopped in, as recent boredom spurred me to look for any form of excitement. He checked the magnetos as we lined up on the grass strip, which had high weeds growing down each side. The width of the east west aligned landing strip was not much more than the wingspan of the little Aeronca. As the airplane lifted off the runway and turned north, he explained the mission to me. The radio in the airplane did not work and there was no way to contact the airplanes in the air. He had ordered a flight of four aircraft to strike a hill that the Chinese forces had occupied. He had made contact with the flight of four 51s and in order to identify the hill, he was going to drop a flare on it.

He handed me three smoke flares and a pistol used to shoot the flares. It was called a *very* pistol and was familiar to all pilots who had ever been on runway control duty and had to stop a pilot from landing with his gear up. Circling the hill, we saw a group of drab light olive figures moving about on it. The 51's circled to the west of us as we opened the door of the airplane and dove down over the hill. The airspeed crept over the red line and the door, propped open by Dusty's foot, caused the airplane to skid from the uneven air pressure. I fired the *very* pistol and a large red flare spiraled down to the ground. We both had our 45's and on the next dive, we emptied the magazines at the figures on the ground. It was a rather senseless action but it made us both feel better to fire at a target that we could see, although it was virtually impossible to hit anyone. Then we moved aside as the Mustangs took over and literally saturated the hill with napalm and machine gun fire. After a lengthy period of inactivity, it was good to be doing something and we spent a long time after we landed talking about the flight and the events that had transpired since we had last seen each other.

Since he was leaving, he asked if I would like to take over his place with the Canadians and have someone else fill my spot with the British, since they needed someone to fly the airplane for the commander of the Commonwealth Forces, Brigadier Rockingham. This offer appealed to me from the standpoint of having an airplane to fly and having someone to introduce me to the people with whom I would be working. In a matter of hours, it was all arranged and all that was left was to be checked out in the Aeronca.

The checkout involved showing me how to get it started and then slowing it down sufficiently to land as I had grown accustomed to coming down final at around 130 mph. Dusty had an interesting experience with the Aeronca when he got lost taking one of the Canadians to a rear area. Running low on gas, he landed on a main road near a small village. The only safe place to spend the night was at the police station because of Communist guerillas in the hills. A short period after this, the guerilla activity became so bad that the air units were diverted to an operation called "Rat Killer" in which our units were sent to hit the hills in the rear areas infiltrated by guerillas. It was one of the few times that a pilot was able to get a combat mission behind his own lines.

I took Dusty back to K-13 at Suwon, the new base assigned to us which was about 50 miles south of K-14 at Kimpo. We circled at the end of the runway opposite traffic and waited for a light to flash signifying we could land. We landed on the taxi strip and parked close to base operations. Bidding adieu to Dusty, I went back to the airplane and couldn't get it started as it had a nasty tendency to flood in hot weather. Finally after much sweat and cursing, the engine caught and I flew back to the front and my new assignment.

When I returned to the Canadians, the unit was being placed in reserve and my job was to be the pilot for the commander of the Commonwealth forces. This duty appealed to me since I would be doing a lot of flying and the job had stature of a sort. The old Aeronca was stationed at a small airstrip along with two British Osters, the British version of the Taylorcraft aircraft but with a large radio installed. It was used for directing artillery fire and observation. The Canadians were a happy lot and even in the middle of the day when I stopped in, they had whisked up squash, a flavored beverage they mixed with whiskey. Many pleasant moments were spent in their tent, which also served as an officers club and a mess.

I shared a tent with other Canadian officers and had been offered a batman but turned it down since I felt if I got used to having a servant, it would be difficult to adjust after returning to my own unit. The officer's mess was a tent, part of which had been converted into a bar, which seemed to be so vital a cog in the smooth functioning of a headquarters. After the evening meal, the officers gathered in the tent where the bar was and as the evening progressed they began to sing some ribald classics such as "Cats on the Roof Top." Vat 69 was the Brigadier's favorite brand of scotch whiskey and his bottle was placed at the back of the bar for his exclusive consumption. This so impressed me that for years afterward, I drank only Vat 69.

I recall waking up in the morning and watching the batman bringing hot water to the officers to shave and wash. The batmen were more trouble than they were worth and of constant concern to the officers they were assigned to. There was also a degree of jealousy among the officers and if one did not have a batman who religiously fulfilled all the demands placed upon him, he was the sly butt of jokes by the other officers. These jokes were to the effect of how he could possibly control his men when he had difficulty controlling his own "servant".

This all seemed a little asinine to me and from my standpoint I questioned the system. However, it may have merits and perhaps I am making a judgment on an isolated observation of the system. In any event, this custom has now been discontinued in the British forces. In the evenings, I would go down to the airstrip and fly the Aeronca for the pure pleasure of getting in the air. There were many landing fields close to the front that were designed for the small Army liaison airplanes and it was a joy to take-off and land in some of these fields. The Aeronca was being phased out of the Army inventory and all the parts were being sent to Inchon for salvage. Consequently the airplane had to be kept in good flying shape or else it would have to be scrapped. One of its faults was that the door could not be locked or unlocked from the inside and sometimes it would pop open in flight much to the alarm of the passenger in the airplane. Keeping the airplane operating required maintaining good relations with the rear maintenance area personnel.

With the faulty door that kept popping open and the tendency for the engine to refuse to fire up when it was hot, it was a wonder that we were able to justify it being airworthy.

Several times, I was called upon to make a flight back to 8th Army HQ in Seoul. This was always an experience, as I had to land on the racetrack. Since I have always added a margin of speed above the normal glide speed on final approach to allow for unforeseen variables, the landings were always hot. The approach, no matter where the wind was from or landing east or west, was above many thatched roofed houses and was no place to suffer a power failure of any kind. The final landing roll was always around the turn of the track. What one would call interesting maneuvers!

One of the airstrips near the First Cavalry division and right on no man's land was a true challenge. The landing approach had to be made over a small hill and then the airplane slipped around or over it to land. With the runway at the base of the hill, either way was difficult. The slips to a circle and landing of my Navy days came into good stead when using this particular strip. The only possible way to take-off was to the south and then follow the valley floor as it rose. It rose about as fast as the Aeronca could climb on a warm day.

One day the equivalent of a battalion commander in the Canadian Army wanted to check over his positions from the air. It was agreed that I would pick him up at this airstrip near the Army cavalry division. He was waiting as I made two passes at the field and when I finally managed to land, the airplane used up the entire runway. Shutting down the engine, we found when we were ready to go that it would not start and finally, when it fired up after much cussing and propping, the door would not shut so we wired it shut and took off. The maximum climb with two on board barely maintained the altitude gain with grade increase of the terrain. After circling the Canadian positions, the landing was the final straw that broke the staunch infantryman's flying nerve. I had to land to the south and the slip over the hill was held until a few feet above the ground and I am sure that he thought that we were going to hit the ground sideways. After that there were no more flights requested by the ground commanders, although they all had great plans to use aerial surveys to improve the set up of their defensive positions. The army men presumably felt safer being ground bound.

One of the Canadian officers had been flying as an observer with the 67th Tactical Reconnaissance Group, when the pilot was badly wounded. The officer, although he had never flown an aircraft before, successfully landed the T-6 at Kimpo. He was awarded the American Distinguished Flying Cross from our forces for landing the airplane. Although he could have bailed out and no one would have blamed him, he elected to try and land since he knew the pilot was still alive. This is an example of the fine showing the Commonwealth forces made during the Korea War and I know that the war was as unpopular with their public as it was with ours. Perhaps even more so.

The time approached for the return to my unit and my relief pilot reported in. A few days before I was scheduled to go, the airplane was used for a mission it was initially intended for. It was supposed to be Brigadier Rockingham's personal airplane and had his star ranking emblazoned on the side, but he used it only once and this was to attend a firepower demonstration put on by the ROKs. The Brigadier was a big man and it was no small feat to safely fly the airplane with such a load on board. We usually wore parachutes but on this occassion we did not because the weight factor was critical.

We took off and I planned to follow the valley to our destination. As I began to fly up the valley he asked why I was not going direct to our destination, which he thought was the primary reason for the airplane. I therefore changed my plan and flew a direct course and since I am lost about 90 per cent of the time when I fly without navigation equipment, in this case I was lost 95 per cent of the time. I finally found the landing strip, lined on both sides with other liaison airplanes of a newer vintage. There was a vicious crosswind and I vowed to make a good landing to impress the Army pilots who were waiting for their respective commanders. I landed with the left wheel touching down and running along the ground. Following airplanes had a more difficult time and the Brigadier commented that "We did a good landing." Little comments can often make or break a man and any form of praise or bit of encouragement is always well received.

My last official duty was to check out my replacement in the L-5. He was a B-26 pilot and no matter what I said or did, he insisted in making his approaches in the same way he flew that B-26 and at about the same airspeed. Finally, I got tired of the hot approaches, climbed out of the airplane and pronounced him checked out.

I returned to the rear areas of the 8th Army and saw something there that surprised me. I had heard that while in the field, the Army commanders lived under the same conditions as their men. But in the rear areas I saw large trailers that were fitted out in good taste and exceedingly comfortable. I thought about the battlefield living conditions of the rear area brass as compared to the front line troops. It simply did not begin to compare to the conditions under which the troops existed.

The trip back to the rear area was routine and so was the rest and recuperation time that I spent in Japan. While I was there I had my 45 chrome plated in the main department store in Fukuoka and with a little apprehension I returned to pick up the government issue weapon. There was no problem, and later the 45 logged many hours in the air with me while I was flying combat.

CHAPTER 10

105 MISSIONS

Every aviator knows that if mechanics are inaccurate, aircraft crash.
If pilots are inaccurate, they get lost – sometimes killed.
In my profession life itself depends on accuracy.
Charles A. Lindbergh

While I had been on forward air control duty, my unit had moved from Kimpo, K-14 to Suwon. It moved about 50 air miles from the original base in Korea because of the deterioration of the runway; one of the major problems for pilots during the Korean War. In North Korea we tried to keep runways out of commission and south of the front lines tried to keep them in a state of good repair, yet they continually took their toll of aircraft and men. During the first year of the war runways were hastily constructed and maintained. For the heavy toll that they took on men and machines it would have been more economical to have had decent runways put in at the start. Good runways at Kimpo, K-55, Taegu and other bases were not built until late in the war.

Upon my return to K-13 at Suwon, I found that the unit was firmly entrenched on the base and a sense of stability had settled into it. Both sides had dug themselves in along a narrow belt across Korea and neither side dared cross for fear of upsetting the delicate political negotiations. Nobody wanted to be killed on the last day of the war and each day might well have been the peace pact. And so the static phase of the Korean War set in. It was no longer a war of movement but a war of attrition and each side set out to make it as costly to the other side as possible without undue losses to themselves.

The runways at K-13 were in good repair; the best in Korea at that time and the pilots were appreciative of this. A wooden tower overlooked the middle of the runway on the east side and surrounding it were the tents and quonsets of the 8th FB Wing.

The summer heat was oppressive and made it difficult for the pilots and maintenance crew to keep the airplanes flying and in good shape. The pilots welcomed the opportunity to fly and escape the heat, since the cooling unit in the F-80C was most efficient. At times of high humidity, ice crystals formed and were blown into the cockpit past the pilot's face and were a welcome relief from the ground bound heat. As the airplane landed and the canopy slid back, we paid for the brief and welcome respite of cold, as the heat settled in the cockpit like a bath of extremely hot water, akin to immersion in the public Japanese bath houses.

Although I had nearly sixty missions logged in the F-80, I once again had to be checked out in it before being allowed back on combat missions. It was the same old Army game of "hurry up and wait" as the training unit was only given airplanes from the squadrons when they were not required for combat flying and thus had the lowest priority on the totem pole. It took many days to complete the number of flights required for getting recurrent in the aircraft. It was the same old story of not making allowances for the skill level of the individual pilot.

A lot of new pilots had been assigned while I had been on forward air control duty. When I first arrived there was a premium placed on pilots. Now there were plenty of pilots and a dearth of missions. Consequently the crews spent much of their time waiting around and the inactivity and boredom took a toll on their initiative and drive. The Air National Guard was heavily represented in the quota of assigned pilots and this caused some sensitive feelings among the ANG pilots who believed that the citizen soldiers were being called back to fight a war that the regulars had got them into. The majority of the Guard had been recalled to active duty and within a very short period of time found themselves in Korea flying combat.

The most flagrant violation of the reservists' rights was represented by the Marine Corp. Many of the pilots fighting in Korea had been in the Marine Corp reserve since the end of WW II and had no active duty training of any kind whatsoever. Within a matter of a few short weeks, and in some cases merely days, they were recalled and sent immediately to Korea. Some pilots had not been in an airplane since the end of hostilities in 1945 and suddenly found themselves flying combat again. There were not many regular officers represented in combat at this time and some, because of their duties, never even flew combat missions, so it caused much discontent among those who did.

A small winterized tent at the south end of the runway was home to the 80thFB squadron unit and operations clerk. It was hot and humid in the tent, particularly the afternoons, which were unbearably oppressive. When it rained and turned humid, it was like a badly ventilated cellar with flies and bugs congregating in the moldy recesses of the canvas. This was the working hub of the 80th FB squadron -The Headhunters.

My old aircraft, 659, "Kismet" had met a warrior's death. Bill Dixon was flying old 659 on a strafing mission over the front lines when he was hit in the engine section. The airplane started to burn as he approached the front lines but she held together until he was over friendly territory. He bailed out and landed in the harbor of Inchon. The rescue helicopter followed him down in his parachute and as soon as he separated from his chute, he climbed into the sling of the helicopter and was immediately pulled to safety. A feeling of sadness came over me when I heard the fate of "Kismet." A feeling probably akin to the way an old cavalry officer felt when his trusty steed finally went to greener pastures. The first airplane, like the first car, is always the one most fondly remembered in ones memory bank.

The missions had slowed down to about ten per month for each pilot and this schedule was rigidly adhered to. If ten missions were flown in the first week, then one could bet on sitting idly on the ground for the remainder of the month

K-13 Korea. Summer 1951 Fischer, Smiley, Givens, Yedmak, Rinehart, Dixon.
(Photo Bill Dixon)

with spare time to kill. Much of my time was spent at the end of the runway watching the activity of the airplanes and listening to the pilot reports following combat missions.

One day as I was walking down to the flight line, I looked up and saw debris coming down and amidst the debris, a parachute. The parts looked like tinsel as they fell earthwards. A group of us watched it and wondered what happened to the engine and if it could have be blown completely apart. The parachute drifted east of the field and the vehicles went in search of the pilot. In the club that evening the pilot, with a red ring around his neck from the Mae West life preserver, became increasingly intoxicated and belligerent. He had been flying north on a mission against the North Korean forces when he had a fire indication. He immediately bailed out of his F-84 and it exploded seconds later. He was lucky to be alive. This was all part of daily life in a war zone.

The squadron orderly room was close to the center of the airfield complex and our tents were close by, each housing from six to eight men. Normally a tent was assigned to a flight. Our flight leader at this time was Bob Given and he had his wife in the Far East when the war broke out. He was a great guy and called his wife in Japan each night via the "hot line" and talked for upwards of an hour. I was the assistant flight leader in this tent.

When I returned from Forward Air Control, many of the new pilots assigned to the unit were from operational F-86 squadrons. It was quite a come down to return to the lowly F-80 after flying the F-86. These men were later transferred across the field to the 51st Fighter Interceptor Wing where they converted back to F-86s, since they already had experience with the airplanes.

The bathroom facilities were primitive and privacy was decidedly lacking. The toilets were the common types called "privies." Around 6pm when the showers had hot water we would get in line. The water for the base came from a small stream, little more than a drainage ditch, which flowed behind the orderly room. The water certainly smelled like a drain and taking a shower merely meant exchanging one stench for another and removing a few layers of brown clay and sweat.

The missions were in support of the front line troops and sometimes an assigned mission for the day would take little over an hour. They did not seem to be necessary or have a purpose and did not give the pilots any sense of accomplishment as the missions from Japan had done.

We once flew a mission from Japan in particularly rough weather. Having been in the clouds for almost two hundred miles, we let down, and under the direction of a T-6 broke out over a battalion of enemy soldiers who were taking advantage of the cloud cover to change positions on the front lines. They were completely surprised and hastily dispersed leaving their equipment on the road, which included a 75-mm field gun being pulled by numerous packhorses. A camel was also identified among the menagerie. It was a day when we could actually see what we were attacking and since we were the only ones to strike a target that day, in bad weather conditions, there was talk of a citation but nothing ever came of it.

Since the truce talks had started, these sorts of missions ceased and by July 1951 the front had stabilized. Many of the missions were in the so-called popular places of attack: The Punch Bowl, Heartbreak Ridge and others that were blooded ground by both sides. The problem was having to follow map coordinates with the attack spot being anywhere within a 30-mile radius. When the front stabilized and flights were sent more often to the same targets, pilots began to identify points without the maps.

The B-29s had been making daily bombing sorties against the North Korean targets along the Yalu River and were usually escorted by the 4th Fighter Interceptor Wing, though few enemy aircraft were ever seen. On a particularly black day for our Air Force, a large formation of 12 airplanes, in perfect weather conditions, flew over the North Korean area with an escort of F-86s. As they pulled off the target, they were met by enemy Mig-15 fighters, who ignored the ineffective F-86 escort, flew in perfect four plane formation on fighter passes and fired their 20 and 37 mm cannon on the B-29 formation. There was little our B-29 gunners could do against these tactics since the aircraft were out of firing range. It was a meeting of WW2 aircraft and the modern jet and the B-29s didn't stand a chance.

Eight B-29s were shot down and the remainder so shot up that they landed at air bases in Korea, unable to make the long over water trek to their Okinawa base. We were assigned to patrol from the friendly islands of Chodo to the mouth of the Yalu River in search of any B-29 crew who might have bailed out of their crippled B-29s.

It was a scramble mission and we flew line abreast along the coast, just a few feet above the waves, to the mouth of the Yalu and back. We eagerly scanned the waves hoping to see a sign of life or some life rafts. Our search time was drastically cut down due to the low altitude that we were flying. Much to our disappointed we had to leave the area without finding any survivors. A "Dumbo" rescue aircraft that was also searching the area withdrew when we did because of the possibility of the MiGs returning. With sadness we climbed for home realizing that tactics would have to change, and that the bombers would either have to have a bigger and better escort, or would have to cease day missions and begin night bombing. It so happened that this was the last daytime mission for the B-29s during the Korean War.

Other than a few units, the Strategic Air Command was never committed to the Korean War, thus none of the more modern aircraft of that time, the B-36 and B-47s were used. Besides the fighters, the only other jets were a few reconnaissance B-45s. There were no targets that warranted a more potent bomber force so the Strategic Air Command was kept in reserve to counter the greater threat of the Soviet Union, which was the major pawn in the international chess game of power politics at that time.

The targets in North Korea were kept well damaged by our Air Force although there were a few areas, including Pyongyang, the capital of North Korea, which the fighter airplanes did not attack. There were two excellent airfields that the Communists reportedly used, Pyongyang east and Pyongyang west, both heavily defended, which our units were never ordered to attack.

To the novice pilot, flak held a particular fascination and a puff of black smoke anywhere in the sky made the adrenalin pump fast. The pilots with WWII experience, particularly those men from the European operations, tended to view the flak in the Korean arena with disdain. It was a matter of conditioning, as the older pilots had seen the heavy concentrations of flak that the Germans put into the sky and here in Korea, the enemy did not have the ability nor evidently the desire to commit too many anti-aircraft guns to one area. They preferred to use a tremendous amount of small arms fire, 20 and 40 mm weapons on our low flying aircraft.

I was nearing the end of my missions and new men were coming in to be trained. On one of these flights a new pilot named Yedmak, with F-86 time, was being groomed for assistant flight leader. The weather was low and the flight had to make a penetration into the overcast, which was the first time that he had led a formation in the clouds. It was not dark so there was not much trouble even though lead was a little rough. A Lieutenant Colonel was flying wing on the lead aircraft and a young Lieutenant was on my wing. The flight broke out over North Korea and we began a search for suitable targets. Our fuel ran low and finally our flight located some truck revetments. Since our fuel was critical and a penetration was necessary back at the base, we signaled to join up for the return with the

Colonel "dilly dallying" around until just before the flight leader led our formation up into the overcast. With bad weather at the base, a ground controlled instrument approach was required. The pattern must have been designed for reciprocating aircraft for the run was aborted when fuel became critical and we let down using the radio compass. Because of the aborted GCA we broke out way south of the field and I took my wingman in to land. We had less than 50 gallons and one go around would use 20 gallons. Pyontaek had 5,000 feet of PSP and we both got in on the first pass. After being refueled, we discovered that there were no starting units at the field. I made a battery start and then pulled my aircraft in front of the other aircraft, and using the jet wash to get the turbine rotating, started the second aircraft in this manner.

It was a routine return to K-13 and nothing was said to the Colonel about his slow join up, but words were dropped on me for landing at Pyontaek because of low fuel. However, it was my duty to take care of my wingman who had less fuel than I did.

Yedmak had some sort of visual advantage that made him an excellent pilot to have on a mission. He must have been far sighted for he could pick out targets that no one else could see. I was leading a mission when he identified a camouflaged truck and tank beside some native houses. I never did see them, but the way our rounds ricocheted off the thatched roofs, there must have been something substantial inside them that warranted the attack.

The railroad tunnels in North Korea hid engines and rolling stock that came out under cover of darkness to haul supplies to the front lines. They were prime targets for us. Ferreting out locomotives became a game as exciting to us as shooting down enemy airplanes. In fact, there were 'locomotive aces,' primarily the B-26 night crews. They flew night missions with no running lights and after detecting a train carrying supplies, would idle the engines and glide down to attack the trains. These locomotive busters claimed many kills. I remember seeing B-26s with all types of armaments, sometimes as many as fourteen forward firing machine guns. The units were stationed at K-9, at Kunsan, and would sortie out of K-13 on their night missions. We heard the activity of their nocturnal missions taking off and landing at odd hours throughout the night. One of the pilots was also their operations officer at K-13 and invited me to accompany them on one of these missions into North Korea.

One evening in early August, with a perfect bombers moon above us, I gathered to be briefed with the pilot, navigator-bombardier, radar operator, and gunner. The take off was scheduled for 2200 hrs. It was a little eerie going out to the airplane in the dark knowing that the entire mission would be flown with the minimum of light in the cockpit. Since I was a day fighter pilot, the idea of flying at night was not in the least bit to my liking. I climbed aboard and sat in the right seat; in this aircraft there were no dual controls for a co-pilot and the left seat pilot was in sole command of the two-engine ship.

It was cool in the cockpit and we wore heavy jackets to combat the cold. The climb to altitude was under the control of the radar site at Kimpo. Crossing over the front lines, flashes from the heavy guns on both sides were evident. Hundreds of thousands of dollars being spent on heavy artillery with men on both sides dying, and the communiqués would read that there was little patrol activity along the front. Again it made me wonder why men fight for ideologies, when in fact they might be compatible.

The crew began a routine search of the area just north of the lines. Toward the end of the mission they saw what they considered to be a truck convoy and decided to bomb the area. Having carefully checked the terrain height for adequate clearance they began the run on the target. When the first bomb dropped, all lights in the vicinity of the target went out as if tripped by a single switch. Whether or not the target was hit, it certainly stopped the truck activity. At 4am the B-26 made a lonely approach back at base. I went to my tent and the crew went to debrief.

Shortly thereafter I suggested that another pilot friend accompany the B-26 on a night mission. His trip turned out to be quite eventful. Upon their return, a heavy fog, peculiar to the area near the coast had come in and blanketed K-13. The B-26 attempted a GCA but with the light on the ground fog, it was impossible to complete the landing. There were no suitable alternate fields as all bases within the range of the aircraft were below minimums. They waited for as long as their fuel held out, hoping for it to clear and tried innumerable approaches without success. It was finally decided to make one more attempt and if unsuccessful, to pull up and bail out. The runway was sighted but the pilot was unable to land. A low visibility approach was attempted, where the pilot turned 90 degrees from the runway heading and then 270 degrees inbound.

Only a few feet above the ground, the pilot successfully completed the 180-degree turn to parallel the runway, but was so low that he struck a gun emplacement protruding about 15ft above ground. The gunner in the gunnery emplacement was killed. The B-26 began to burn immediately. The rest of the crew escaped, but all were hospitalized with serious injuries and burns. Needless to say, upon investigation, all further flying with other units on combat missions, ceased.

Our quarters were moved from the partially winterized tents, to tents with more exotic refinements such as boarding along the side of the tent walls. A stove in the middle of the tent provided heating. The latter part of fall was spent wrapped in a sleeping bag, huddled close to the stove, as there was little else to do. The food was nothing to get excited about, with ration noodle soup being a regular menu item. Hence any C rations that could be scrounged were highly prized, as they were at least palatable. Whenever I went to Yong Dong Po in the jeep I loaded up C rations from the Army depot and rushed them back to the base to share with our flight. Many nights were spent around the stove heating up cans of food, spaghetti and meatballs being a favorite. One of the squadron Sergeants never ate in the mess hall as he created his own splendid culinary delights; pheasant cooked in wine was a specialty of his.

There were very few white women in Korea, and those were mainly nurses stationed at the Army general hospital in Yong Dong Po about thirty miles away. There was a Red Cross detachment in a building close to the main runway at K-13 where the girls dispensed coffee and doughnuts. Some of the girls were older and not particularly attractive. One of the Red Cross girls was petite, attractive, blonde and rather thin. She took up with one of the pilots and they made a cozy twosome sitting at the bar each evening sharing cigarettes. One day her pilot beau failed to return from a combat mission and she was alone for a time, until a new Captain who was just checking out in a combat airplane, began to pay attention to her. Soon he was occupying the same spot at the bar of her previous beau, and when the bar opened at 4pm they would take up together in the corner next to the door.

There was a rock in the sea just west of K-13 that the pilots used to dive bomb during combat training. It was deceptive as there were no visual references for the pull out and the distance above the water was difficult even for experienced pilots to judge. On one of these bombing missions the young Captain did not pull up in time, and the seat next to the Red Cross girl was once again empty. The pilots began to wonder who would next warm the seat for by this stage it was regarded as an unlucky spot. Not much is said about superstition among intelligent, capable combat pilots, but there is always apprehension of the unknown that is not transgressed. So no more officers approached the Red Cross lass, and soon she left Suwon.

The missions were coming to an end and my total, with the B-26 and L-5 missions, came to 105. This was five more than the required duty tour of 100 missions set by headquarters and it was the criteria for returning to the ZI, the United States. The old hands fondly referred to stateside as USA Jima or the Island of the United States. When leaving the shores of the USA for combat missions there is always a thought of possibly not returning.

My 100th jet mission in the F-80 was not much of an event. There was a time when pilots were allowed to buzz the base on the last mission, and would call the tower and beat up the field. But one intrepid warrior, in an effort to impress his fellow pilots, exceeded his flying skills, crashed and killed himself. This put an end to buzzing the field and pilots were limited to a low-level pass down the runway, if traffic permitted, and not below 500 feet. On my 100th mission above the lines, I broke from the formation and requested a pass over the airfield. It was delayed and my low fuel became a problem but after repeated calls, the request was finally granted. The run down the active runway was at the maximum speed possible from the old F-80, which was .82 mach. Then a pull up to a normal entry into the traffic pattern for the final landing. I had logged 240 combat hours in a little over six months and had dispensed literally hundreds of tons of bombs, napalm, rockets and 50 caliber bullets on the North Korean countryside. What my personal contribution was toward the United Nations objective is impossible to assess and could only be matched against that of the average combat pilot assigned to the Far East. Certainly, in my mind, my contribution was above the average expected of the individuals assigned to combat.

With the completion of a 100th mission a pilot would foot the bill for a party at the club, with much merriment, toasting all around and a good many ribald songs were belted forth. As I looked around this group of friends and fellow pilots, I wondered who among them might not be going back. Ernie Dunning, Sid Millican and many others.

One of them who would not be going back was an ex-sailor. We became very good friends at Lackland AFB, had gone through Williams together and among other experiences had climbed Superstition Mountain. He was on the verge of going far in the 35th FB squadron. While flying on a target of opportunity mission and strafing an ox cart, he hit a high-tension tower and the impact literally tore off the leading edge of his right wing. He had three trusses lodged in the main spar of his wing and how he ever managed to maintain control of his aircraft was a mystery to everyone. Somehow he righted the airplane, and with full power was able to get two hundred miles per hour. He flew back to K-14, landed the airplane and later said that it stalled at 180 mph. We talked over his experience and he mentioned that his wife had been writing him upsetting letters about a boarder in the apartment next to theirs. The set up back home with his wife and boarder might have been casual but it troubled him. He was killed a few days later going in on a target. He apparently never attempted to pull out and crashed into his intended victim. He may have suffered from what pilots know as target fixation. There were a number of factors, which had they been known, would have been cause for grounding him. Firstly the fact that he thought his wife was being unfaithful to him, either in thought or in deed, but enough to cause mental distractions and secondly, the fact that he had such a close call a few days before which inwardly shakes one up. No one knew what psychological anguish he was coping with and were baffled at what might have happened to him.

Missions began to be 'just another mission' and with my 100th not far off I began to wonder what lay in store for me and if I should return to studying or try and further my Air Force career. I had investigated moving up to group or wing HQ, hoping for a promotion or further job opportunities. Around this time a request came for someone with combat training to work at Far East Air Force HQ, in the combat crew branch of personnel. This sounded like a relatively good job, so I applied for it and when I was interviewed at Fifth Air Force headquarters at Taegu, they encouraged me to apply for the job and forwarded my name. I was interviewed and got the job, starting after the completion of my missions.

Returning to Suwon I prepared to go to my new assignment. A Captain had wanted me to remain and work with the 8th but I opted for the more sophisticated atmosphere of Tokyo.

My departure was in wing's C-47 with Colonel Tipton, the wing commander, who was going to Japan. My worldly possessions were packed in a black painted rocket storage case, with my name painted in yellow. My good friend Dusty Hays was just leaving on one of his last missions and I crawled up on the wing to say goodbye to him.

It would be the last time that I was ever to see him, for he applied for an assignment in Germany as soon as his tour ended. On a training flight in Germany, he was making a pass on two British Meteors and hit the second one. He bailed out but his parachute streamed. And so a very good friend was lost, one who had been concerned and compassionate about old people and oxen being shot up during his combat tour. He was killed in an accident over which he had little control.

As we climbed aboard the C-47 for our departure to Japan, a mission was set for take off. The morning was still, clear and cool with heavy dew still on the grass. As a fitting climax to my tour, on take off one of the F-80s dropped his 1,000-pound bomb half way down the runway. The bomb tumbled, rolled and skidded to the end of the runway, coming to a halt opposite the C-47. The other aircraft took off over the bomb and continued on their mission. Once the roar of the F-80s died down, the C-47 lifted into the air and as soon as it leveled off, I crawled into a sleeping bag and awoke as the airplane began its letdown into Haneda airport, Tokyo, Japan. It was the beginning of a new assignment.

CHAPTER 11

RESPITE

*I am an American fighting man
in the forces which guard my country and our way of life.
I am prepared to give my life in their defense.*
Code of Conduct

The C-47 touched down at the Tachikawa airfield, a field close to the outskirts of Tokyo. During the war the Japanese had an underground aircraft factory at Tachikawa and when the war ended they flooded the entire underground installation. When the occupation troops took over, they did nothing with the underground facility other than putting up steel gates to keep curious onlookers away.

The approach to the single runway was over a high fence. Tachikawa was on the west side of the field and the Far East Air Material Command on the east. Each side had a base commander, and for all I know, their line of authority ended in the exact center of the runway.

I had been to Tokyo a number of times before and on the drive into the city center I was still a little shocked at the indifference as to where the children excreted and relieved themselves and how close they were allowed to walk to the road.

The spacious billets at the Riverview hotel in downtown Tokyo were excellent with clean sheets, maid service, laundry facilities, restaurants, and a bar where a combo played almost every evening. It was unnecessary to leave the facility other than to go to work. It was a paradise for the officers on rest and recuperation leave from the front.

My job was in combat crew assignments and my boss was a Captain Ballinger. The Far East Air Force HQ building was in the old Meiji building that had been taken over by our occupation forces after WW11 and had never been returned. It was a spacious building with enough room for several units to function efficiently. However, the impact of the Korean War was noticeable by the many partitions that had been erected in the various offices to adequately house the higher ranking officers. Before the war the Meiji building had belonged to an insurance company, which was supposedly eager to get it back. The Emperors palace with a moat surrounding it was right across the street and a little further down were the former headquarters of General MacArthur. He had been "sacked" by President Truman for his eagerness to carry the war to Manchuria.

After a few days at my new job I began to feel extremely tired and while holding out my hand in being introduced to someone, everything went blurred and for the first time in my life, I passed out. The next thing I was aware of was someone holding me up. The flight surgeon checked me over and prescribed some pills. The next day comments were made to the effect that Tokyo nightlife should be indulged in just a little less freely. I remained constantly weak, very tired and developed an insatiable thirst.

One morning I almost passed out while shaving and while relieving myself, looked down in amazement at coca-cola color urine. I ran, not walked, to the nearest flight surgeon and was promptly whisked off to the Far East Air Material Command hospital in a big Cadillac, certainly a prestige car to be used as an ambulance! The driver had to stop a few times as I threw up. Upon my arrival at the hospital, I was put to bed immediately.

There was no desire to do anything but sleep. Food was of no interest and a few bites filled me. The nurse brought in what I termed the "iron scarecrow" which held a quart bottle of intravenous fluids. The drip was started in my right arm but within a few minutes the arm began to swell as the needle dislodged from my vein. The nurse had difficulty finding a vein, as they appeared to collapse at the touch of the needle. I was a mess. Half hearted comments were made about this being an indication of a dope addict, which did not amuse me. Finally, with the aid of a doctor they managed to get a needle in and a quart of fluid. I told the doctor that I would eat all my food if they ceased to torture me with that fiendish device, the "iron scarecrow"! I thus made a valiant effort to force down food that was presented to me. Half an hour before we ate, all of us suffering from hepatitis were given 12 pills of various shapes and sizes, which ruined any appetite we might have had; but eating kept the 'scarecrow' device from my bedside. A few bites of food had me off to the bathroom with a feeling of desperate nausea. This was a new turn of events for a healthy robust farm boy with a large appetite

There was a cute red head nurse who had the eyes of all the troops following her as she made her rounds. True to her red hair, she was feisty and her temper was triggered by the slightest infringement of the rules. She was the one who uttered the caustic remarks about me being a dope addict.

Finally I managed to get up at a decent hour and shave, brush my teeth and comb my hair. The hospital rules dictated that this had to be done within a few minutes of wake up call when the orderly turned on the lights. I was still very weak and allowed to lie in bed until after breakfast, before trying to get down to the bathrooms to shave. On occasions I was too weak and had to use my electric razor and shave in bed.

There was no bed for me in the officer's ward so I was placed with the enlisted men. I enjoyed their company so much that I decided to remain with them when given an opportunity to move to the officer's ward. The enlisted men seemed to appreciate having an officer who did not pull rank, who received the same treatment and participated in their conversations.

A month went by and my health slowly improved. Being bed bound became torture and to alleviate this boredom I spent some time working on a model of the old Republic F-47, the Thunderbolt. It was a u-control gas model that I was reluctant to fly after completing it.

I started to believe that being in prison would be preferable to incarceration in a hospital. Later I was to find out that a hospital was infinitely preferable, in fact veritable luxury, compared to prison life.

Christmas Eve of 1951 was spent in the hospital with orders to remain in bed. Those were difficult rules to adhere to, and I got a reputation from the nurses as being a bad patient. One of the nurses would regularly give patients a back rub and rumor had it that she would give them much more, but this favor never happened in my case.

There was talk of airlifting the patient's home to convalesce in hospitals near their families. I heard about this while my records were being processed and refused to be sent home; a request that was granted, and a decision that finally allowed me to achieve a goal that I had been seeking of being an ace. However, the decision was made with a number of psychological reservations pertaining to personal matters, but the war was in this area and that foreshadowed all personal reasons, and I elected to remain in this theatre.

Finally the doctor said that the size of my liver was almost back to normal and I was granted a few hours of freedom from the confines of the hospital. I took a taxi into town and the life of a flyer on R and R commenced. Tokyo is exciting with round the clock entertainment always available. It was good to be away from the hospital.

The first place that I visited was a coffee shop right on the Ginza frequented by Japanese businessmen. Every conceivable flavor and blend of coffee was available, from the thick syrupy Turkish coffee to the mellow South American type. From there, I went to a small restaurant and had some "sushi", raw fish on rice cakes with mustard sauce. Once adjusted to the idea of eating raw fish it was good, tasty food. The next stop was at the Tokyo Onsan, where one could take a hot bath with a Japanese maid to wash one down. The joys of a day and night in Tokyo were utilized to the fullest and when my ten o'clock curfew rolled around, I was ready to return to the hospital, and so was my liver.

The results of that little jaunt into the center of Tokyo set me back severely as my liver enlarged again and resulted in an extra month confined to the hospital. It gave me a new understanding of what was wrong with me and how a liver worked.

Eventually I returned to work with the intention of remaining permanently distant from all hospitals. My job was very interesting and informative and I discovered a plan that higher headquarters had for the rotation and requisition of personnel. The needs of the units were predicated on a crew and a half per aircraft. Since the fighter units were the ones mainly used in Korea, the idea was to have ideally, 37.5 pilots for the 25 aircraft assigned to a fighter squadron.

Many of my friends from the 8th called up to request their assignment when they were ready for rotation. It was one of the advantages of being at HQ and made me aware of the benefits of being on the 'inside' where decisions were made. That conviction has remained with me to this day; the higher the headquarters, the better the duty and the more chance to benefit from duty assignments. Besides the obvious advantages for better promotions it also broadened ones basic background to work at HQ and made one aware of the premise that "all debris rolls downhill" certainly applied to HQ duty.

It was good to be involved with flying again and the first airplane I was checked out in was the venerable old C-45, in which I was to see most of Japan from an altitude of about 50 feet. It was surprising how the scars of the war had not been erased from the outlying districts around Tokyo. Bomb craters were still in evidence at some abandoned airstrips as were the remains of bombed out buildings. An airstrip north east of Tokyo was still serviceable and once in a while I landed the T-6 there.

Having always been a little cautious of instrument flying, the conditions around Tokyo gave me good experience with bad weather flying. The C-45 had an undeserved reputation for having bad characteristics on instrument flight; but it was this wonderful old airplane that truly taught me the art of relying entirely on the instruments. Many times at night, when bad weather grounded other pilots, I would be up there in the soup, building time and proficiency in that sturdy old 'gooney bird'.

Cars had always interested me and the purchase of a jeep and later a Crosley sports car added much enjoyment to my stay in Tokyo. With personal transport I managed to see many sights around the vast metropolis of Tokyo, which at that time, in spite of the fire bombings, was still the third largest city in the world. With delight, I located the places where the locals shopped. On one excursion in northern Tokyo, I came across a leopard skin being sold for the equivalent of $35 in military script. I would have liked to have purchased it, but never did.

As far as nightlife was concerned, Tokyo and Hong Kong were the R and R centers of the Far East and any pleasures that one desired were available. It was with erotic pleasure that I observed, but did not partake of the various pleasures. Many a time my roommate at Riverview hotel had his bed warmed by two bodies. His girl friend was a civil service worker in the Tokyo area and they were living it up. A highlight of the week was Sunday morning brunch comprising solely of scotch and milk that was held at the women's civil service billets. The white girls and dependants of the servicemen held the Japanese women in the lowest esteem, but in most cases they fought a losing battle as many of the men had well established Japanese mistresses long before their wives came over to join them.

I witnessed the frightening scenes of the 1952 Tokyo May Day riots. Early in the day, there had been a socialist meeting addressed by Norman Thomas. Communists, who led the workers on a march to the plaza in front of the Emperors palace, where a mass meeting was scheduled, supposedly broke up the meeting. I saw the marcher's dog trotting four abreast down the street and waving banners.

The police were out in force awaiting the workers as they turned into the plaza and tried to remove their banners. It was impossible to gather them all and the banner poles were effectively turned into clubs and used as weapons. A leader began to harangue the group, inciting them to demonstrate which provoked the police to use tear gas and clubs to disperse the crowds. Waves of skirmishes occurred and after each a few bodies remained on the ground, either unconscious or seriously hurt. Soon automobiles, and later a bus were turned over, and cars set alight. Rumors ran rampant that Americans had been killed or injured and several servicemen were thrown into the moat surrounding the Emperors palace. Armed American soldiers with bayonets in place surrounded the Meiji building.

The police chased the dispersing crowd along the sidewalks close to FEAF Headquarters and looking down we watched them striking out at the protestors including women and those lying injured on the ground. Later that day, walking back to the Riverview Hotel, I carried my pearl handled 45, with a live clip in the breech and a round in the chamber.

During this time I witnessed a fire in the heart of Tokyo, near the hotel where I was staying. One of my roommates had been a B-29 pilot and a participant in the firebomb raids of Tokyo during WW 11. He said that on one raid, he could see the fires from 200 miles away. The houses were built so close together that it was almost impossible to isolate a fire to one dwelling. During my stay in Tokyo I witnessed one such fire, which, before it could be contained, burned to the ground an entire row of houses that were built along the banks of a stream. It gave me a little insight into what occurred during the height of the fire attacks on Tokyo during the war.

Having recovered from my lengthy bout with hepatitis, and settled into my new job, once again the lure of combat and the talk of the jet aces began to excite me. Major Whisner, an ace, stopped by the office and stated that experienced pilots were desperately needed and that with diligence, I could become an ace.

This was again an opportunity to fulfill my life long dream and also enable me to better serve my country; though a trite phrase, I believed it implicitly. In another era, another country, and a different allegiance, I might well have served the Fuhrer and believed in the master race. With the prospect of returning to action, I requested that I be sent back for another combat tour, which was turned down by a very kind and dignified gentleman, Col Prohazka, who I believe had my best interests at heart.

Instead of returning to combat, I was allowed to apply for a fighter unit at Johnson AFB, not far from Tokyo, where the squadron commander, James Stewart, was a personal friend of mine. It was with the understanding that I would remain for the minimum time and then reapply for a fighter unit in the active theatre. He was gracious enough to agree to this and with the contacts at FEAF headquarters, the skids were greased, so to speak.

The stay at Johnson AFB allowed me to check out and become proficient again in the F-80. There were some excellent pilots in the squadron who were far above me in almost every phase of flying ability and reality struck as to how vital it is to remain current in an airplane to retain peak proficiency.

It is only the pilot himself who can truly, and with honesty, judge his proficiency although to others he might appear to be better skilled than he really is. I had been away from fighter aircraft for a few months and my rusty skills showed when I flew with other men who had been getting their daily kicks in their machines. Their techniques were far superior to mine and it gave me cause to wonder about my own pilot proficiency and a determined will to improve and get myself back up to scratch and well honed again.

There was an old fighter strip close to Johnson AFB that was used during WW 11. It was rumored to be the base where the Japanese Kamikaze pilots were trained and where many took off on their last flight against the allied forces during the latter stages of the war. It took me many years to understand their motivation.

It was interesting to note that there were elements during the Korean War of Japanese people who protested, sometimes violently, as in the case of the May Day riots in Tokyo, against the American forces in Japan. Protest demonstrations took place very close to the Johnson AFB. Our policy was to let the Japanese handle these problems, as they did during the Tokyo demonstrations, without American interference.

While at Johnson AFB, I purchased and sold a Frazier automobile to a Japanese, at quite a good profit. The payment had to be in yen and in order to convert the yen to script, I had to exchange it with Americans needing yen. There was a base at Niagata, across the island from Tokyo, where yen had not been available for some time. So, arranging a flight to Niagata, I stuffed my flying suit with about $800 worth of yen and considering that there were 360 yen to a dollar, all the pockets of my flying suit were stuffed with currency. When I landed, an announcement was made over the public address system that a money exchange would take place at the snack bar for anyone interested. Within a matter of hours, I had all the yen exchanged for script, with the NCO and officers club taking a lot of it. The men who were keeping their mistresses and girl friends were desperate for yen in order to support their ladies in the manner to which they had become accustomed. The black market in script was non-existent; the men needed yen and I needed the cash. I valued cash at that time, and the thought occurred to me that I would have probably gone down with the aircraft rather than risk losing all those yen over Japanese territory.

There were still F-51s at Johnson and hearing them roar overhead with the pilot adjusting the pitch on those mighty Merlins always sent a thrill coursing through me. Perhaps it is a failing of getting older to yearn for something that is so close but always unobtainable. So it was with the Mustang. Perhaps my passion for the airplane would have dwindled, had I had the opportunity to fly it.

Two small incidents marked an otherwise uneventful stay at Johnson. One occurred while I was on a flight to the gunnery range. On the let down to the range, I looked over and saw that one of the tip tanks was missing. I had no knowledge of loosing it or when I had last noticed it, except that it had fuel in it on my preflight check. A lengthy investigation was conducted and a search party was sent out to try and determine where the tip tank might have dropped. Another incident was when our flight was sent up on an air-to-air gunnery mission over the sea. We flew at 20,000 feet and our patterns and scores were appalling. Out of 200 rounds on board the only one I managed to put on the target appeared as if it had been fired at right angles to the target, when the desired angle between the path of the bullet and the target should be between 20 to 45 degrees.

It was at Johnson AFB, that I witnessed the eternally dreaded fear of all pilots, a gear up landing. One of the pilots came in, touched down beautifully, and slid most of the way down the 5,000-foot runway on the Jato hooks, flaps and the front part of the fuselage. He was an excellent young pilot, though inexperienced, and with much embarrassment admitted that he no idea how he could have forgotten about the gear.

My inherent bias against regular officers was reinforced at Johnson AFB. Having seen the attitude of many officers while fighting in Korea, I was well aware of the fact that more than a few were reluctant to be in the active combat zone. There were two regular officers, in fact flight commanders at Johnson, who made no bones about wanting to remain in the safety of Japan while the war was going on in Korea. They were the types who liked their overseas duty in the Far East well removed from hostilities, in a cozy safe haven. It seemed to me, that wherever possible, the regular core officer should be doing the actual fighting and the reservists placed in combat ready backup support squadrons.

Some idea of fighter against bomber tactics was impressed upon me while flying a mission to intercept and make passes on a B-29. The interception was easily accomplished with radar vectors to the airplane. However, at the interception altitude of above 20,000 feet, the speed of the B-29 and the F-80 were uncomfortably close. It took a great deal of time to fly abreast of the B-29 for the conventional fighter pass, and then as the turn into the aircraft was begun, the rate of closure was so slow that it was uncomfortable knowing that the "enemy" gunners were shooting from the moment one came into range. Between the two aircraft, bomber and fighter, it would be a toss up as to who the victor would be and get to land back at home base. It gave me a new perspective into the tactics of air-to-air combat.

Eventually all my endeavors to get into an active fighter unit and the many long over water flights between Haneda AFB and Korea, were about to pay dividends. It took another three flights to the 51st FIW in Korea to lay the final plans for my eventual transfer to their unit. The group commander of the 51st gave me every assurance that I could be used. The orders were finally received and my assignment to Korea was confirmed. The talk of aces and aerial combat once again captured my imagination. The opportunity for fulfilling a long held dream now lay before me.

CHAPTER 12

INDOCTRINATION

Nor law, nor duty bade me fight,
Nor public men, nor cheering crowds,
A lonely impulse of delight
Drove me to this tumult in the clouds.
W.B.Yeats

I again found myself traveling the same road that I had done on my initial arrival in the Far East. I came through FEAMCOM and then an airlift to Suwon in Korea, the place where I had finished my last missions. There is a theory that everything travels in circles and I had done exactly that by stepping off the airplane once again in Suwon. It was September 1952.

Fall was in the air, with pleasantly warm days and cool nights with frost. The climate was much like Iowa and it reminded me of the cool fall days of corn picking and combines harvesting the beans. Now instead of a cold tractor cab, I had the heated cockpit of a jet.

There were six squadrons, comprising a total of two wings that were utilizing the base. Across to the east was my old wing, the 8th Fighter-Bomber Wing, still flying F-80s. On the west side of the runway was the 51st, flying F-86s, which at that time were the most advanced of our jets and the only modern aircraft we had in the Korean War. All other types of aircraft were obsolete compared to the standards and performance of the enemy aircraft. In some cases the MiGs performance made the F-86 appear obsolete. Both sides matched themselves in combat supposedly to save this small part of the world for democracy or tyranny, depending upon which side one supported.

The F-86 was designed and built by North American and financed wholly by them, since the basic research for the airplane had taken place right after the Great War of the 40s. North American gambled on the fact that a need would arise for a high performance fighter and interceptor, along the lines of the famous Mustang.

It was rumored that the F-86 came from a common parentage with the MiG. At the end of WW 11 and the disintegration of Germany, the Americans obtained the designs of the swept wing aircraft that the Germans had intended to produce. The Russians got the German design engineers and the Americans got the plans. So in the Korean air war, the two aircraft with common ancestry but sporting different tail designs, met and waged combat in the name of freedom for both sides, in the cold skies over North Korea, to supposedly decide the fate of a nation.

Having arrived at the 51st, I got the chance for much needed rest while waiting for the necessary orders to be cut sending me back to Tsuicki where pilots went through a F-86 ground school. My days were spent reading, sleeping, thinking about the situation we were in and listening to the roar of the F-86s taking off and returning from missions. A number of pilots achieved their ace status around this time and it was inspiring to be around them, listening to them talk and describing their missions and combat tactics and also meeting and talking to the ground crews who tended their airplanes.

After a few days at the base I became familiar with the squadron, and the orders were finally cut sending me to the reserve base at Tsuicki, where the mobile training unit was situated and where the rear area maintenance facility was located for the 51st FIW. Tsuicki, on the southern most island of Japan, was where all the troops were sent to become familiar with the weapon of the moment, the dauntless F-86.

Tsuicki was close to the sea and the approach to one runway was made over the water. If one hit short, it would be on the shoreline, or in the water. The main runway was of pierced steel planking with only a few thousand feet of actual cement. It was with much interest that I went to Tsuicki to check out in the new airplane and learn the new systems. One lad who was teaching in the school was an enlisted man from my hometown back in Iowa. It made it more enjoyable having someone there whom I knew and was pleasant company.

There was not much to do when not attending class. There was a little town, about three miles from the base that was the main center of entertainment. It had a dance hall that also happened to be a center of prostitution. The hostesses were there to be danced with and slept with in an adjacent hotel where all the "call girls" stayed. This establishment and the hotel were the mainstay of the economy in this little community. The other source of revenue seemed to be from the GI's wallets as many kept their "cobitas" or Japanese wives here.

It was here that I bought a light and efficient Japanese bicycle to get around the area when not in class, as it was preferable to walking. It ended up on a C-119 as part of the cargo when I returned to Korea, where it provided many hours of time saved in walking. I used it for about a month until the days became chilly, whereupon I sold it to a Sergeant in the 51st FIW.

The systems of the F-86 were diffuse, complicated and according to all reports, highly efficient. We sat through a week of school covering all aspects of the airplane. It was interesting, informative and I was amazed at the complexity of the various systems. It seemed to me that unless the ordinary pilot was an engineering officer, that he had no more need to know all the intricate details, which were soon forgotten, than he would need to know why a 4th of July skyrocket goes up when a match is held to its fuse. It would be nice to know everything about an aircraft but practically impossible to retain all the information without constant study and repetition of the material in the pilots handbook.

The F-86 was an airplane conceived of by free enterprise and it was in competition with the best that the Communist world had to offer in the skies over a country that few people had any inkling of its existence until world news headlines brought it into public focus. It was a tribute to mans irrationality.

As a diversion, I often went down to the line and watched the work being done on some of the gallant birds that had done yeoman service in the skies over Korea. These were the aircraft that had been able to fly back to the rear base in Japan to be repaired. Many other aircraft were too badly damaged to make the long flight over water to Japan and were salvaged in Korea. Then, of course there were always the airplanes that had left their mark as a burned patch on the ground with nothing left of them at all. These accidents were inevitable and usually happened in accelerated peacetime operations and were now more prevalent because of the additional hazard in flying combat missions and also the psychological factors of fear taking its toll. In times of stress, the best and the worst traits are brought out in men. Fortunately, stress brings out the best in the majority of men. In the Tsuicki maintenance hangar, there were airplanes that had been damaged by the enemy but there were far more airplanes damaged in non-combat situations by the pilots who flew them.

At the completion of the school, we had to put our names on a schedule to get ourselves back to Korea. After a lengthy wait I finally managed to cadge a ride on a C-119 bound for Suwon, that had picked up supplies for the base.

The place looked much the same, still dusty, with a few new buildings adding a more permanent look to the airfield. There were more gun emplacements and more aircraft. The area had the look of over two years of war in a stationary area. The men's need for a sense of security was apparent in the permanency of the structures and in the fine officers club that was built on the 8th side. Because of the additional aircraft, there was almost constant activity, with the runways in use at all times. There was a flight of aircraft landing as we arrived and the leader had a dirty black nose from firing his guns. That night the world might read of another enemy aircraft shot down or damaged. If the pilot was one of those who already had a number of victories, then his name would be mentioned in the dispatches and perhaps even a feature article would be written about him. That was the reward the victorious pilot would reap for doing his job well.

After attending the school and the mobile training unit, I was ready for my checkout in the F-86. But first the inevitable questionnaires on the aircraft had to be completed. This was paper information indicating on my records in the event of an accident that I was at least familiar with the airplane and systems. There was a distinct lack of urgency in my checkout due to the backlog of pilots that had been assigned to the squadron. I was assigned to C flight of the 39th FIS and a member of this flight took me aside and helped me with the questionnaire answers and went through the procedures for a field checkout. One of the requirements was a front seat and back seat ride in the T-33, the two-seat version of the F-80. I had no problem with that since I already had approximately 240 hours of combat in the F-80

As the impending checkout in the F-86 approached, I developed an entirely irrational mental quirk. The F-80 had straight wings and the F-86 had swept wings.

I thought that looking out of the cockpit and not seeing the wing in the usual place would be a mental barrier and deprive me of one of the visual references that I had become accustomed to when flying the F-80. After a lengthy verbal briefing and a blindfold cockpit check, I was ready to be launched into the wild blue. With more than slight trepidation, the crew chief helped me start the airplane and the pilot waved me away. Roaring down the runway, the airspeed rapidly accelerated and easing back on the controls the airplane immediately became airborne. Since the Sabre accelerated so fast, it was imperative that the gear be retracted as soon as possible. As I reached for the gear, the airplane started porpoising up and down in the air. This was the classic indication that a novice was flying the airplane. The Sabre rapidly accelerated and the indicated rate of climb speed absolutely amazed me. The manner in which the airplane headed for the wide-open sky was exhilarating and life was worth it just to be a part of the airplane for that moment. After becoming acquainted with this new machine in the local practice area, I attempted a landing, which did not feel right, so did a go around. The first flight was completed. It felt good.

After my initial introduction to the F-86 there were flights to familiarize me with combat formation and tactics. The last flight before being assigned as combat ready was north of the 38th parallel up and around the Chongju River in order to familiarize the new pilots with the front line and the combat area. I was finally able to say that I was now combat ready in the much vaunted F-86 and ready to seek the foe. It was an interesting situation, to finally be here and ready for the goal that I had dreamed of for so long. It was now within in my grasp; that of being in combat with other aircraft and being given the opportunity to shoot or be shot at or as the ancient Greeks have been quoted as saying, "I will return either with my shield or on it." It was harvest time. I had striven for this chance and the time would not be wasted. A golden opportunity lay ahead of me.

The final flight of the combat crew training school was crossing over the lines which never failed to give me a peculiar feeling of being completely dependant upon the engine. It was a time of realization of ones total dependence upon things mechanical and ones senses became fine-tuned and more acute listening with rapt attention to the roar of the engine. I was always aware of the quickening of my pulse as the front lines passed beneath me. This final flight was the key that opened the door to the main combat arena, where we bartered our lives against those of enemy pilots.

Having finished the combat crew training program, I was placed on alert status ready to make my mark. It was squadron policy to fly a new man in the flight on a combat mission as soon as possible after graduation. And so within a few days after being combat ready, I was on my way to my 106th combat mission. The flight was uneventful with the leader giving me valuable guidance. Because this flight was an indoctrination flight not very far north of the fighting line, and not where the flights tangled with the enemy, only two aircraft were sent aloft.

Usually the leader of a two-ship flight was a combat veteran who just had a few missions to go before returning to the states. During my flight, the leader called off the various areas, such as the mouth of the Chong-chon River, and the capital of North Korea, at Pyongyang. From 30,000 feet he pointed out the site of the peace talks, Kaesong; areas where aircraft were prohibited from flying over; the Wonsan harbor, where the Navy held court and were responsible for the territory; and areas where the Air Force seldom flew.

The front lines where the United Nations men were fighting and dying were not apparent from above. The newspapers always extolled the virtues and accomplishments of the pilots and did not pay proportionate enough heed to the Queen of Battles, the infantry, the artillery, and the rear echelon troops. To the media, to die in the mud appeared mundane but to die in the air thousands of feet above the ground, was heroic and the warriors supposedly went to Valhalla. My thoughts and admiration often went to the ground troops battling in difficult conditions away from the comparative comforts of home base.

My flight leader was a young Lieutenant, who refused have his hair cut by the Korean barbers as he did not like the smell of kimchi, the strong fermented cabbage the Koreans were fond of and thus considered it beneath his dignity to have them cut his hair. He would only have it cut when he was back at a base in Japan. The squadron commander eventually ordered him to have his locks cut and I hardly recognized him with a shorn head. He had valiantly tried to seduce the enemy but in all his missions was only able to claim a few damaged aircraft. He had but a few missions to complete and before I was able to get adjusted to combat, he completed his tour of duty and the command was turned over to an exchange officer from Canada, Squadron Leader Douglas Lindsay.

The new Squadron Leader was one of those extremely rare individuals truly dedicated to getting the job done. Because of his belief that results were more important than the methods used to obtain them, those who, so to speak, sat at the head table, looked upon him with disfavor. He was my first flight commander and it was he who taught me to fly combat.

It is usually the first people who introduce one to life and procedures who have a marked influence upon their later reactions and actions to particular situations. So the flight leaders trained their men in the image of themselves and if the flight leader was good from the standpoint of aerial combat, the men were invariably good, having taken on the mold of their leader. If the leader were mediocre, invariably members of his flight would be likewise. It was apparent that little could be done once a pilot had been indoctrinated. Even a change of flight leader would not help once he has been molded and stuck in a set way. Effective pilots are made or broken in the initial training given by their flight leader. I would not have scored and had the success that ultimately came to me in combat situations had I not been trained as I was by this new Canadian squadron leader in the art of aerial warfare.

Douglas Lindsay RCAF Korea 1952
(Photo Douglas Lindsay)

Doug Lindsay had flown Spitfires in Britain during WW2. He had finished one tour, almost completed another, and was an ace against the Germans. He remained in the RCAF after the war and flew a Norseman aircraft on skis and floats around the Canadian Arctic, establishing gas caches, flying the RCMP, the Indian Affairs doctor and survey teams to the numerous northern outposts. A Corporal mechanic was his flying partner who serviced the aircraft, did the refueling and the maintenance, and sometimes even flew the rugged Norseman. Their relationship was somewhat different under these conditions than the strict rank based friendships found on a base. Doug Lindsay was a sterling man of good judgment and conviction and had a great influence on me.

He took me on my first actual combat flight north of the Chong-chon River, which bisected the area north of the front lines. Our fight ended up on the Yalu River with a number of other aircraft at 40,000 feet. My position was wingman and I stuck as closely as possible to the Squadron Leader as we circled around in the thin air. Other airplanes become visible as the flights approached each other in their orbits. The basic strategy was that one flight would follow another in a gigantic orbit over known landmarks, making a huge racetrack pattern. The theory was that if any Communist aircraft attacked one flight, the following flight would be in position to render assistance and disperse the attackers. This bright idea was conceived by armchair strategists who were intent on thinking of ways to increase the score of our side and believed that this might be one way of doing it. But the paradox of this strategy was the fact that it was based on both offensive and defensive thinking. All of the aircraft were committed in one area, each protecting the other and the tactics were merely an extension of the old Lufberry circle of WW 1 fame and merit.

During this maneuver from the mouth of the Yalu River to the Suwon reservoir, all the aircraft of the 51st FIW assigned to the mission began the huge racetrack pattern. Even the airspeed was prescribed since too high an airspeed would cause one flight to overrun another and leave a gap in the circle. As our flight neared the mouth of the Yalu river another flight of F-86s decided they would position themselves and begin an attack on our flight. As they moved into position, our only alternative was to break since any flight at this position was potentially dangerous. Our flight broke to the left. Being nervous and having very little experience at high altitude and following through a break as hard as that one, I lost the flight. We were briefed that if we got lost, to head for a point about fifty miles south of the Yalu river.

Since I could not identify the specks on the windshield as part of my flight, I called that I was proceeding to the rendezvous point at the predetermined altitude. Reaching the area, I set up an orbit to the right as briefed and soon three airplanes appeared. I rather sheepishly joined up with them and we returned to the battle area. There were no enemy fighters in the air that we could become engaged with, which made the verbal dressing down that I expected for loosing my flight, easier to face. As it turned out the flight leader merely stated that I had done the right thing in going directly to the rendezvous upon being separated from the flight. I sheepishly apologized for losing him in such a crucial area. It was a lesson that I never forgot.

I was my own worst critic and was hard on myself. Since I held the flight commander in high esteem, the fact that he might have been disappointed with my mistake was probably more effective than real voiced displeasure by someone else. I thought about that mission for a long time.

Fuel had always been a concern to me when flying the F-80s. It seemed to fairly gobble it up particularly when the fuel gage registered less than 100 gallons or 600 pounds of fuel. This fear of running out of fuel became an obsession, which was dispelled after an experience on a mission flight, led by Doug Lindsay. On this particular mission I was again flying number two with Doug. In the air over the mouth of the Yalu, number three and four became separated from us and we were on our own. We were in the combat area and the air controller near the island of Cho Do had called out bandits. (Cho-do was actually under UN control but north of the battle line.) A thrill always surged through me hearing the radar controller over the air saying, "Heads up in ...." or "A bandit train is reported north of the Yalu River", or "There is a bandit train reported in the Suwon reservoir area." Usually there was no warning at all and suddenly the high tailed swept winged aircraft of our enemy would appear. I am sure that it was as much of a surprise to the Communists as it was to us to appear in the same airspace. Sometimes these meetings were as fleeting as a chance meeting on a street in a Christmas crowd and sometimes the contacts were prolonged for hundreds of miles, before either one was victorious or the engagement was broken off.

On this particular day, the Communists had been reported in the area, specifically around Ta-Tung Kou, an airfield about 30 miles inside the Manchurian border. The bandits had been reported taking off from here and dust could be seen rising from the airfield even from the distance we were flying way over the Yalu River.

Suddenly, Doug turned his airplane northward and headed toward the Ta-Tung Kou airfield. Over the Yalu River, our aircraft floated into the sovereign territorial air of China. This was an infringement of the official written rules but certainly not of the pilot's unwritten rules of aerial combat in this theatre. Crossing the forbidden territory of the Chinese mainland, a thrill coursed through me, similar to the feeling I had when crossing the front lines. I was flying the number two position and as always it was a pleasure to fly this position on the Canadian. I prided myself on my ability to fly wing and I endeavored to remain line abreast to him, both to cover him better and to be sure that I was also covered. A few miles south of Ta-Tung Kou, we could see the alert aircraft take-off and disappear over the terrain at the end of the runway. We dropped down in a steady descent assuring us that we would overtake any aircraft and also that the rate of closure of any aircraft attacking us would be minimal. In my mind his intentions were to attack the aircraft formations as they were joining up. I kept radio silence as much as I could until I saw an aircraft at about 20,000 feet heading due west and climbing. He had evidently lost the rest of the aircraft or was an observer. Calling out the aircraft, which was about at the nine o'clock low position to our two airplanes heading north, Doug acknowledged. The sun was at the mid-afternoon position and we let down into the slanted rays of the sun. Excitement was at fever pitch and I would not have traded this moment for anything in the world

As Doug began a gradual let down to the left, he gained the ideal fighter pilot position at the six o'clock slot or right on the tail of the MiG. Our speed was so great that in order to remain in this excellent position, we reduced our throttles, a tactic not recommended in the combat area. Approaching from the six o'clock position, I called Doug clear as he approached the westbound flying MiG but he delayed his firing. I expected him to begin firing when the airplane came into the optimal range of 1,200 feet. Calling him clear again, he still delayed his firing. I thought he would never fire but when he was within 150-200 feet of the MiG, a short trail of smoke from his guns indicated that he had squeezed off a few rounds.

This was very different to what I had imagined. I had seen film where the aircraft had been literally blasted out of the air, with many of the bursts not even hitting the airplane. As we zoomed to gain altitude, we still had considerable airspeed and we both looked back at the MiG. It began to turn to the left and gradually started to spurt puffs of smoke. Diving down at about a 45-degree angle, it appeared that the MiG would crash into the ground at this angle. Just before it hit, the entire aircraft turned into a flaming orange torch and then leveled off momentarily. It was a doomed aircraft.

We now had problems of our own, though not as devastating as the problems of the unfortunate MiG pilot, but certainly one that could claim either or both of us. We were extremely low on fuel. The let down to 20,000 feet had played havoc with our normal fuel reserve. We were 200 miles from home, in China, and with a minimum amount of fuel. I had advised Doug of the low fuel situation before the attack and there was no need to bring it up again. The concern of the fuel situation led me to display little emotion over the fact that I had been in on a "kill". Some pilots flew entire tours without even seeing an enemy aircraft. No matter how the end occurs, memories cannot be done away with or the emotions connected with them.

As the aircraft that we had attacked crashed, I was asked if I had seen it go into the ground. This was standard procedure, for to be awarded a kill, someone had to have actually witnessed the aircraft crash. If this did not happen, it was very difficult to have the aircraft officially recorded as destroyed. The best one could reasonably hope for was that the airplane would be considered a probable and this carried no weight when the tally was considered for ace status. I was able to verify the kill.

Flying southbound, Doug asked me the quantity of fuel on board. With 100 miles to go, I had 100 gallons or about 600 pounds of fuel with the way the fuel gates on this particular aircraft were calibrated. He had about the same, which was comforting because normally the leader will have more fuel since he does not usually vary his throttle setting as much as the wingman does. The trepidation grew as we let down to the traffic pattern. The fuel gage registered empty as we pitched over the end of the runway, the throttle was not adjusted as we flew the traffic pattern since there was little we could or should have done had the engine quit. With a sigh of relief, our F-86s touched down on the runway. As my F-86 rolled into the revetment area, it ran out of gas. As frightening as the consequences could have been, it was the finest indoctrination experience that a pilot could have had so early in his career. After this experience, I was no longer afraid of low fuel, but always kept a close eye on consumption rate, the basic fear of jet pilots.

While debriefing in intelligence, I talked with my fearless leader and congratulated him seriously on what I had considered to be a daring bit of flying. He smiled when I told him that the crew chiefs were concerned as to why I did not taxi all the way into the area and follow their signals. They were a little amazed, and also amused when I informed them that I was out of fuel. While we were pinpointing the kill on the ground, which for record purposes was somewhere just south of the Yalu river, the armorer for my Canadian friend and leaders airplane came in and stated that only nine rounds of ammo per gun had been expended on the enemy aircraft. This was a lesson that I was to follow all the way through my combat flying; that of conserving ammunition in case of need.

I had witnessed my first kill very early in my aerial combat career. With very few missions I had learned the important lesson pertaining to this type of warfare of knowing just how much fuel would be needed to return safely, which in fact was much less than recommended or ordered in the briefings and also the value of conserving ammunition and the small amount needed to justify a kill. Those who panicked or nervously sprayed the area could easily burn out their gun barrels with continuous firing of 1800 rounds.

This was my early lesson, before there was time to develop undesirable habit patterns. The experience with Doug Lindsay had left an indelible impression on me and from this time on I became an advocate of the Lindsay type of flying, the kind that produced aces.

Soon after this experience, I was able to fire back at the enemy. It happened when I was flying number four in a four-plane flight. As the flight was orbiting in an oval pattern, midway between the front lines and the Yalu River, bandits were reported heading south over the Yalu. These reports came over the ground control interception channel utilized by our wing. They tracked and identified the enemy by the lack of responding equipment from them or by monitoring voice reports, which gave their position. I never determined if language experts actually translated their position reports or if direction finding equipment was used, which would depend for bearings on the voice emission of the MiG pilots.

Suddenly, the voice from the GCI station called, "Heads up in the Chong-jo river area", and almost immediately MiG fighters appeared at our three o'clock position and began an attack on a flight that we could see ahead of us. As they broke, the MiGs passed in front of us. The number four man in the MiG formation was behind the rest of his formation and I saw that he would pass at a position ninety degrees to me at about 2,000 feet directly ahead. Pulling the nose of my airplane up, I estimated the range and lead and fired about 100 rounds. The lead was correct but the range was apparently off. When I got back to the base, I talked to the flight leader and belatedly asked his permission to fire. A wingman had to have the flight or element leaders permission to fire and I had not done this. With the possibility that a few of my rounds might have struck the MiG, I claimed a damage based on film assessment.

CHAPTER 13

FIRST KILL

There are pilots and there are pilots; with the good ones, it is inborn.
You can't teach it.
If you are a fighter pilot, you have to be willing to take risks.
General Robin Olds USAF

I eagerly awaited the film while the entire reel was run off. The first frames were of other pilot's claims. In some cases the film had jammed or was over exposed. In many cases film was the only proof that a pilot had of kills, damages, or probables and it was disheartening to see a pilot depend upon it for his claim to fame only to find that his gun camera had not worked adequately. Finally my name came up, a few blurred frames appeared and in the distance a swept wing aircraft came into view. My tracers reached out for the high tailed MiG-15 but passed about 25ft under it. The lead was correct but the range was wrong. I saw that there was no possibility that any of the rounds could have struck the airplane. However, there had been an outside chance for a claim, if only for a damage. At least there was a record that with only a few missions I had fired my weapons in anger. Some pilots had not had an opportunity to fire at the enemy during their entire tour of duty.

As the missions progressed, my desire for a real kill became an obsession. A chance came while flying a mission with a very young blonde Swede from Minnesota, Lt Johanson. It was his hundredth and thus last mission flight. He had excellent flying skills and because of that spent almost his entire missions on tour as a wingman for the brass who came down to fly with the 39th squadron. He had probably participated in more battles and watched more airplanes being shot at than any other pilot of his age, rank and flying experience. When a wing commander wanted to fly, Lt Johanson had always been assigned to the Colonel's wing. It was still the prerogative of the flight commander to give permission for the wingman to fire and with the speed of jet combat, once permission had been granted, it was too late to fire. Also with high rank leading the flight, who would dare to ask permission to fire his machine guns as this might be construed as a reflection of the flight leaders ability and there would also be the squadron commanders to reckon with once the flight had landed. Thus his 100th mission rolled around and he had not even a damage to his credit.

There was a great deal of sympathy for any pilot who, because of his superior ability had been limited to flying wing to protect senior ranks; he had been too good for his own good. The intention was for him to get his MiG on his last flight, so Swede was placed in the lead and given a mission where the possibility of encountering the enemy was greatest. I flew his wing, Doug Lindsay flew number three and a southerner, Smiley, flew the number four position.

It was a clear afternoon and we knew that the enemy had drawn their monthly supply of fuel so the chances of contact were good. We were definitely in a mood to support our flight leader and it was truly commendable of our Canadian leader to lend his support to this flight. Many of his rank would have been too intent on building their own careers to bother with the feelings of a young fighter pilot who had diligently done his job.

As we climbed into the bright sunlight of this late September day of 1952, bandit tracks were reported near the island of Cho-do and tension increased, for a victory by Johanson would be a victory for each of us. We were all ego driven and this could easily have been one of us flying our 100th mission without a victory to take home and show the folks. The publicity would be good for the victor, as it would appear just prior to his return for a thirty-day home leave. We all wanted that for Lt Johanson and as the flight winged northward, our number three monitored the channel assigned to the 4th FIW. The controllers were more inclined to help the 4th than the control unit assigned to the 51st; hence we monitored the 4th channel as well. There had been occasions, when bandit information was known and actual battles on the go with nothing reported to the 51st.

Upon reaching the area where the bandits were reported we almost immediately spotted the flight of MiGs above and crossing our flight path to the southeast. We turned, intending to follow them, but in the turn, we lost distance and fell to about a mile behind the flight. They were our only hope and the Swede knew that, so we cleared him and he began to fire very short bursts at the airplanes ahead. I suddenly spotted four MiGs slightly to the right of our element, with my position being between the MiGs and Swede.

Informing the leader of the situation, I said that I thought that we might have to start a turn to the left but that I would inform him when. Alternately looking at lead and the MiGs, I saw them move into position at about 6 o'clock high and called a turn. They began to fire and I thought that they were not pulling lead when suddenly there was a dull "thlop" type sound and I knew that I had been hit. Calling a break as I went into it, I proceeded to make the most unorthodox break in the history of aerial combat. It was a combination of a turn, roll, split "s" and control reversal. The moment after the break is hazy and the next thing that I can recall is going straight down toward a deck of clouds below, and seeing a spinning aircraft. Disappearing into the clouds, I came out at about 3,000 feet and saw a swept wing aircraft. I was over my fright and began to get mad that I had been made a fool of, by myself. Believing it to be a MiG that I had seen spinning into the clouds, I banked around to fire on the aircraft when I discovered that it was another F-86 element. There was a spiral of smoke on the ground, all that was left of the MiG and pilot.

Suddenly a light in the cockpit struck me, indicating that my main hydraulic system had failed and that I was operating on the emergency system. Since the F-86 controls were all hydraulic, if the system failed completely there was no way to control the airplane and necessitated a bail out. Looking out on the right wing, I saw a jagged hole where a 20-mm had penetrated.

I now had problems of my own; the fact that my emergency hydraulic system might not last and I would be faced with a bailout over my base, an alternative that about froze my blood. I called that I had been hit, and began a climb to the south for home base, which was only about 150 miles away, and about 100 miles from the front lines. I still had power and rudder control so if the hydraulic system failed I knew that unless another eventuality occurred, there would be no great cause for concern. I was escorted back by the three men in the flight. They peeled off and landed while I made a straight in approach to minimize the use of the controls.

Having pulled into the revetment after landing, I inspected the hole in the wing. The missile had passed about a foot over the canopy and entered the right wing at an angle causing me to lose both my fuel and the hydraulic fluid. Altitude was the primary reason for the aircraft not catching fire. Doug came over to inspect the damage and casually suggested that it looked as if Swede got his MiG and we should give him this one because there would be plenty of opportunities for me later. This was a little disappointing to me because normally in these cases, the kill is given to the one who spins him off and I had a damaged aircraft to prove it. In some cases the downed aircraft is shared but logic prevailed and the kill was given to the one who really deserved it.

Before the debriefing the flight commander said, "You will get your MiG" and with his words stuck in my mind, very soon the moment every fighter pilot dreams of did indeed occur.

I can remember every detail of the mission and re-enacted the aerial battle in my mind a thousand times over. The thrill that occurs over ones first kill is almost impossible to describe.

My position was number two and our flight was over Kang-Ye, a point almost at the source of the Yalu River, the furthest distance from our home base, and almost to the outer fringes of MiG Alley. Doug Lindsay was the flight leader. Nearing the end of the mission, the Communists used their familiar tactic of sending their aircraft into the area when our aircraft were low on fuel. According to radar reports, bandit tracks were spotted and trains were pulling out of the station. I was pumped up and tense with excitement as I eased my aircraft up above the normal position for a wingman. This was my moment and I was prepared to move. Our flight had been given freedom of action and if I saw a bounce or attack, then the initiative was mine to take. Being determined to make the move I was mentally prepared when suddenly the air was filled with MiG aircraft like goldfish in a bowl with us being in the center of the bowl. There had been nothing but blue sky all around us and in a flash there were aircraft everywhere. With aerial combat at high altitude, it takes training to become a seasoned airman with sharp air eyes and many pilots never developed the skill of searching out and locating aircraft in the air.

It was a marvelous opportunity and though a perfect bounce was not evident I feared that the flight leader would make an attack before I had the chance, so called that I was going in on one of the enemy. I had a feeling that Doug was delaying in order to give me an opportunity to attack first. As soon as I called a bounce, I turned to the left, surveyed the scene for a moment, and saw two MiGs passing below me at about 1500 feet. Thinking that they probably would not see me, I took a chance, paralleled their course and allowed them to disappear from view. It was a tense moment when I lost sight of the MiGs and my imagination worked overtime as I visualized them zooming up and attacking my vulnerable six o'clock position. But my fears were unfounded as I spotted them going at a high rate of speed toward the Yalu River. I began my attack.

As I eased down from my higher altitude I fell about a mile behind and the loss of thrust that I experienced by allowing my aircraft to slow down for the MiGs to overtake me was difficult to rectify at this altitude. The enemy airplanes were about 4,000 feet away, and since my radar gun sight would not work at this distance, I moved the selector to the fixed position, raised the nose of the airplane, giving me a chance of hitting the MiG, and fired. Even though I was out of range, I fired for no other reason than to justify my initial bounce.

The tracers reached out in a large arc and seemed to fall around the two airplanes. The chance of hitting the airplanes appeared to be slim and they seemed to be pulling away from me. Squeezing off two long bursts, I was ready to stop the attack as we were approaching the Yalu River sanctuary. Then an amazing thing happened, the wingman who was on the left began to turn to the left and slant downward. Excitedly I called Doug, said that I had one going down and was following him. He called back and said that he would have to leave me since he could no longer clear me and that I was on my own. He told me later that he turned into two enemy aircraft clearing the deck for my action. There was nothing behind me so I continued the attack. Squeezing off bursts in an attempt to hit the MiG, I slowly got closer to it. Finally, it seemed to slow down and leveled off deep in Communist China. My airplane was bucking and rolling from the high-speed dive at full power and when I gained control of the aircraft, I fired.

At about 2000 ft AGL the MiG slowed down and began a gradual climb, which enabled me to close rapidly. The wing roll began to diminish, indicating that I was out of the critical mach airspeed area and giving a stable gun platform to use, for the range was now the optimum of about 1,000 feet. Two of the bursts went right up the tail pipe and the impact caused the tail section to light up. There was no doubt in my mind that this was now my airplane, nothing could survive the deluge of lead that had penetrated it. It seemed to fairly stop in the air as I closed in. Giving one last burst of ammunition, I rolled around the MiG to dissipate my airspeed and not let it get behind me. This also gave me the advantage of keeping him in sight at all times. Since my speed had dissipated, the radius of roll was very small and as I rolled to the right around the MiG, I got a big surprise, as the canopy was missing from the aircraft and the pilot had obviously bailed out at some time during the chase. I had been closing on a derelict aircraft, that had no pilot; an aerial "Flying Dutchman." It had obviously recovered from its prolonged dive when it reached the more dense air of a lower altitude. I dropped my speed brakes and watched the aircraft crash into a rocky mountainside in North China.

A fear reaction then set in, for during the excitement of the chase, there was no time for any thought about what might be on my tail. I knew that the flight leader was no longer covering me and I was on my own. During the chase, I had not looked back and once I had seen the MiG go in, I checked my tail. Another doubt entered my mind, as to who would confirm my first victory. This concerned me and the only thing to do was to take a picture of the smoke and strewn wreckage on the hillside. I turned and fired a burst into the hillside thus taking a picture of the area, as the gun camera operated when the weapons were fired.

This area was barren, desolate, and brown mountainous countryside without any sign of habitation. A very lonely feeling came over me. Applying full power the F-86 responded and began a rapid climb to altitude heading for home and the safety of our lines. At about 20,000 ft I spotted a white object in the sky, which turned out to be a pilot sitting back in the risers of his parachute, floating earthwards.

There wasn't time to pull the gun circuit breaker, so aiming to one side of the pilot, I squeezed off a short burst as I went by in order to register the chute on my film and get to verify my kill with certainty. I had absolutely no intention of strafing the pilot or harming him in any way but I am sure that the pilot hanging in the straps of his parachute thought that I had taken a shot at him. Moving a 100 feet to the right of the pilot, I took a good look at him. He was dressed in a wool flying suit bedecked with fur, winter trousers similar to the trousers that we were issued, and fur lined boots. His parachute was of paramount interest in that it was a ribbon parachute, similar to the German ones used during W 11. This particular chute apparently eased the opening shock and I am sure that this pilot bailed out at a tremendously high altitude. As the MiG fighter began its long journey to earth, I thought that I had seen something disappear from the aircraft, but the range was so great that I could not verify what it was. Dipping my wing as I passed, I literally grabbed for altitude with just enough fuel to get me safely home and not enough to give me any leeway in getting there.

Crossing the front lines with a feeling of elation, I contacted the flight leader verifying that I was all right. He briefly asked if I got the MiG and stated that he too had gotten one. This was team work of the best kind and though not following the accepted procedures, it certainly produced very fine results, which impressed me

Landing with the nose of the aircraft black was a sign that the pilot had fired back in anger and usually caused excitement to those on the ground and our crew chiefs. Doug met me at the airplane, asked for the details of what had transpired and shared my delight about the kill. He had taken one of the airplanes off my tail and had gotten a picture of the pilot who had bailed out and thus also claimed a victory. So we had each eliminated an airplane from the Chinese inventory.

Doug said that it would probably be impossible for me to sleep that night. His first kill came while he was stationed in England flying Spitfires and he said that he could not sleep that night and relived every detail of the battle. He was quite correct; I too could not sleep and relived every moment of the flight, every reaction, every fear, and joy was engraved upon my conscious mind with no way of being erased. That first kill made my second tour all worthwhile and the goal of becoming an ace improved by 20 per cent!

During debriefing, Doug indicated that the aircraft he claimed had been spun off and the pilot bailed out. I verified his airplane. I then waited on pins and needles for the claims board to meet and verify my film to determine whether or not they would award me the MiG I claimed. If the film was not clear the claim would be denied but there was always a possibility of being awarded a probable since it was difficult to be awarded a kill on film alone without verification from another pilot. After an indeterminable period of time, they finally made a decision. As I rolled over the aircraft, the film ran out, so there were no shots of the impact area and none of the parachute. But it did show two extremely good sections of film where the entire tail section lit up from the impact of my fifty-caliber ammunition striking directly up the tail pipe. My first kill was verified.

There was a strong possibility that the parachute I would have had on my film was the pilot who had bailed out from the MiG I destroyed but also possible that it could have been from the MiG destroyed by Doug. Thus both of us claiming a kill from the destruction of one aircraft. It would be interesting to equate all claims with the loss figures of the opposing forces. In all likelihood there would be many under and over claims.

(Further information with the figures from the Russian files has been published in "Red Devils on the 38th Parallel" by Col A.A.Germon, a Soviet fighter pilot from the Korea War era. The data in the book was taken from official archives and personal pilot reports from the Soviet airmen.)

The F-86 was a very dependable machine but on occasions malfunctions of the aircraft scared the hell out of the pilot. On one of my very early missions a mechanical malfunction gave me a real scare. I was flying the number two position on a morning mission. As we broke ground on take off, I reduced power to keep from over running the leader and nothing happened. I moved out to the side, tuned to another channel and reported to the lead that it was impossible for me to reduce power. I had no option but to keep climbing above the field, for in the event of a flame out, I would still be in a good position to bail out. The flight leader had no advice to give me so I switched to operations frequency, where the operations officer, Will Crane, said that if I placed the fuel switch in the emergency position, that I would be able to manipulate the throttle. Easing on the fuel switch, the engine immediately reduced power and gave immediate indications of a flame out. It was a touchy situation but the rpm stabilized and as long as I held the emergency fuel switch on, I could control the power. However, the fuel switch was above the throttle on the left side of the cockpit and in order to adjust the power I had to hold the stick with my knee and use my right hand for the manipulation of the throttle. It was a little awkward to do this but I managed to fly over an area where I could drop my tanks before coming in to land. With great difficulty I finally managed to make a long low approach. On landing, I switched the throttle off completely and rolled into the revetment area and off the runway.

Right after my first victory an opportunity arose for a flight to Tokyo as one of the airplanes had bellied in and they needed a pilot to ferry it to the Far East Air Material Command in Tokyo. The crewmen had raised it with hydraulic jacks and cranes and then lowered the gear. After an inspection they determined that it was flyable and requested a ferry pilot to deliver it to Tokyo. Had it remained at the Suwon base it

Hal walks away from his F-86 marked with nine of 10 MiGs he downed before capture.

would have been used for spare parts and it had more value than that. It was impossible to determine the exact damage to the aircraft so the flight was restricted to day and visual flight rules. I filed a flight plan with reported good weather conditions.

I noticed with surprise on take off that the airspeed indicated about 40 knots and my first thought was that the pitot cover was in place. I distinctly remembered removing it, as it becomes second nature to check the pitot cover. Back in the United States a good friend had failed to remove his, and ran off the end of the runway. Two hidden fears that pilots have are a gear up landing and taking off with the pitot cover on. Discovering in this case that it was only a faulty airspeed indicator, and realizing the length of time it would take to burn off fuel before returning to base to have it repaired, I decided to press on and land at Tsuicki. The runway at Tsuicki was not desirable, but would present no great problem since it would be possible to have someone scrambled and allow me to fly his wing and so gain an indication of my airspeed on final approach. Another factor that I had to contend with was that the fairing doors had also been removed and thus the airplane would require a greater power setting than normal.

The clouds began to build up over the Japanese home islands. Approaching Tsuicki, I began a let down through an almost solid overcast. Breaking out, the coast was ahead of me and I decided to make a no airspeed indicator landing without the aid of another aircraft. Since no one knew about the airspeed indicator, I was not obligated to have it fixed. That is, not obligated to anyone but myself. Making a wide passenger aircraft approach, I set up a long power final. The only indication that I had was the feel of the airplane. The runway was short but I made one of the best landings of my short career with that aircraft.

I did not want to remain in Tsuicki so asked the crew chief to see if he could locate the trouble but not to write up a report on the aircraft form. I went into base operations and filed a flight plane to Tokyo. The weather officer said that there was a thick overcast in the Tokyo area but should break out at about 2,000 feet. This was encouraging to me since a let down with no airspeed indication would have been precarious and only attempted under the best instrument flight conditions. The crew chief had done nothing to rectify the problem so I took off and set course for Tokyo along the shoreline.

I was able to get the airplane up to 37,000 feet before it stopped climbing economically. The lack of fairing around the landing gear made itself felt and in reducing the throttle, the airplane began to mush and did not maintain itself on the step, the attitude that gave the best distance, horsepower, fuel combination. With applying 98% power, I was able to maintain the 37,000ft.

I approached the Tokyo bay area around 4pm and below me, over the entire area, was a thick overcast. I requested an immediate let down from the Tokyo approach control though I preferred the armed forces radio station, which was the strongest station in the area, and besides, using their frequency one had the pleasure of listening to music as one made a let down; it relieved the tension. So, listening to the radio, I reduced the power, dropped the dive brakes and commenced the descent into the thick murk. It always gave me a thrill penetrating overcast and going from bright sunlight one moment, into dark cloud that sometimes looked like a solid brick wall. I could only monitor the rate of descent and the altitude to determine whether or not the let down was proceeding satisfactorily. It seemed like ages, before breaking out over the Japanese countryside at a scant 2000 ft AGL and I still had the problem of landing at the destination airport of Tachikawa, with its 5000 ft runway sporting high fences at both ends.

This was one landing that I would not attempt alone so contacted an F-80 that was flying locally from Johnson AFB, a few miles from Tachikawa. Explaining the situation to him, I requested that he lead me into the field for a landing. Joining him just south of Johnson AFB, I took his left wing, and in a large circle to the left entered the traffic pattern at Tachikawa. He called out the airspeed as he dropped his gear and I followed suit, quickly followed by the flaps. Over the end of the runway, just over the fence, I cut the power and the airplane settled and touched down immediately. I was extremely happy with the landing and I recalled an instructor during my early flight training, covering the airspeed indicator thus allowing the student to judge the attitude of the airplane by the sound of the wind rushing between the wings and wires of the old biplane.

With relief I delivered the F-86, changed my clothes and went to the club for some of the excellent food and service unavailable in Korea. It was always a refreshing change to come to the comparative civilized atmosphere of Japan where waitresses served fine food and tables were laid with crisp, clean, white linen. There were excellent bars, with dance bands where one could get thoroughly clobbered if so desired. I knew a pilot who had dragged out a ferry flight duty such as mine into two weeks. He landed at Johnson and was unable to get his aircraft repaired to his satisfaction, and when it did finally check out, the weather turned bad. So for two weeks, he wined and dined a nurse at Johnson AFB. It must have been interesting for each night they spent together was supposedly his last night. From all reports it was a torrid romance.

Johnson was a favorite stopping off place for many pilots and there was one civilian worker who boasted that she had slept with every Korean ace. From my experience later, she may well have slept with every Korean ace, except one.

This interlude included a visit back to the hospital to speak to the doctors and nurses who I had known while a patient there. It was actually a bit of egotism because I told them of my recent victory, to which they patiently listened as I spelled out the fight details and enjoyed another moment of triumph.

In putting together Hal's story, I had so many questions. I once asked him what it was like to be a wingman. This is what he said:

WINGMAN (Korean Air War)

A wingman is always in transition, with exceptions. After a certain number of missions flying wing, for instance 25 combat missions, an airman progresses to element leader. After another 25 missions he may be flight leader where he is qualified to lead four aircraft. With four qualified flight leaders, the flight can be its most effective when each can call out an enemy aircraft and take the bounce (attack). The other three support the attack. Depending on their position, a flight leader can become a wingman. He remains as a wingman until the results are concluded, either a kill, damage or an aborted attack then the original formation is again maintained.

It is almost always more advantageous to have new pilots out of flight school and gunnery school for it is easier to mold them into a team. Beware the dreaded multi-engined pilot.

A wingman can be too good. Chosen by the commanders to fly their wing, their chances for survival are good, since commanders are protected usually by other flights and element. However, few commanders share kills or permit a wingman to commence an attack.

RULES FOR A WINGMAN.

1. Choose your flight assignment if you can. It is better to go into combat with someone you like and respect.

2. Learn about any flying idiosyncrasies the flight leader might have. For instance making left turns off targets fostered by being right handed.

3. Take copious notes during briefing, it not only keeps you awake, but you might be the only one coming back. You may have lost the leader.

4. Maps can be your best friends. There is no place to stop and ask for directions.

5. Spend time at the bar and listen. What you learn there might save your life later.

6. When you walk out to the airplane, leave all the problems you might have on the ground.

7. Cultivate your crew chief, for he is the most important person in your life when you walk out to the airplane.

8. When you get back from a mission, have a personal way to release tension.

CHAPTER 14

ACE

Other people's errors in judgment and/or incompetence
Should have taken both of us out a long time ago.
Everyday is just a bonus my friend.
Tom "Spook" Weeks

The Official "Ace". Five Fingers held high.

Time rolled around for me to return so I caught a courier aircraft back to Korea. It was good to be back and time to try my skill at gaining more victories, and with the past experiences, others might come more easily. The vacation had given me time to reflect on recent events and I now wanted to listen to the latest war stories. It was of intense interest for me to spend my time in this way, because I could learn from each situation and re-enactment of the victories the pilots talked about. Since the men who were involved wanted to talk, it was easy to recreate in ones mind the situations they experienced, then possible to analyze the reactions and actions of the enemy. One of the most interesting speculations of the war was whether or not we were fighting oriental or Caucasian pilots. Further impetus was given to these speculations by the fact that one of the pilots had damaged an aircraft and, seeing that it was helpless, he had moved up to the side of the airplane to look at the pilot who had not bailed out. The pilot had jettisoned his canopy so our pilot was able to look very closely at his adversary. He stated that the pilot was large, had red hair, was definitely not Oriental and shook his fist at the victor.

This lent credence to the report that there were other than Orientals flying the MiG and other aircraft. We even speculated that there might be Americans who had been with the Chinese and were now flying with them and against us. This rumor was buoyed up by some of the pilots who had been flying in the Far East at the end of WW 11 and had been offered money to fly for the Communists. Speculation was that the Chinese were still paying them or that they actually believed in what they were fighting for.

Another fact the pilots were concerned with was that there seemed to be a great deal of disparity in the performance of the pilots encountered in the Korean air war. Some were excellent, and some were novices. A few of the pilots in the enemy forces had abandoned the airplane immediately when fired upon. This ludicrous action occurred regardless of the airplane having actually been hit by enemy fire. Flights that adhered to this peculiar fighter style were called "jackpot" flights. In some cases these pilots took absolutely no evasive action when fired upon and continued to fly straight and level with another airplane firing at them from the six o'clock position at the ideal range. The range varied from pilot to pilot, some preferred to be at a much closer range, from 200 to 500 feet. The kills from a "jackpot" flight were just as important to an pilot as a victory over the enemy's best planes flown by their top pilots. Roy Brown, a WW I pilot, was credited with only one victory. He downed Von Richtofen, and it was a very important victory.

Then there were the apparent masters of the game. When we came in contact with them, they would usually be doing the firing and when we managed to counter attack we were lucky to make a mark on the enemy.

Several pilots returned literally white with fear from encounters with these superior pilots. A good friend of mine, Lt Sam Darby, who would have made ace twice over, once had one on his tail. He literally did everything in the book to evade, and the only thing that he could finally do was to put his airplane into a violent forward spin and hold it until he reached lower altitude. When he did this, he had to spin through a literal barrage of cannon fire, and he was lucky that he did not hit any of it.

His basic problem was not his flying skill but the fact that the airplane he was flying was an F-86E model that was not capable of attaining the altitude of the 86F. A minor modification to the F-86F also gave it a few hundred more pounds of thrust so it performed slightly better than the E models. He and his wingman struggled to get the aircraft up to altitude, where he was usually able to break up into a fighting unit. However, once there, he did not have the necessary airspeed to either divert an attack or make one. So he was almost always on the defensive, which seldom allowed for a quick change to an offensive action. He was probably the most shot at man in the unit: and not only by the enemy. The group commander was about as MiG happy as anyone I have ever known. He always kept his airspeed up and chased anything that had swept wings all over the sky. Since he had a visual problem and a great desire for shooting down MiGs, he was dangerous to have anywhere in the six o'clock position.

Hal and crew chief Bert Simms

Darby and his wingman were emerging from the sanctified hunting grounds of China when the group commander, seeing two aircraft heading south from across the Yalu, assumed them to be hostile. He made an attack on them, firing all the way, in spite of Darby calling over the radio for him to find a MiG, and not shoot down one of his own for target practice. At the last moment Darby turned, then reversed the turn, and recognized the familiar markings of the group commander's airplane. He was almost mad enough to shoot him down but restrained his initial impulse to do so.

Since he was an ANG troop he verbalized exactly how he felt about being shot at by his own Commander. Apologies were profuse, the Colonel's film was destroyed immediately and my friend was a little more careful where and when he crossed the border. The fact that he was caught crossing the border by the group commander tempered his outburst a little but it certainly did not increase his respect for the colonel's eyesight. It is bad enough to be shot down by the enemy but a lot worse when done so by your own commanding officer, who probably would have claimed the victory as an enemy MiG fighter.

Now that there was one kill officially credited to me and having been involved in innumerable skirmishes with the enemy and listened to many verbal encounters, my chances were greater of making another kill. I returned from the first kill with a minimum of radio chatter. Another pilot on that mission was so excited that he gave a detailed account over the radio to his wingman, down to the smallest detail. I was complimented on the fact that my microphone button had remained inactive; better that it remained that way for some of the things said in the cockpit are best left unheard.

When heavy breathing was heard over the air, it indicated that a pilot somewhere was under strain, and inadvertently had depressed the microphone button. Under heavy combat engagements I always breathed heavily and usually returned with a sore throat and had to drink vast amounts of water. The sore throat was due to the rapid intake and expulsion of 100 per cent oxygen at high altitude.

My position had changed from wingman to assistant flight leader. Squadron Leader Douglas Lindsay recommended that I take over the flight when he left. It was a recommendation that I honored greatly and was very appreciative of. Our Canadian was nearing his fifty-mission mark that was considered a normal duty tour for the Canadians. He was leaving with two kills but had the hope being the first Canadian jet ace.

The flight was turned over to me but not without its difficulties, as there was a lot of pressure to have a more senior ranking man assigned as flight leader. I was a First Lieutenant and when I had initially arrived, there were only Majors leading flights.

One of the Majors who had been assigned as the operations officer was on exchange duty from the Royal Air Force and had pulled many strings to be assigned to a combat tour in Korea. He was one of the truly fine officers in the corp and was extremely well liked by the men under him.

During one of the missions that the Major led, Andy Mckenzie, the replacement for Lindsay went missing. It was a black day for the Major, as he was unaware that Mckenzie had been lost until he returned from the mission. In such cases, it was customary to send up a flight in search of the remains of the aircraft or the possibility of finding the pilot. Since the Major had led the flight, he was turned around and given the lead on the search flight for McKenzie. Just as his airplane broke ground, the fire warning light came on in the cockpit and his wingman shouted that his airplane was on fire. There was nothing he could do but pull up and bail out of the airplane. His chute popped a scant few feet above the ground. His flaming aircraft hit the ground a short distance away. He was an extremely lucky pilot and fortunate that he was such an able one, to have survived this catastrophe. It was bad enough losing a man in the flight but the second streak of bad luck left him badly shaken up. He was renowned for taking off his parachute in the air so that he could look around with less restriction.

Following this incident one would have thought that he would be given a degree of praise. As it turned out the wing commander made an illogical and arbitrary decision and decided to send the Major back to England. He stated, "We cannot have someone with such bad luck around."

The Canadian who had gone missing, was tentatively programmed to take over the flight after he had completed a number of missions and was considered competent. His loss ensured that the flight would remain mine for the time being. Not a trace of him or his airplane was found. Everything pointed to the fact that he had been killed and assumed that he would never be seen again. It so happened that I was to meet him again later in the war, under the most unusual and difficult circumstances.

Since I now had the knowledge of how to gain victories in the air and had been involved in a number of skirmishes, it was inevitable, with a little luck that I would score again. While waiting down at base operations one afternoon, a call came for a flight leader to hurry over to the group briefing room for a 'hurry up' mission to search for a downed pilot reportedly crashed near the Yalu River. Four of us received the sketchiest briefing and since time was of the essence, we were scheduled for an immediate take off and headed toward the northwest.

There was a lot of activity reported both north and south of the Yalu and again a feeling of intense excitement pulsed through me. Being subject to migraine headaches at times like these, I would get the first indication of one by getting distorted vision in my right eye. I always dreaded the possibility of getting a migraine in flight, but fortunately it never happened while I was flying in Korea.

As soon as we passed the Chong-chon River, we saw contrails approaching us from the south, well above our altitude of 40,000 feet that we had just reached. Evidently the Communist ground control interception stations were operating effectively. Assessing the likelihood of impending action before getting to the area to search for the downed pilot, I called for the tanks to be dropped. Seven of the eight tanks fell away, glittering in the sun as they dropped. It was standard operating procedure for an aircraft with a hung tank to be sent back to base with an escort. I ordered my wingman to escort the number four man with the hung tank to home base. This left the element leader, Archie Tucker, and myself alone to face the foe. It was our opportunity to find the wily MiG. Archie had gone through class 49 C and had more experience than I had in this game. He often talked of his reluctance to check out in the F-89 at the stateside base that he was assigned to. He delayed it for so long that finally his overseas orders were cut and he came over to the F-86 unit. He was one of two pilots I knew who had survived a spin on final approach. He had spent a long period of time in hospital as a result of this but it had not dulled his desire to fly.

About twenty miles north of the Chong-chon River, we suddenly found ourselves in a gold fish bowl with MiGs all around us. Fortunately when they appeared there were none in a good firing position, so we immediately started a turn to keep our tails clear. The Communists had a tendency to fire at our aircraft if their nose was pointed vaguely in our direction. Since there was little likelihood of hitting our aircraft, it was no more than a little disconcerting. Both of us decided to at least squeeze off a few shots to upset them and discourage their attack. Consequently, when the opportunity presented itself, both of us fired a few tracers in their general direction.

Several opportunities arose in rapid succession for attacks on the MiGs but as soon as I started firing, Archie would call a break to fend off other MiGs attacking us. In a matter of minutes we attacked and defended many times with neither side gaining the advantage. It was only a matter of time before both sides had to withdraw. Evidently the MiGs had less fuel than we did so their superiority waned as they gradually withdrew. This gave us more of an opportunity to pursue our determined attack. Turning to the left, our element dropped down on a flight of two that were heading north to the sanctuary. We were at about 40,000 feet and for the attack positioned myself directly behind the MiG at the ideal range of about 600 feet. Before I could settle down to fire, the MiG pulled up and over in an almost perfect loop. My F-86 floundered around the top of the loop and only made it because of the excessive speed of the initial attack. I squeezed off a short burst to prevent my airspeed from diminishing from the recoil of the guns. At just this time during the attack, Archie called out that he was down to minimum fuel. Having no intention of abandoning the chase, I told him to leave when he had to, but to call me before he left.

The MiG executed consecutive loops and in so doing the advantage to me became greater as altitude was lost. Just over the Yalu River, the MiG straightened out momentarily and I prepared to fire a long burst when an object going by my aircraft diverted my attention; it was the canopy, followed immediately by the pilot in the ejection seat. He had bailed out, evidently having given up on shaking a determined aircraft that had no doubt been reported to him as being unable to follow a MiG in a loop at altitude.

During the time that I had been firing, I had not seen a hit register through the loop and the only reason that I had fired was to disconcert him as much as possible. Archie had turned a few moments before heading for home. On the ground, we talked over the mission and I told him that I had gotten the MiG and he said that he would verify it. It was later confirmed, as the pilot ejecting past my aircraft was captured on film. In this case it appeared as if the Communists had deserted a fellow pilot in trouble and this happened many times during the air war.

This second victory, besides helping to cement my position as flight leader, now instilled in me an even more impassioned desire to become an ace, especially following so close on the heels of the first victory.

The flight that I took over had many personalities in it. There was a musician, a psychologist, a farmer, a pilot who had gotten through flying school because his father had connections, and an architectural engineer. Each had particular desires and motivations for being there. It was a young flight, all of the pilots having graduated from flying school within two years, including myself. The total flying time averaged less than six hundred hours including the time spent in flying school. We were being trained in this political war that was a police action for the big show that could possibly develop. All of the men were young but there was certain maturity about all of them. That maturity happens fast with the reality that ones life is on the line. They were young and malleable and from them could be created a potent fighting force.

With this in mind, I began to form them into a team. The basic premise that I started with was to make every man a leader. The element leaders would be trained as flight leaders and the wingmen as element leaders and then as soon as they had their prerequisite number of missions flown, for everything was covered by regulations, they would be checked out in the next higher position.

Everyone was also to be checked out in the T-33. Having these men trained for the next higher position and getting them checked out in the T-33 made for a more efficient fighting unit. Consequently our unit was asked to perform more details than the average flight and it placed the flight in a position to ask for more of the good missions, such as ferrying aircraft to Tsuicki and other areas in Japan. The operations officer stated that he levied more details on our flight because we had more qualified men.

For a while, I was one of the few T-33 pilots who was also an instructor pilot in the aircraft. The operations officer scheduled me for morning, afternoon and night training periods in the T-33 as well as the required combat training that I was giving to pilots. As far as I can recall, he never wore a hat, possibly because he had such an enormous head that the size would have been accentuated with a hat. He was pushing me so hard that the next F-86 ferry flight to Japan I literally flew the coop and left him to it. When I returned, he apologized; evidently realizing that the amount of flight instruction he was loading onto me was excessive. He was one of those typical regular officers who fixated entirely upon his career.

The Colonel of the base had done such an inefficient job while based in Alaska that he was relieved from his assignment and put on the first overseas shipment. He had an air base wing in Alaska and now he was placed in command of a fighter wing in a front line area. He was literally kicked upstairs for inefficiency. One of my friends who handled the assignment of Colonel's in FEAF told me of this. The reason he was assigned to the 51st FIW was merely because a vacancy arose in the 51st around the time he was relieved of his position in Alaska. It was not until later that his records were reviewed and they found out what a miserable job he had done in there. When this was discovered, there was a campaign for his removal but he had already reported in and was in the process of taking over his new assignment. A Negro Colonel had been assigned to the air base wing, and that nettled him no end. He did much damage in his position and he lasted purely because he had good men working for and under him.

Around this time there were a lot of "The Brass" flying with the 39th FIS because we had the best airplanes. It was almost impossible to get to lead a good mission because of the time-honored tradition of giving the lead to the ranking man regardless of his ability. So it was that I was given the element lead to the wing commander on a good mission. A good mission was one between 10am and 3pm when the enemy were flying their MiG's. A good time for activity always seemed to be around the 1st of the month. We theorized that the Chinese received their monthly quota of jet fuel around this time via the single rail line connecting Russia to the airfield around the Yalu River.

It was difficult when flying with a ranking leader to do what was termed "boogering off" or getting away from the control of the Colonel so some real hunting could be accomplished. The ranking man or the "over-fed, over-head" preferred to have an extra element around, flying cover for his big fat tail. For some, I would literally go through hell, but for others, I would not deign to give them a drink on burning desert sands. Some are deserving of immense respect and allegiance, but there are many who deserve only contempt.

Being assigned as flight leader to the wing commander was a political task, given to me because he needed to be taken care of. It was what the system demanded. Our element kept dutifully in place, while the flight entered the combat area and followed the Colonel as the bandit tracks were called out. As he began a turn to the north, a flight of MiG's passed over us heading south. This was our chance, but it was not a privilege that had been given to us during our briefing. Calling lead that I was initiating an attack, I turned my element around and headed toward the south. Although the MiG's were not in sight, I estimated where they would turn north. We were lucky for the MiG's appeared in the distance, having completed their racetrack pattern. Setting up an interception turn, our element joined up with the MiG's and we opened fire. One element broke away, leaving our flight behind the other element. It was an ideal situation until they utilized tactics that were especially designed for their type of aircraft; they began to zoom up, taking advantage of their lighter construction. There was little we could do but to attempt to follow them. As their altitude increased, our aircraft began to mush under full power and it was impossible to raise the nose of our aircraft without stalling out. As their aircraft neared the Yalu River and our fuel became low, I pulled up the nose, squeezed off a burst, stalled and turned for home.

There was a light twinkle on the other aircraft's wing and tail but he continued on. I claimed a damage, the only damage that there is on my record, since there is little reason to carry anything but kills. I damaged many aircraft but this was the only one I bothered to claim for. Incidentally this was the last time that I was asked to fly with this particular Colonel.

Under similar circumstances, the third aircraft was claimed destroyed, and verified. On this occasion, the MiG ahead of the me was either fuel heavy or the pilot was not skillful, for he opted to go down after he had tried to zoom away. Evidently he was psychologically defeated. As soon as he started down he was lost, as the fifty calibers chewed up his airplane. I did not see him bail out and the MiG disintegrated on ground contact. At this point there were about 33 F-86 missions credited to me and two more aircraft to go before my desired goal was reached.

Bill Bowman was made assistant flight leader, chosen because of his high missions and his eagerness to seek out the enemy. It was a pleasure to have him working with me. He had some unusual ideas, and thus added much to the flight. On the missions that we were assigned, I liked having him as the element leader, particularly when action was expected.

On a particularly good mission, around the first of the month, Bill was given the position as my wingman. The enemy aircraft were flying and the weather was good, a perfect situation to make contact with them. Our flight had freedom of action, which meant that if an attack presented itself, the wingman had an equal right, if he saw the opportunity, to make the attack. We were a potent fighting force. In this situation, the stigma of being a wingman was erased, and thus allowed the unit to function as a team. On this mission, we were flying to the Yalu River and as soon as bandit tracks were called out on the other side of the river, we turned off our IFF equipment and crossed the Yalu into China. We knew that there would soon be aircraft letting down and landing at the airfield close to the river.

Bill and I had been on a mission before that demonstrated the teamwork so necessary to claim victories. We crawled up to the highest altitude that we could get, which was around 43,000 feet. This was in the area around the mouth of the Yalu. Struggling up to that altitude, we let our airspeed diminish and were virtually standing still in the thin air. This was inviting attack and was one of our ideas, and precisely what we hoped and planned for, in encouraging an attack.

Suddenly, to our left a flight of two MiG's appeared and immediately made an attack on us. At this altitude a turn would often suffice rather than a break to remove the potential threat from our tails. Calling a turn to the right, we reversed the turn under my directions and telling Bill to pull up his nose and fire, he was able to get some good hits on the MiG. The only problem was that at our low airspeed and acceleration capability, the MiG was easily able to outrun us. Our only hope was for the MiG to have been hit severely and forced down. We were unable to do this and the MiG disappeared into the high, clear blue sky.

It was a little like vectoring Bill on a GCA run since he could not see the other aircraft when he reversed his turn. The MiG had actually been in a firing position on me for a very short period of time and the fact that we were able to get into a firing position or turn the defensive into an offensive situation was reward enough for our element. Bill was given a damage and with better luck, it would have been a kill. This was the teamwork that the flight strove for.

The next encounter Bowman and I were engaged in as a hunting team was a little more successful. This time, we snuck across the border behind a flight of four MiG's who were letting down to land. As we crossed the border, we turned off our IFF to prevent our own side from picking up our signals. Although the official policy forbade the crossing of the border, it was unofficially recognized that there would be occasions when it would be necessary to do so.

We dropped down at a great airspeed behind the flight of MiGs, who appeared unaware of our presence. They were making their approach a long distance away from the airfield, to preclude our forces from attacking them as had successfully been done in the past. I chose the number four man of the four-plane flight. Letting down at a tremendous rate of speed, almost over the top of the MiG, I squeezed off a burst at about 400 feet. It struck the aircraft and the tail cone lit up with a bright flash. As I settled down for a further shot, I hit the jet wash from the airplane in front of me. The jolt was so great that the binoculars around my neck shattered when they hit the stick. To cap this, while I was firing, the gun sight went off and my guns ceased firing. For a moment, I thought of ramming the aircraft, hitting the high tail with the inboard section of my left wing.

This was not a random thought, as I had been giving much thought and consideration to using this tactic. The high tail of the MiG was notorious for having on occasion separated from the fuselage while under excessive G forces. There were reports of the aircraft losing the cumbersome tail and this lent credence to the fact that the MiG tail was vulnerable to attack. With this in mind, pilots had discussed ramming the airplane and considered that the inboard part of the wing was the most logical portion of the airplane to come into contact with another aircraft. It was surmised that a force applied to the tail of the MiG would disable it completely yet still render the F-86 flyable.

Thus the thought went through my mind about ramming the MiG rather than letting it get away. The thought plus opportunity presented itself as I drove my aircraft, the Paper Tiger, toward the ill-fated MiG. At the last moment, my wing slid about six inches past the tail. I did not have the nerve to complete the final action. Rolling around the airplane, which was rapidly losing speed, I checked my gun switches on the console positioned between my legs. It was off. The force from the jet blast rocking my airplane had broken my binoculars and knocked off the cover of the gun switch. Turning it back on, I completed my roll, dropped the speed brakes, reduced power and literally blasted the MiG out of the sky. The aircraft immediately caught fire at an altitude of about 2,000 feet and I waited for the pilot to bail out.

The airspeed of the MiG was literally turning it into a gliding derelict and impossible to stay behind it. Closing the throttle completely, I slid my aircraft alongside the doomed aircraft and then briefly slid in front of it. For a moment, if the pilot of the dead aircraft had fired his weapons, he could have hit me, as the range was about 100 feet. I looked back and saw the burning MiG and the surprised pilot looking down and to the side at me. The huge number on the right side was 341, and with much pleasure, I reported this fact to the intelligence officer on debriefing.

Bill called, asking for a shot at the MiG, but before I could answer, the aircraft went into a hillside in China, close to the landing field. The pilot of the doomed aircraft did nothing to save his life, for the canopy was not jettisoned, nor was he attempting to land. Evidently he was so panic stricken that his basic survival reactions froze up on him.

This kill was a certainty and mentally I was painting another red star on the side of 958. But the battle was not yet over.

Turning the element over to Bill Bowman, I joined up on his wing so that he could lead us into battle. I had had my turn, now it was his. Climbing, we saw MiGs all around us but in positions that did not invite attack. Climbing over Antung, Bill saw a group of MiGs going into the landing pattern. He called that he was taking a bounce and started down. I was right with him all the time calling him clear to reassure him as he let down into their traffic pattern. He let down, entered behind a MiG that was in trail formation and fired when his terrific closing speed brought him in range. He was going so fast that he had little time to fire and there was no chance for him to slow down and keep behind the MiG. He hit the airplane and ran since our fuel was getting very low. The airplane headed for the ground and I am sure that it crashed but I did not see it hit the ground. His film later showed a great flash of fire at the wing root of the MiG and he was given a probable. If he had said that it crashed then I would have confirmed the kill, but he too was not sure of it. The tally for the day ended up with one kill and one probably destroyed. This was my fourth kill and the fifth was not far off. I now had 45 missions in the F-86.

The fifth kill came sooner than I expected and with it a great deal of mental anguish. I have never been able to hate an individual of the enemy but I could hate the ideology that controlled them and in which they believed. Consequently, I could fight well against the ideology which was threatening our system and way of life, but man to man, I felt compassion and this fact was brought sharply home to me on my 47th mission.

A lanky southerner from Mississippi, Biffle Oscar Pittman was flying my wing. He had a great natural flying ability and had been through gunnery school at Las Vegas. It was Pittman who witnessed my fifth kill.

On this day, our flight had again been scrambled on a search mission. The only way to conserve fuel in the search area was to climb to altitude and then let down, so our flight went to 40,000 feet. The ground controller, who had been silent after we had checked in with him suddenly came on the air and told us to take up a heading due west.

We were over the Chong-chon area, about 100 miles south of the Yalu River, progressing up to a point about 25 miles from the Chinese border to see if it would be possible to find the remains of the airplane that had been reported down. A flight from the other squadron was also proceeding north with us at a different altitude, when we received the word to turn to 270 degrees.

The controller was remarkably precise. He must have been one of the very best available for he said that the enemy would be at our altitude and 15 miles ahead and that he was setting us up for an interception. Having little faith in the usual instructions, this controller inspired confidence. To my amazement, four dots rapidly became larger and merged into a flight of four MiG's on a southerly heading. It was a perfect vector and the only one I received while active in the Korean air war.

Our flight set up an interception turn and we fell in behind the four MiGs heading south. It was perfect: four aircraft behind four others. If we were lucky, everyone would take home a kill. Just as we were ready to fire, the MiG's utilized their favorite tactic — they zoomed for altitude. As they began to go up, the number two man evidently panicked and his aircraft wings rocked back and forth. Either he could not continue the climb or he chose what he considered to be better evasive action. Three aircraft went up and the fourth went down. I fell in behind the fourth and ended up about 4,000 feet behind him.

Looking through my gun sight, he appeared to be too far away for the radar gunsight to operate. So the logical action was to turn it off and use a fixed gun sight. There was only one thing to do, and so squeezing off short bursts at the aircraft, I hoped to slow him down so that I could join up with him and finish off the encounter. Judging what I thought would be the proper elevation for the range, I spasmodically fired a few rounds. This went on for a while, with no indication that I was hitting the mark. Once a spark lit up on the aircraft ahead and I called out to Pittman that I had finally hit him.

There were only two of us now, since the other element had chased the other three MiG's. For what seemed like an agonizing period of time, my aircraft gradually drew nearer to the MiG. We had been in a slanting dive for miles and were well into the northern reaches of China now. There was no one else around except the two of us at a lower altitude and Oscar Pittman at a higher altitude clearing my aircraft. It was an eerie situation.

Gradually a light began to grow in the tail of the MiG ahead of me. First a small pinpoint of light developed, like a candle on a dark night. Then it grew until it enveloped the entire tail of the aircraft. By the time I drew within ideal range, there was no need for me to expend ammunition. It was a dying aircraft.

The rate of closure was fast, and the entire fuselage was a flame holder for the now fiercely burning aircraft. Rather than fire on the MiG again, I pulled up alongside the aircraft to look at it. I wish that I had not done so for the pilot was beating on the canopy, trying to escape. The heat must have been intolerable for the canopy was changing color and the smoke was intense. Up to that moment the enemy had been impersonal, each aircraft a target that had little meaning and not associated with flesh and blood. But the sight of another man trapped in the cockpit of a burning aircraft with no power and with no place to land was impossible for me to forget.

Seeing me, the pilot attempted to turn his aircraft toward me and ram me. It was easy for me to evade him by moving out to the side. There was only one thing for me to do and that was to put the pilot out of his misery as quickly as possible. Sliding behind the MiG, the molten metal of his airplane came over me like a light rain shower and partially obscured my windshield. I pulled up the nose to fire and squeezed off a few short rounds before something happened to my aircraft.

Suddenly the sound changed and three of my guns quit firing, my left rudder pedal went to the firewall and my heart went to my mouth. My first thought was that I had been hit. But this was not the case since I knew that Pittman had been clearing my tail and I had complete trust in him. Pulling away from the doomed aircraft, I tried to assess what had happened. There was no logical explanation and I turned for the long trek home. Looking around, I saw Pittman conserving his fuel about 10,000 feet above me. He was doing his job and doing it well for there was no telling how far the chase would have continued into the sky of China.

As my aircraft continued to climb, I realized that I had lost pressurization and the effects became obvious. My stomach gases began to expand and my life raft became as hard as a rock. The change in sound of the aircraft had been due to the loss of pressurization. I was concerend that my rudder pedal was useless and the landing would have to be made without brakes.

Pittman preceded me on the flgiht home and we agreed to rendezvous over the homer at Kimpo, but his fuel was so low that we decided he would go in before I did. It was difficult to talk at high altitude without pressurization and my left shoulder began to hurt from the bends. Due to expanding abdominal gas I also had to loosen my belt. I tried everything to relieve the pressure, which included belching and breaking wind but my stomach remained as hard as a rock. It was extremely uncomfortable but the elation of coming back from the fifth kill made the pain bearable.

When I believed that I had been hit, my thought was, "Well, this is it!" and a momentary feeling of apathy overcame me. The different sound in the engine made me presume a power failure but when I discovered that I had power and the aircraft was controllable, there was something I could do about it.

I let down over the field and called the control tower saying that I had something wrong with my left rudder pedal and that I might not have rudder control and also that there was a strong indication that I would have no brakes. The fire trucks were alerted and the traffic cleared from the area. As much traffic as possible was landed before I made my approach since there was a possibility that my aircraft might block the runway for a period of time. Gingerly touching down and controlling my direction before touch down with aileron, I stop cocked the engine and hoped for the best.

Hal is congratulated by members of his squadron after downing his 5th MIG, earning him the right to be called an ace. He became the 25th jet ace.

For the first 1,000 feet down the runway, there was no problem since the momentum of the aircraft kept it going straight, following the principles of Newton's law. Since I had no rudder control, the only control left to me was the brakes. I could turn the aircraft to the right by using the right brake, but there was nothing that I could do to turn the aircraft to the left. Taking a chance that my brake on the left was still operative, I stretched my leg as far as I could and touched the moveable left rudder. By pushing it as far as I could, I was able to work the toe brake and to my immense relief, it operated.

My problem over, and using only the brake to keep the airplane straight, the F-86 rolled off and stopped at the far end of the 9,000-foot runway. Waving away the fire trucks and climbing out of my parachute, I let myself down to the ground where a jeep with the intelligence officer, public information officer and operations officer met me.

The word had already spread ahead of me that I was a new ace and a group had gathered to congratulate me on the fifth kill. Psychologically it was my finest and best hour. Everything that I had wanted, and dreamed of had been achieved that day. With an immense amount of pleasure, I went to debriefing with Oscar Pittman and described what had happened. This was all that I had ever wanted, nothing more, nothing less. I had made Ace in 47 F-86 missions. The day before, Dolph Overton had made it in 48 missions. Both of us had previous combat missions, he in F-84s and myself in F-80s.

23rd January 1953. Two aces, Dolph Overton and Cecil Foster congratulate the newest ace. Overton got his 5th MIG the day before.

Quotes from Algona press January 24th 1953

"He loves the F-86 and he loves to fly," Mrs Fischer said. "He says that flying the F-86 is fast and furious, but that the enemy MiG's seem to be wonderful planes, also." She reported that in his letters her son "says he thinks the Russians may be flying some of those MiGs over there and he wishes more of them would come out .They're so hard to get when they stay up in Manchuria"

Mrs Fischer said that she does not know the plans of her son for the future but that "as long as he can fly, I believe that he'll stay in the air force"

At his base in Korea Saturday, Fischer was quoted as saying: "I just like to fly combat. It is the best flying in the world. Being an ace feels pretty good, but I think the first one is the big thrill"

The Swea City Fischers learned of their son's latest air exploits not by letter or telegram, but by radio news and newspapers.

Their rural telephone line was kept busy all day Saturday with calls from friends and well wishers, and calls from state newspapers, radio stations and wire services.

Mrs Fischer was quoted as saying she thought her son will probably "write us about it but he doesn't say much."

<u>From a speech given by Col Harold Fischer USAF (ret)</u>
<u>July 25th 1988</u>

As I look back on the reasons why I was successful and others were not the following variables come to mind.

1. I had the itch, the fervent desire to be an Ace. This was with me from the first time I read those stories about the WW1 Aces.

2. An early experience and lesson with military life which showed me that goals could be accomplished irrespective of rules and regulations.

3. A cautious disrespect of authority unless it was based on accomplishments and judgements.

4. The knowledge that air power is part of the team effort and is inefficient in deciding a conflict alone.

5. Being trained by a "warrior", in my case Squadron Leader Douglas Lindsay caused me to become an Ace. If I had been trained by an American with the prevailing mentality of the 50's it would have been difficult if not impossible.

6. Conserving fuel and ammunition for when you need them is paramount.

7. Obey the rules that meet your needs and always have an explanation for whatever happens…that's the most important.

Iowa's leading newspaper, The De Moines Register, not only reported Hal's success in Korea, but it's chief cartoonist, Bob Artley also penned tributes to him.

*Iowa cartoonist, Bob Artley's depiction of Lt. Fischer.
February 1953.*

CHAPTER 15

BAIL OUT

I just like to fly combat. It is the best flying in the world.
Being an ace feels pretty good, but I think the first one is the big thrill
Hal Fischer ...Jan 24th 1953

I had achieved all that I had originally dreamed of. Now it was time to assess just what I wanted to do. With the acedom had come a telegram from Lt General Barcus commander of the 5th Air Force wishing me success in my endeavors and hoping that I would continue the good work. Publicity was circulated and I found that I was the 25th ace of the Korean conflict, within 47 combat missions. It was difficult to guess how many more aces would follow. Had I had my way, and had I been a free agent to choose just what I wanted to do, I probably would have gone home at that time as I had achieved exactly what I had striven for and there seemed to be no more reason for me to continue to fight. It would make no difference to the general outcome of the war if I shot down more MiG's. The aerial war was a bonus, so to speak, the MiGs did not have to fly and their activity did little to further the Communists ends in the war, since they never supported the front line troops. The only reason the MiGs were flying was to give the Communist pilots combat experience, which was precisely what the United Nations were also doing.

Dolph Overton got his 5th victory the day before. He was famous for the fact that he got four MiGs on his last four missions. But it was the way that he got them that was disconcerting to some, particularly the base commander, the Colonel who had been kicked out of Alaska. A photo was taken from the wing of Dolph and another

27 Feb 1953. Smiles at a debriefing after a mission.

ace, Cecil Foster, congratulating me. Dolph told me that he did not know if his victories were going to be confirmed by the wing commander. This was a surprise to me since the publicity had already been disseminated and wired back home. It transpired that the wing commander had indeed recommended that Overton's last two kills not be awarded to him. Fortunately the recommendation was turned down at 5th AF headquarters.

The tactics that I discovered were being used by the aces and other members of the flight was to fly together to the border, separate, and then go into battle alone. This was a dangerous method and considered by most pilots to being a foolhardy action. When they returned, they would report their kills and the others, who went into battle with them, would vouch for them. The results certainly were spectacular and their tactics were ideal for getting results. A flight of four could cover only one area at a time if they stayed together, but separating, they could cover four different areas. The wing CO became aware of these tactics and thus did not wish to recommend or award Overton his victories.

When 5th AF HQ turned down his recommendation he wrote such an stinging report on the ace, that upon his return to the United States, Overton was asked to resign from the service. This was a great loss to the USAF of a very fine and effective fighter pilot and was a classic case of the ineffective destroying the effective.The most dangerous man is an incompetent, ineffective individual of high rank, for the system protects and rewards his inane mediocrity.

Another future ace, Joe Mason, was transferred to the 39th FIS from one of the other squadrons in the 51st FIW. He was assigned to take over a flight and he came with high recommendations by all who had flown with him. Joe took over D flight in the 39th and I had C flight.

I decided to continue with my missions and to do no more than any other pilot to seek out the enemy. It would be easy to do, just follow regulations and they would protect you completely. The majority of the pilots were doing just that, getting their missions and abiding by all the rules. If the enemy attacked or were in a position where I could easily get a kill, then I would do so. I would take the easy ones and let the difficult ones go and not take any chances or put myself at risk in any way. In this manner, I could go home honorably. If I had expressed the desire to go home at that point, there would undoubtedly have been snide remarks that I had got my kills and was running out.

I was also given the opportunity to have an actual flight command and the idea of controlling from eight to ten pilots on a day-to-day basis delighted me. I could guide and mold these men with some experience into excellent combat pilots.

At about this time, an interesting event took place in the squadron. It was designated to get a gas free diet that included steak, fresh salads and all the fresh milk the pilots could drink. This was because we had the new superior high altitude aircraft. Actually, our aircraft could only get up about 3,000ft higher that the F-86E models that the other squadrons were using. It was rubbing salt into the other pilot's wounds for us to first have a superior performing aircraft and then to have our squadron served a better diet. The food that was served in the mess hall was not of the best. The food that was given the 39th was equivalent to eating at a gourmet restaurant as opposed to the dime hamburger shop across the road. Since we had better food, the brass saw to it that they ate with the 39th squadron.

From a press report by M/Sgt Dick Bartlett
February 1st 1953

A group of guinea pig pilots of the 51st wing are eating their meals without onions these days. Their meat is broiled and roasted and their eggs are poached. All of which boils down to a special high altitude diet.

The F-86 Sabre jet pilots have just completed a 90-day trial period during which their menus were planned to give them food that eliminate meteorism or altitude cramps.

At high altitudes expansion of various gases in the digestive system causes extreme pain to a pilot. Pressurized cabins reduce this pain but do not eliminate it entirely at altitudes above 30,000feet.

In an effort to eliminate this psychological distraction to flying an entire squadron of 51st pilots was chosen to undergo the special diet test. All gas forming foods, high residue foods, excess carbohydrates and excess fat have been removed and fresh vegetables, fruits and abundant salads have been added to their diet.

The pilots submitted monthly reports on weight gain or loss and the effects during flights. Wing Flight Surgeon Capt Frederick Hinman said that the most immediate result of the diet was the upsurge in morale among the group. "We also noted an increased performance of the study squadron during that period and there has also been a marked reduction of altitude cramps and pain attributable to diet. I sincerely recommend this diet for all high altitude combat crews"

1st Lt Harold Fischer, newest jet ace in Korea, said: "During the last war German pilots were fed a special diet, and we've known about these gas pains for some time and what caused them. I am glad they finally decided to test the diet theory. I don't know if it was directly the result of this diet or not, but I know that I shot down all five of my MIG's during the test period"!

The result of us having better food was that pilots who were closing the bar bombarded our squadron barracks with beer cans at all hours of the night. We retaliated by showering their quarters with rocks and cans and occasionally someone would fire a 45 through the roof of the barracks. But this type of action was rare and certainly did not conform to the rules of good or acceptable behavior.

A few missions went by and the lack of excitement on them was boring. I began to take a little more interest in my work and started to look for attack opportunities again and became intent on getting two on one day, or on one mission. Only one other pilot had done this and it seemed like a fine challenge, which was certainly possible to achieve.

Two flights of the 51st were on alert, C and D flight of the 39th FIS. Alert was normally in two shifts, morning, evening or afternoon shift. The morning shift was from 30 minutes before sunrise and the evening was 30 minutes after sunset. My preference was for the morning shift when I was at peak efficiency, then retire in the afternoon for a siesta and again be fresh for the evening mission. This gave me an advantage, in that I could sneak a nap when there was little chance of being bothered.

The alert schedule occurred every four days for the flight but it was broken down so that one member of the flight would only have alert every eight days. On this occasion my alert time fell in the afternoon. Going down in jeeps to the alert area at the south end of the runway, we arrived on station and relieved the flight at the normal time of 12:30 pm. It was a beautiful day. I was in command of my flight, and along with the other flight commander, Joe Mason, we looked forward to a peaceful afternoon, reading, playing cards, sleeping or just talking. Placing our equipment in the airplane cockpits we went into the operations shack and waited for the klaxon to sound. Suddenly the blare of the buzzer went off motivating everyone to instant action. Pilots and crew chiefs sprang to their airplanes, the motors for the APUs roared to life as the pilots strapped on chutes and their safety belts. There was a lot of excitement and action.

Within a matter of minutes the aircraft were rolling out toward the end of the runway and making no checks immediately started the take-off roll. There was no waiting for the wingman to get into position and he kept up as best as he could. My wingman, Dick Knowland was a young pilot, fresh out of flying school and it was his second combat mission. Normally on alert, nothing much happened so it was a good time to use the new troops to fill slots. So it was with this young man, who had a lot of aptitude considering his experience. He fell in beside me on the left as our formation climbed out. It was warm in the cockpit, since I had on a heavy arctic parka, with a huge hood that projected above my helmet and hindered my vision to the rear.

Our job was to patrol the Chong-chon River from the mouth to a point about 100 miles inland. We set up a sausage-shaped patrol and edged our aircraft higher, making turns so that our flight path came increasingly closer to the Yalu River and "MiG Alley," a name so familiar to the readers of newspapers back home. The controller kept calling our flights back to the patrol area and grudgingly we eased back to the intended area. This tug-of-war went on for what seemed a lengthy period of time. My position was over the entrance to the Chong-chon River and Joe Mason's flight was positioned at the other end of the orbit.

Without warning from ground control, Mason's flight began to call out bogies. Suddenly they were also calling breaks. A decision had to be made whether to progress to the scene of the battle or to wait for them to complete their sweep, which would take them into my flight's area. As soon as the information came over the radio, the element leader departed as he had freedom of action and that left me alone with my wingman. Climbing as high as I could, I turned the flight to the east, hoping that the MiGs would come below me to the right and at 90 degrees to my course. For once, like the books say, the planning paid off.

A flight appeared from the right, then another, and the last flight flew right underneath me. Choosing the number four man who passed under me, I turned left and dropped down line abreast with him. I did not want to commit the same error that I had done on my first kill. This time, I almost misjudged my position the other way. Line abreast with a MiG, with only a few hundred feet separating us was an ideal situation and an excellent opportunity for the classic dogfight of WWI. No matter who won this encounter, it would be a fight to remember.

In the best traditions of Mannock, Udet, Bishop, Nungesser and the heroes of the WWI dogfight, the situation unfolded. Immediately both of us started to scissor, in other words, each tried to get on the others tail by turning into and then away from each other. The flight paths of both our aircraft resembled an interlacing pattern. For a few moments, the situation was static, with neither of us gaining the advantage, and then I took a calculated risk. One of the things a pilot theoretically should not do is to drop his speed brakes, for this reduces his speed and since speed could always be converted into altitude, the one who had the altitude had the advantage. But this stalemate was going on longer than I wanted and there were so many other aircraft in the area to tangle with.

Briefly dropping the speed brakes, my airplane fell behind the MiG. Seeing that the advantage was on my side, the MiG headed for the border just a few miles away. His aircraft was forming heavy contrails, and I was 600 feet behind. The contrails were so heavy that when I pulled up to shoot, my canopy entered them. The radar gunsight was working marvelously, and the first burst of a few seconds caused his aircraft to light up almost from wing tip to wing tip. It appeared as if every round found its mark. Before I had a chance to fire again, the canopy went by followed by the pilot. My wingman, Dick Knowland, verified the kill immediately, for number one of the day.

I looked over to see Dick's position and he was off to my left and slightly higher. Looking at him and at the MiGs in front of us, I saw him fire and the right wing root of the MiG sparkled with an excellent hit. It was his first mission deep in enemy territory, and he was already a success. Before he had a chance to press his advantage, we turned and he called on me to break, since I had a MiG on my tail ready to fire. Looking over my shoulder I shivered, because there, about 1,500 feet out at about my seven o'clock position was a single MiG. I recalled the tales of the professional hot shots who flew alone. Rolling up and over, I pulled as many inverted G's as I could without stalling the aircraft and losing my airspeed. Then doing a split "S", I called again, although it was hard for me to talk, with the force of the G's pressing my body to the seat. I asked if the MiG was still there. My wingman called and stated that he wasn't there the last time he saw me, but that he had lost me and was heading home. Checking my own tail, I took up course for the front lines.

Looking above, I saw a lone aircraft heading to the south, which I presume, was my lost wingman. He was following instructions that if lost, to get the hell out of the area. But behind him was another aircraft about 3,000 feet directly astern of him. It was a single MiG evidently out to avenge the aircraft lost and damaged in this particular fracas. Now it became the hunted stalking the hunter as I took up a position about 3,000 feet behind the MiG. Calling Dick, I reported the MiG behind him, and that he should level off, build up his mach number and run for it. He acknowledged and I saw his airplane ease down, and with it, the MiG fighter. I told Dick that I would tell him to turn when I initiated my attack. I assured him that there was little danger to him, since the range was great. Knowing the MiG pilot would have to turn I was in an excellent position for my attack, although for the moment out of range. Also knowing that the MiG pilot would not continue his attack without firing, I called and notified Dick of that.

Nearing the Chong-chon River, my range had decreased. Looking back I saw that I was also being followed at a distance. It was easy to determine attackers and attacked since our airplanes were not in the heavy contrail area. Finally, squeezing off a few bursts, the MiG in front of me either became aware of the aircraft behind him or one of the Communist pilots warned him by radio. He began a turn to the left and I fell in behind him, in a turn to decrease the distance between our two airplanes. The MiG pilot tried their successful tactic of zooming, but in a turn this was not successful and I ended up at 300 feet behind him almost in a full stall. The MiG in front of me was a beautiful silver color and it looked as if it was just off the assembly line from a Russian factory. At this range, I could not miss and since my guns had already been tested for accuracy, I squeezed the trigger of the 50 calibers.

The burst hit directly behind the cockpit and caused it to light up in an encircling glow of light. The MiG immediately snapped into a spin and there was nothing to do but to spin with it. Both of us went into a spin at 38,000 feet and squeezing off a burst in the spin, I was able to register another hit on the wing tip of that beautiful airplane. It was a spin that continued all the way to the ground. Joe Mason's wingman verified this kill.

As soon as the second hit registered, I pulled out of the spin and looked around. On my left there was the MiG that had been following me and attempting to do to me, what I had done to his comrade. But in this case, his position was not as good as mine had been. Turning into him, he slid on by and I again turned so that I was behind him. His speed was too great and he pulled away rapidly.

When both of our speeds stabilized, he was out of normal range at about 4,000 feet. Other kills had been made at this altitude and at this distance, so I concentrated on firing at the fleeing MiG. By this time, my wingman was calling that he was getting low on fuel so I told him to hold on a moment more and I squeezed off a burst. The MiG was in heavy contrails and they deceived me into thinking that I was getting hits and perhaps he was on fire. Calling my wingman to leave, I fired all my ammunition at the MiG and finally left him as he crossed over into Manchuria. Both sides retired to calculate their casualties..

On the way home the controller was ecstatic over the results of this day's mission. Over the radio, I had heard Joe Mason calling to his wingman, Wally Green, to verify the pilot bailing out of the MiG he claimed. The total claims for this eight-plane flight were three aircraft destroyed and two damaged. Later the results awarded by the claims board, were three kills and one damage. The damage that I had claimed was not verified and had been submitted only to indicate the magnitude of the battle.

Back on the ground, I praised Dick for his good work. It looked as if he would have a great future. He was another of the very young pilots assigned to be trained in the police action. Joe had a little difficulty with the verification of his kill. When his wingman finally did verify it, he then agreed to verify my kill, the second one that my wingman did not see. So with no further ado, both my aircraft were confirmed and this gave me a total of seven kills, two more than I had initially dreamed of getting and two on one mission, which was my next dream.

During this time, I took an interested in learning as much about the Korean and Chinese people as I could and trying to find out why the Chinese revolution was successful. During alerts, I read about the Koreans and their culture from books that I found in the base library, but they did not answer all my questions, although gave me an insight into the people, their culture, aspirations and national purpose.

It was during this time that I read about the Powell's and their decision to stay behind in China under the Communists and the fact that they verbally supported the Communists through their newspapers. I wondered why they had done this. There were books by people who had lived with the Koreans, or who had dealings with the population through being assigned to Korea. A husband and wife team who had been members of the state department and assigned to Seoul wrote a book that was critical of our state department. They pointed out the fact that our messages were not getting to the people and that we basically misunderstood their national aspirations, and that the great amount of money we were spending on the support of the Korean government was being wasted. Very little was being used where it would do the most good and going back to people. Again, there was the problem of corruption in high places. The so called common people were deriving little benefit from the money, and the way it was spent on them made it degrading. They pointed out that more good could be done by presenting information in the Korean language in a way the people could understand, rather than the many important missions to government leaders. It was the old story of our government dealing with the leaders of the country and not with the people. And this is the basic fault of our government's approach. The United States and the Western world deal with the governments; and the Communists deal with the people. For, after all, the people are the backbone of the government.

During this period of serious reading, I read a book concerning the new regime in China. In a passage, the writer referred to the Americans as "paper tigers" and from this, I chose the name for my aircraft, the Paper Tiger. The basic reason was to show the enemy that not all Americans were "paper tigers."

My next victory was the most dangerous one and also fraught with mistakes. It began again with a new wingman, who had been a professional musician and played the clarinet beautifully, especially 'Rhapsody in Blue.' The flight often sat around and listened to him play. He was my number two man, as I took the new men out on my wing for a few flights to assess them, and to get them combat seasoned. This pilot was not as good as my previous one who got a score on his first mission.

Our flight was late getting into the air and the battles had already begun. The fight was taking place about fifty miles northeast of the mouth of the Yalu River. As we came into the area at 40,000 feet and climbing, having dropped our tanks, we saw a great panorama of contrails and visible aircraft in the blue sky. Through this melee, two MiG's flew on a course northward. Like a pack of dogs after two rabbits, the full complement of the flights in sight turned and immediately gave chase. One F-86 pilot must have used up every bit of power to attain a tremendous altitude and in making his attack, came straight down through the MiG formation. He had evidently under estimated the recovery time at this high altitude. He probably recovered when the airplane was at about 10,000 feet below the target.

After these two MiG aircraft stole the show, four more in the standard fingertip formation came in behind them. There were four aircraft right behind them though at a great distance. Although not in the same formation, we were so close that we almost ran into each other, as each would not give way to lose an advantage. It was an interesting situation that had developed. There was little use of extensive firing, for the MiG's knew that we were behind them and the range was too great to be effective. We were now over China.

There was an undercast below us and it was unusual for the MiG pilots to fly in weather conditions such as this. They were letting down and so were we, into the thick overcast. Guessing where the aircraft were going, I continued with my element. Occasionally I saw the MiG's disappear, only to re-appear in and out of the moderate cloud layer, but it was easier to follow the contrails of enemy aircraft as they passed through the overcast.

Suddenly we broke out, and seeing the four aircraft in the flight to our left in a turn, it was easy to almost drop from the heavens and join up with the MiG's. In fact the join up with the number two man, who was on the inside of the turn, was too good and I was too close to fire effectively. My wingman called me clear, but before I could fire, an enormous amount of cannon tracers went by my right wing and canopy. It gave me a tremendous fright. Immediately after the fireworks had passed within a few feet of my canopy, the wingman again called me clear. Thinking that the man behind me had negated his attack, I continued with mine. Just as I was getting settled down again, another burst of fireworks passed over my right wing and canopy. Not looking back, and before I had a chance to break off the attack, my wingman again called me clear. I was most apprehensive but not once did I look behind. The reason that I was probably able to escape was the fact that I was so close to the MiG in front that it was impossible for the MiG behind me to get a good shot without hitting his comrade in front of me.

Finally the barrage of fire ceased and I thought I was clear to fire. It was no problem dispatching the aircraft ahead of me once I got my mind settled down. A few good bursts and the battle was over. The aircraft was on fire and the pilot bailed out. As I pulled up and looked around I saw two F-86s pull away. Evidently they had been observing the kill that I made. But where was my wingman? When the other F-86s departed, it was suddenly very lonesome. Calling my wingman, I searched the sky and he answered that he had me in sight. I looked around frantically, but could not see him anywhere. There was no place to go, but to head home. Over the Yalu River, I heard my wingman call that he was low on fuel and intended to go into an island off the coast, which was friendly to us. It then became apparent to me that he had joined up with another aircraft during the melee.

There were a million questions on my mind as my wingman called that he was going into the strip at Cho-do. When had he lost me? Was it before the enemy aircraft appeared on my tail or was it afterwards? All these questions raced through my mind as my course led me back to the strip at K-13. I had no real confirmation of my eighth victory but this was not really of great concern to me for there were other matters on my mind and serious questions to be answered.

Taking my parachute, survival gear, helmet and maps into base operations, I turned them into personal equipment that shared the same building. As I walked up the incline to squadron operations, the operations clerk said that I had a call from a Lieutenant Colonel from K-55. He said that both he and his wingman had witnessed my kill so there would be no problem of confirmation. He also said that he could not understand how my aircraft had not been hit in the face of such a close range attack and the quantity of ammunition that had been dispensed at me from the MiG on my tail. I wholeheartedly agreed with him.

The more I thought about it, the madder I got at the wingman who was supposed to be flying my wing. I thought of all types of action to take and he was exceedingly lucky that he did not land at our base at the same time as I did. It was bad enough losing your leader, but to call him clear when he is under attack is tantamount to murder. The timing of the entire situation appeared more ludicrous than tragic.

The next day, the courier from the island of Cho-do brought back the wayward wingman. I was waiting for him in personal equipment where he had to turn in his equipment. His aircraft had been left on the short strip and it had not yet been decided who would go and get it. The beach was about 5,000 feet long and suitable only for emergency landings. The approach to the runway was over and around mountain approaches. All in all, it was a poor choice for anything other than an emergency landing strip. Whenever an aircraft was in trouble they headed for the friendly island either to bail out or land on it. It was a haven and used by all United Nation forces.

A British Fairey Battle from her Majesty's forces once made an emergency landing on the strip at low tide. The aircraft overturned and trapped the pilot in the cockpit. The tide slowly rose and in spite of all the efforts of the personnel stationed on the island, the pilot drowned. This story alarmed me and I began to carry my chrome plated .45 right in front of me, so that it would be immediately available in a similar emergency. I could shatter the canopy and break out or if I ever got into a position where I was immediately below a MiG fighter, I could crack the canopy and fire up at the Mig. There were cases in the war where this might be feasible and I didn't want to miss any chances.

I was waiting for the musician wingman when he walked in. I had alternately stewed and fretted and mentally went over what I was going to say a hundred times. I finally took the approach of calm outrage. This fitted my personality more than other approaches.

When he walked into base operations, I asked to talk with him. Explaining just exactly what had happened, that I was being called clear when I was actually in the process of being fired upon, I impressed upon him the fact that but for a great deal of luck, I would have been left up on the cold China countryside. I was just getting wound up, really racking him up one side and down the other, with calm cold contempt, when an unusual scenario occurred: tears came to his eyes. There was nothing else that I could do but dismiss him and encourage him that greater mistakes had been made. All my rehearsals came to naught and that was where the one sided interview ended.

There was a degree of official concern over this mission by the squadron commander. As soon as my wingman landed the CO asked to see him, and that he wanted to see him alone. Taking the wingman over to the CO's quarters, I did not give him instructions as to what to say. There were certainly things that he could report that would not be in my best interests. For instance we had done the fighting in China and other operations of the flight, such as the minimum fuel that we returned with. Many of these matters were in contradiction with the orders of the brass. They were not practical down at the working level, but they did add validity to the operation of the mission.

As a result of not only this occurrence but also other incidents, the CO took me aside and gave me a very stern warning. These included the warning that if I ever lost a wingman, that I would be relieved from my flight. As he talked, he made further stringent statements that if I ever lost, or had a wingman hit, then I would lose the flight. This was probably because he was not doing too spectacularly himself, and also due to the fact that my many skirmishes with the enemy placed my wingman in more dangerous positions than those of other flights. The matter closed there.

There was no animosity toward the wayward wingman. I recommended him for First Lieutenant and this evidently surprised him, for he thanked me and indicated that he had not expected it.

After the squadron commander's warning, I was placed in an awkward position for bad luck could so easily relieve me of my position as flight leader. This was naturally of concern to me, since I was happy with my job. Soon after this warning, one of my wingmen was hit. It was on a flight where I was flying as the element leader and the squadron commander was the leader with one of my best wingmen, Stanley Fisher on his wing.

In the battle area, we immediately encountered a flight of MiGs heading south and turning. I immediately made an attack with the squadron commander's element following mine. Just as I reached an excellent position on one of the MiG aircraft, there was radio chatter from number two saying to break and then very rapidly stating that he had been hit. This occurred just as I was about to fire, and for a split second I debated on firing a burst or checking on the element. This was a momentary hesitation and I immediately broke off the attack and looked for Stan Fisher.

Down below I saw a lone F-86 heading for the deck and for the friendly off shore islands. Above were two following aircraft. The squadron commander was with Stan Fischer and shepherding him all the way and giving him advice. Stan was probably the calmest of the flight. When he was hit I had a tremendous sinking sensation for he was a good troop and his loss would be mourned by all who knew him. Deciding to keep my height, which would allow me to conserve fuel and to be of use if the MiGs attempted to attack, I followed them home along the coast and over friendly water. Not once did we cross over land until we were south of our lines. Then a long approach was made to the field with the squadron commander giving the final instructions before landing to bail out if anything untoward happened. Stan Fisher made a good landing.

Expecting the worst now that one of my wingmen had been hit, I dreaded talking to the CO. But his first words were that it had really been an interesting mission. This would be a great story that he could tell the wing and group commanders that he had personally shepherded home a wounded eagle and saved him for another day. Not one word was said about me being relieved from the position of flight commander. But if he had not been along on the flight, and not responsible for the wingman, then I have no doubt that he would have carried out his threat and dismissed me. The fact is that as soon as my element made the attack there was no other recourse that could have been taken.

The MiGs that we ran into were reported to be from Czechoslovakia. They were a dull green color with red noses and supposedly one of the crack units of the satellite nations. They were identified by their peculiar paint color. They certainly had to be crack shots or else very lucky to secure a hit on Stan Fisher's aircraft. This was the first time that it had been confirmed that there was actual participation by the satellite nations in the actual conflict. Stan was shaken up by the incident, for there is a thin line between being hit and being shot down and the pilots who flew daily, were readily aware of this.

There began to be a great deal of pressure in the organization now that I had secured a number of kills in a relatively short period of time, to more or less sponsor me and thus assure that I would be the leading ace of the theater. There was talk by the wing and group commander of giving me choice missions and with a wingman of my choosing. This scheme was dropped probably because there was little reason to be given preferential missions, since I was able to gain victories without "selected assisgnment."Anyway I was not keen on someone else dictating my goals, which might not necessarily be the ones I wanted. It was akin to the gun fighters of the old west, where someone else encouraged the gun battle just to be around to say they knew the gun fighter. To these types it was irrelevant if the fighter survived the dual.

Around this time I was picked to fly with General Barcus, the commanding general of the theater. It is to his credit that he checked out in the F-86 and it was further to his credit that he actually flew two combat missions against the enemy. Both he and his executive officer elected to check out with the 51st and the 4th. Because the 4th was the unit that had received preference in the past, the General decided to give the 51st the added prestige of flying with them. Certainly the fact that he was going to check out had a far-reaching impact on the organization as a whole.

Reverberations were felt down to the lowest ranking airman as the base was made ready and cleaned up. General Barcus arrived in a De Havilland Beaver aircraft, flown by his personal pilot. Having heard so much about him and about his fierce nature, we expected to see a veritable monster step from the airplane. As it was, we watched a white haired elderly gentleman, who was kindly to his subordinates, but harsh to those who did not produce as he desired. His checkout had everyone running around and he had the wing operations officer, the wing commander and the executive officer helping him into the cockpit. My job was to help him get his parachute on and to monitor his start. When briefed on the traffic pattern, the standard rectangular pattern detested by fighter pilots, and for which he was personally responsible in the combat area, he calmly stated, "I will fly my own pattern." He probably had the largest ever entourage of any pilot, wishing him well and waving to him as he taxied off.

General Barcus had put out an order that there would be no more aircraft accidents while he was associated with the training command and a story did the rounds that shortly after he put out the 'no more accidents' ruling, that he landed at a base just before the following aircraft in the traffic pattern made a wheels up landing. The base commander was promptly relieved of his command.

Shortly after he checked out he made the unprecedented decision to join a combat sortie. This decision was made after he decided to boom 5th AF HQ. To do this the aircraft was flown to 40,000 feet and pointed straight down over the intended target. With full power, the F-86 would sonic boom the installation below as it went through the sound barrier. Other pilots did this particular performance when intent on giving vent to their frustrations or stress factors. However this was the first time a commanding General had done it. He had given the staff at Seoul plenty of warning so I imagine that it was successful, whether they heard it or not.

The day the General decided to go on his combat sortie the weather was clear and he was sent up on a patrol of the Yalu River. It was an ideal time for the enemy to be active. Ten aircraft were aloft with the General leading. The wing commander was flying the General's wing. My squadron commander led his element with Stan Fisher as his wingman. Stan evidently engendered a feeling of pride in the squadron commander since he theoretically saved and shepherded him home after he had been hit. On the Generals left, there was another element composed of the operations officer with an excellent wingman. The other two elements were led Joe Mason, flight commander of D flight and myself. It was a heavily loaded unit, with two aces leading the trailing elements. Before take-off, we were both given the word that our main job was to protect the General. We were both determined that nothing would happen to him even if we had to ram.

The flight continued north across the Chong-chon River and up into MiG Alley. The situation was ideal. Two patrol circuits were made right on the Yalu River and all eyes were turned toward the north hoping that there would be some indication that we would be intercepted or that some MiG's would cross over the river. After the last circuit the General let down to 20,000 feet to access the Chinese airfields across the Yalu. The urge came upon me to transmit over the radio hoping the Chinese would be angered enough to divert a flight. A verse ran through my mind, "I hope that Stalin dead, the world would be better off with one less red." All in all, the mission was a disappointment. We let down over our lines and followed the General in to land.

Shortly thereafter, General Barcus asked for a flight over the front lines and into the Wonsan area accompanied by only a wingman. I was selected for this mission and again I was pleased to be given the chance to fly with him. I took off on his wing and followed him around the sky. He was not he easiest person to fly with, since he used high power settings. However, he did make a great number of turns so that I was able to keep up with him. Over the front lines and Wonsan area, the communications with the ground became increasingly difficult and I imagined the ground controller responsible for the communications being very ill at ease as the General used his call sign and repeatedly made calls. The flight itself was uneventful and this was the last flight the General made for he was forbidden to fly again over the front lines, as he would have been too valuable a prisoner.

The issue of flying across the border varied from time to time and at one time, we were not permitted to fly closer than 20 miles from the Chinese border. Then it was allowed if in hot pursuit. On one mission we were briefed to patrol 30 miles inside China to protect F-84 and F-80 aircraft that had been given the mission to attack the Suiho Reservoir, which was on the Yalu River, the border between China and Korea. Our wing had the mission of medium cover thirty miles north of the Suiho Reservoir and the 4th was given the mission of high cover. Special tactics were necessary since protection would be minimal while we were directly over the border. However there was no enemy activity on the mission.

A man whom I was to meet later was directly involved with me in another air battle of far reaching importance for both of us. Our flight took off and headed into the combat area. There was no activity on the legal side of the river but there was a great deal of activity on the other side. We could hear the pilots reporting breaks and being cleared, presumably for firing. Down below us we could see aircraft contrails. Our flight had used up a great deal of fuel pursuing MiG's we had seen below us. Our elements had separated and we had fuel for one more attack. Seeing the activity below and to the north, I decided to attack one aircraft and hope that it was the enemy. Picking out this speck in the sky, I began to dive with full power. Gradually the speck grew, which happened to be at right angles to our course, and from the puffs of smoke coming from the cannon, he was firing short bursts. This issuance of smoke indicated that it was a MiG and that it was firing on an F-86. Although out of range, I began to fire hoping that it would frighten the MiG away from its quarry. The MiG was zooming up behind the lone F-86 at about 1,000 feet range. When the MiG pilot saw or felt my attack, he turned toward the north and I fell in easily behind his aircraft. It was an easy task to get the MiG burning and the pilot bailed out. It was my ninth kill. Turning from the doomed aircraft I was puzzled to find that I had two wingmen.

On the return flight, I discovered that the extra wingman was from Col. Ed Heller's element. Ed did not return from the flight. His wingman stated that I must have shot down Ed's MiG attacker. This curious relationship was to continue as Heller's life later became intertwined with mine under difficult circumstances.

Heller, 33 years old, was one of America's top fighter pilots in two wars. He got 5.5 kills in WW 11 and 3.5 kills credited to him in the Korean War. Only the day before he had taken off as a Major, blasted two MIG's out of the sky and landed at his base to be presented with orders promoting him to Lt Col.

The film, when developed, showed a MiG attacking another aircraft which could only have been Heller's and the next frames showed the same MiG dead ahead of my guns, with the trigger lever indicating that I was firing and my hits scoring their marks on the aircraft.

Shortly thereafter, the tenth kill was credited to me on a mission similar to the other kills. By now there was little thrill in a kill other than painting 10 MiGs on the side of my own F-86, 958. The now old aircraft, "The Paper Tiger,"still had the tiger's teeth that we painted on her, but they required frequent retouching as the ravages of weather and high speed took their toll. My crew chief, Bert A Sims and I loved that airplane and we both felt that it was the fastest aircraft in the unit. Other pilots tended to agree with us. He did a sterling job and kept it in peak condition.

I soon learned to be careful what one said to reporters. I mentioned that the radar gun sight had worked but once, and that the system I used was comparable to Kentucky windage, in that I would adjust my fixed sight in relationship to the tracers that I fired. This was picked up by the wire service. While on R&R in Japan I purchased a copy of the Nippon Times, the English daily printed in Tokyo and glanced at an article on the front page that mentioned Kentucky windage. It was almost verbatim my statement with my name attatched to it. I was a little taken aback to read about myself in the Nippon Times where I least expected it, on a Japanese subway train in the heart of Tokyo.

Returning to the unit, the group commander called me in and asked about this article as some individuals in air material command had questioned him about the radar gunsight and my comments. I fully expected to be called upon the carpet about it, but this was not the case. However, it made me aware of how little one could say to the gentlemen of the press.

<u>Press report on the front page of Des Moines Tribune</u>
<u>March 23rd 1953</u>

Fischer's Secret
"Shot MIG's Like Ducks": Iowa Ace
The usual reason why F-86 Sabre jet pilots completely outclass Communist airmen over North Korea is the secret radar gunsight.

A shy 27year old fellow from an Iowa farm who has destroyed 10 MIG's in only 66 Sabre missions confided today that he shot down eight of the Red jets without even using that gun sight.
Blue eyed Capt Harold Fischer looked a bit worried. "I sort of hate to let the air force know about this" he said, "but I shot those eight down like you would shoot ducks. I used what I called 'Kentucky windage'—just lead those MIG's enough so they'd run into the

bullets, like you do a flying duck.

"I get up pretty close and shoot real short bursts of tracers. That way, I see what I am doing and set up my Kentucky windage. When I am set, I let 'em have it"

"But I sure want to say something about the fine radar gunsight. It's a wonderful gunsight and I wouldn't ever want to be without it"

Fischer is the man everybody is betting on to become the leading jet ace of the Korean War. Three more MIG's and he will top the mark set by Col Royal Baker who rotated home to McKinney Texas this month, after flying more than the standard 100 missions.

And what does Fischer think? "I'm really not shooting for a record" he said, "I'm just trying to do the best job I can".

"With more than 30 missions to go, how can Hal miss?" a brother officer asked. Ground crewmen echo the sentiments.

"He could break that record in a Piper Cub," said Airman Alcino Almeida of Cranston .

"Give him a glider and he could do it", Airman F.E.Dawson of Mansfield corrected warmly.

During this time, there were reports that the Chinese were massing jet bombers in the Mukden area and that they had been seen on the airfields of north China. These reports generated the fear that the jet bombers might attack our own airfields so each evening we moved a number of aircraft to other airfields in the area as protection from a surprise attack. This was the United Nations reaction to the Chinese having a twin-engine medium bomber near the Yalu River and thus caused the UN to expend tremendous amounts of resources and energy in ferrying aircraft to other bases each night, only to return them the next day.

It was my duty to lead a number of these flights to Taegu and to K-9 at Kunsan and then return the next morning The quarters we stayed in overnight were most inadequate and the result of this ferrying action was that the pilots were tired for the next day's missions.

On one of these flights to Kunsan I met my old instructor from advanced flying school and it was good to see him. He cautioned me about my flying, in particular the bit about ramming the MiG aircraft. He began the subject by saying that he thought it had been incorrectly reported in the press and the journalist had obvioulsy misinterpreted what I said. During this conversation, I explained the theory behind the concept of ramming and after some minutes at the bar, he began to see my point. However, as he left he still cautioned me to be careful and said that he had not taught me to fly in that manner.

The next day fog enveloped the field and we had to delay the take-off until it cleared. We talked to the crew chiefs and they told us of an F-84 that had crash landed just off the runway and when they got to the aircraft the pilot was gone and there was apparently little damage incurred in the accident. They attributed the disappearance of the pilot to the guerrilla activity that was so predominant in the area around the field. There was also talk of aircraft blowing up on take-off and all in all the morale on the base was very low. It was the home of the locomotive aces, the pilots who flew B-26s and 'killed' trains at night. As soon as the fog lifted, we took off and climbed into the bright spring sunlight. It was the 7th of April 1953.

Raising the gear handle to the up position, there was no response as I had neglected one of my preflight checks, which was to reposition the switch in the nose gear compartment. It was the beginning of a very bad day.

Arriving at K-13 with my gear already down, I landed and spent some time in base operations. An application for a regular air force commission had been delivered by the commanding General's aide which I had to fill out so it could be hand carried by General Barcus when he returned to the USAF HQ. It was a virtual assurance of a regular commission, which was something that I had wanted yet when the crunch came, I was a little hesitant about filling it out. Perhaps it was a way of rebelling against the military system that I liked, and yet was keenly aware of the many defects within the system itself.

Our flight was scheduled for a mission later in the afternoon, which I was to lead with Dick Knowland as my wingman. Oscar Pittman was the element leader. Our flight was briefed to break up into elements as soon as we reached the area. On our climb we saw circling contrails in the center of Korea opposite Wonson. Occasionally two contrails, obvioulsy enemy aircraft, would head north. I called number three and requested that he investigate while I held my altitude. By the time three and four had approached the area, the aircraft had climbed up and disappeared from the contrail level.

Continuing our flight northward alone, I saw a flight of four aircraft come across the border pulling contrails. Positioning my element above as they passed 2,000 feet below us, we attacked. As we gained our position, the flight began to zoom. Before they got the advantage, I fired my guns. At 1,000 feet my shots were off 200 feet to the right. This was because I was flying an aircraft that had not been bore sighted from the mission before when all the rounds had been expended upon an enemy aircraft and subsequently shot down.

It was policy to bore sight the aircraft after every mission when the guns had been fired for the very reason I was now facing. The aircraft was given to me because there were no spares and I had only myself to blame for I had accepted it. I cursed vehemently at my predicament.

Before I could correct for this error in the guns by adjusting my sight pattern, we were attacked by four following aircraft that were above the contrail level. There was nothing we could do but to break off the attack. It was not a break in the true sense of the word, but was a turn and then a reversal of the turn so now we were again the attackers. But it was of no use for the MiG's were traveling too fast. Rather than pursue them in a hopeless chase, we set up our course for the mouth of the Yalu and then home again.

My wingman had a tip tank that had not fed, because he called that he was getting low on fuel. At this point three aircraft came across our noses, heading north. It was an ideal situation. I called a bounce and my wingman called that his fuel was getting lower. I made the wrong decision, telling him to head out and that I would follow him as I had done before.

I continued the attack but now there were three aircraft, one straggler behind the two in front. Choosing the straggler, I dropped down and closed with him at a tremendous rate of speed. Getting off a shot, I made a gigantic roll around him, and then fell in behind him. The MiG in front accelerated and was now even with the other element that I was rapidly overtaking. I rolled over on the number two MiG in the formation, and this time my guns were calibrated. I let him have a long burst and stopped his engine.

He dropped back, giving me an opportunity to hit the lead aircraft. From about 1,200 feet, all six .50s literally tore the aircraft apart. Debris came flying back toward my aircraft in large pieces, and I ducked as pieces went by. There were two choices, either to go down under the MiG or go over it. I decided to go over the airplane because I did not want to be in front of the MiG, as I had been one time before.

At this time the throttle came back into my hand, the engine instruments read that I had a dying engine on my hands, and my speed began to decelerate so rapidly that I was pushed forward against my shoulder straps. I thought of calling, but did not, because it might have been interpreted as a cry for help. The mouth of the Yalu was reachable, but I knew it would be at zero altitude and the F-86 was not known for good ditching capabilities. If one hit just right, it would not sink immediately but predicting a good ditching was a gamble. I decided to risk it until I smelled and saw smoke coming into the cockpit. Fire, the dread of all pilots. If I wanted to live, I now had no choice, except to bail out, for the aircraft would probably blow up. Reaching down for the left handle, I jettisoned the canopy. With the right handle pulled up, I leaned back in the seat, put my feet in the stirrups and squeezed the trigger. The altitude was 2,000 feet and the airspeed, 450 knots.

Des Moines Tribune April 9th 1953

To Fischer Danger is Old Friend
Here's the story of his Tuesday flight over Korea...
By Gordon Gammuck...war correspondent
A jet base in Korea. Just before Capt Harold Fischer of Swea City Iowa took on his seventieth mission Tuesday afternoon, a strange ceremony was performed. Pilots lifted their bright yellow caps, bowed slightly toward Lt Dick Knowland of Goshen Mass. and held their caps over their hearts. Knowland was going to be Fischer's wing man and this mock gesture of sympathy always was extended to pilots about to fly the double ace's wing.

It meant this....the kindest, quietest guy in the world until he took after Red MIG's, then was a ferocious tiger, stopping at nothing until he had killed. Danger always rode with Fischer on a MIG prowl and his wing man had to share it.

With Lt General Glenn O Barcus, 5th air force commander, piloting a small plane, I flew to Fischer's base Tuesday. En route the General said of Fischer, "I dont know when I have known a finer young man". Then it was from Knowland that I got the story of Fischer's ill-fated flight over North Korea.

New York Times July 1953
Captain Fischer was singled out by communist radio commentators from Peiping in broadcasts that followed some of his early publicity at home. They told him that he was recognized by the MiG air groups as an especially juicy prize and he was warned in broadcast after broadcast that the MiGs would get him. Probably Fischer didn't even know of such psychological warfare but in Tokyo some of the army's facilities monitored Peiping constantly and reports of this taunting and warning were made to his squadron leaders.

Hal's comment in January 2001 to the above report was: -The regular pilots never got this information from radar tracks, or any of the voice communications monitored by our Security Service. I knew nothing about it. They are probably still locked up tight in untouched files. The Australians were reported to have had excellent communications intelligence about what was occurring but it was only given on a "need to know basis".

The official USAF publicity photo and news release of the double jet ace, which was featured extensively in the US media including the cover of The New York Times Magazine March 29 1953.

HEADQUARTERS
FAR EAST AIR FORCES
APO 925
(22 March 1953)

BECOMES DOUBLE JET ACE

FIFTH AIR FORCE. KOREA – Capt Harold E. Fischer Jn of Swea City Iowa, an F-86 Sabrejet pilot with the U.S. Air Forces 51st Fighter Interceptor Wing, became a double jet ace, Saturday, March 21, when he shot down his 10th enemy MIG-15 in an air battle over North Korea. It was the 13th time Captain Fischer has scored against the Russian-built jets. He previously destroyed nine MIGs and damaged three, having become history's 25th jet ace on January 24 when he destroyed his fifth MIG. His latest victory came on a day when Sabrejet pilots shot down six MIGs and damaged seven others. Since the start of the Korean War, Far East Air Forces aircraft have destroyed more than 630 MIGs.
(U.S. Air Force Photo) (AF 2780-4)

CHAPTER 16

PRISONER OF WAR

As the years go by, fighter aviation truly weeds out men. You can't lie to yourself when you fly fighters because you would not last, you can't lie to your wingman because you'll kill him. It is terribly unforgiving but it builds 'character', and that character is why we are all here today.
Hal Fischer
From a speech given on July 25th 1988

The 37-mm shell that activated the seat gave me a terrific impetus upward. It caused me to momentarily black out and when I recovered, wind was rushing around me as I rapidly rotated in space. Pulling the ripcord, I waited for the tremendous opening shock that I expected but surprisingly there was no major jolt. I had followed all the well-rehearsed procedures. First the safety belt is unstrapped , and then one steps away from the seat, and pulls the ripcord. When the parachute opened, there was a slight jar and I looked up to check the panels. Bar one, they were all there

Looking around for other aircraft in the vicinity, I saw a derelict MiG trailing a stream of flame as long as the fuselage. It turned lazily toward me and I thought that it would fire at me. Other than my chrome-plated .45, I was defenseless. But the MiG turned just as lazily away from me, and I turned my attention to landing. The MiG was one of those that I had fired at, and the pilot must certainly have had a desire for revenge. Fortunately he did not pursue it.

The terrain below me was hilly with scrub brush and trees growing on the side of the rocky crags. As I gradually drifted toward the side of a hill I wondered where to land and was certain that at the very least, I was going to break my leg on landing. The stillness around me was surprising, but I could hear people shouting on the ground. Their voices seemed to come from all directions.

The next surprise was the landing. Expecting to break a leg or injure myself in a worse way, I simply drifted on down and my landing was cushioned by the canopy of the parachute snagging in the branches of a scrub tree, which saved me from a hard landing and rolling down the rocky hillside. I released the harness of the parachute, lay back for a moment and evaluated the situation.

There was a lot of blood on my scarf and gingerly feeling my ear I found the source. Evidently when my helmet came off, it had torn my ear rather badly. Although it was fairly cold, my body was completely soaked with sweat, and a feeling of utter weariness came over me. I tried to climb up the hill, but I could not get up, so started to crawl. I checked my watch and found that it was 5:20 pm. If I could hide until dark, there was a possibility that I could elude my pursuers, whom I could hear all around me, and make my way down to the Yalu River. Not wanting it to be obvious where I started from, I dragged my parachute out of the tree and began to move off, intending to put some distance between me and the landing site. My handgun was still tucked in my flight suit.

Crossing a small ravine, I approached the crest of the adjacent hill and if there had been a suitable place to hide I would have dug myself into the hillside, but it was rocky and afforded no shelter or hiding place. I was about to cross over the crest of the hill when I heard voices on the other side, so crouched down and decided to sit tight and await my fate.

Soon a Chinese man dressed in typical farmer's attire came down the ravine from whence I had just come. He was unarmed and reminded me of a farmer who was out trying to track a lost cow or stray horse. I had my .45 in my hand, but there was no cause for concern, as he posed no obvious threat to me. I had heard that there were many friendly agents in this area, and the thought went through my mind that perhaps this man was a friend, not foe.

He was within 20 feet of me before he saw me, but gave no indication of surprise. I decided that he must be a friendly agent and that he would lead me to shelter where I could hide. Putting all my trust in him, I followed him down the ravine and he in no way indicated that he was anything other than friendly towards me. We were suddenly confronted by a large group of peasants carrying every type of agriculture implement imaginable including a few old rifles. I'd had it.

The group of about thirty Chinese milled around me and inspected me as if I was a creature from another planet. They were not in any way hostile and they directed me to a little hut and indicated that I should lie down and rest. I saw evidence of confusion in the group as they bickered away among themselves, probably trying to figure out who I was. Was I an American or another of the white pilots who were flying from their bases?

A plan formed in my mind and I made it as plain as I could that I wanted to go to the nearest air base. I reckoned I might be able to pass myself off as a Russian MiG pilot since the peasants probably didn't know one uniform or one foreign language from another. I got up and indignantly told them in dubious sign language that I was returning to my airfield at Feng-cheng, a MiG base I knew to be about 15miles northwest. Then I pushed my way through the throng, walked out of the hut and started down the road. The dumbfounded Chinese followed about 50ft behind me in a large knot, still arguing among themselves, with the usual number of children trotting closer behind me than the adults. I thought about running, but the regulation immersion suit that I was wearing prevented this. It was only good for staying afloat and even in that respect there were conflicting reports as to its effectiveness and worth as a life preserver.

I might have gotten away with this ploy, but a few minutes later I rounded a bend and came face to face with a regular Chinese soldier. He instantly recognized me as an American, leveled his gun at me and took charge. The civilians wanted me to go in the direction of the airfield and the soldier wanted me to go the other way. Both began to push and shove with me in the center, and for a moment, the issue was debated quite violently.

By this time, there were two guards with rifles who were uncomfortably close. Escape was now a thing of the past. One of the militia, evidently the leader, secured some wire and I thought that I was going to be strung up immediately so I submitted and sat down by the side of the road. One went to a road side guard shack, put in a telephone call, and several minutes later an American jeep with four Chinese regulars roared up to collect me.

With more force than was necessary I was tossed in the back seat and driven toward the airfield I was heading for. About a mile further, the remains of my aircraft blocked the road. The last time I saw the plane, it was circling around me and disappeared behind the hill. In front of me lay the remains of about $700,000 of beautiful airplane that was now merely scrap. The "God" that failed.

The jeep stopped and a rather hostile Russian soldier came up along side of the

Hal and crew chief B.A. Simms with "Paper Tiger". This is the picture Hal had in his flightsuit on the day he was shot down. The Russians removed it from him with all his personal possessions. The Soviet archives still hold the original print of this photo.

vehicle. Behind him four Russian soldiers were loading the remains of my plane onto a truck. It was no real surprise to see Russians here since we knew they were helping the Chinese in Manchuria. I foolishly had some identification with me, and this evidently had been reported to him, because he came up and at gunpoint ordered me out of the jeep. Four Chinese soldiers held me down as he grappled with me and took the identification. I have never seen so much hate in an individual as I saw in that one. I was glad that the encounter was relatively brief, for we moved around the wreck of the aircraft and went directly to a nearby village, which must have been the headquarters of the Chinese army in this area.

Four guards took me into what appeared to be a large meeting hall with a rough dirt floor, and ordered me to sit on a chair in the middle of the room. There was a telephone in the corner, which was being used to determine just what to do with me. Chinese soldiers of all shapes and sizes peered through the door and windows at me.

One of the braver soldiers brought my portable oxygen cylinder to me and asked what it was for. I pulled the activating pin and he almost fainted with fright. To no avail he made frantic attempts to shut it off, and looking back it was almost comical. I also saw my .45 on the hip of a Chinese, who was now the very proud owner of the weapon.

After innumerable telephone calls, a squad of Chinese directed me into another American army vehicle. Squeezed in between two soldiers, we went to various villages, where the local population viewed the American pilot who had been shot down. Conspicuous in these villages were the youth groups, the pioneers. I was already a political prisoner.

On entering the confines of a large barracks area, I was blindfolded, taken to a large building and immediately placed in a dormitory where many soldiers in nondescript uniforms were lying on beds or sitting at tables. One of the men who appeared to be in charge indicated to me that food was available and also that I would not be shot. This was a pleasant relief to me!

One man spoke a little English and asked for the number of my airplane. I had no idea what it was and when they insisted, I made up a number that seemed to satisfy them. An omelet arrived for me to eat, and even under these circumstances tasted very good. Hoards of curious onlookers peered through every window until finally the windows were covered up.

After what seemed like forever, a man came in an asked me to remove my undershirt. I did this with the assistance of the guard and then was allowed to put it back on. I had no idea what they had in mind other than to perhaps check if I was armed. I was then taken across the street and put in a room with a bunk bed.

The soldier on the top bunk briefly woke up, eyed me up and down and then went directly back to sleep. I was given a blanket and told to sleep. A guard sat on a chair in the middle of the room watching me. You would think that it would be impossible to sleep under these circumstances, but sleep came easily.

Around 4am, four soldiers came and woke me up. I stumbled to my feet not knowing where I was and the horrible reality of my situation dawned on me again. I was taken out to a truck with an open flat bed and forced to lie face down in it and close my eyes. An extremely rough ride followed over appalling roads. Two soldiers rode up front in the truck and two guarded me on the back. After at least four hours we stopped in front of a barracks type building where my blindfold was taken off, and I was introduced to the place where I remained for a week while they decided what to do with me.

I estimated this place to be about 15 miles from the border. I had not been extensively interrogated up till this time with just a few questions asked. But now the real interrogations were about to begin and continued intermittently for the next 27 months.

There were about ten barracks-type buildings that were situated in the valley formed by two low ridgelines. It was evidently a training ground area for troops being sent to Korea. I was taken to the second floor of one of the buildings, put in a tiny room and guarded by Chinese soldiers with Russian submachine guns. The room was bare other than a board, which was to be my bed. A guard gave me a bowl of rice and millet mush, an unappetizing dish that I was to know well in the coming months, and a piece of unleavened bread called *mantou*.

On the second day a tall, well-built Chinese officer came in, beaming and slapping me on the back, behaving like a member of the county Chamber of Commerce. He offered me a cigarette and introduced himself in the normal English manner as Liu. He asked about my family and generally made it plain that he wanted to be friends and it was obvious that he was an intelligence interrogator so I got on my guard. He said that he had been a flyer with Chiang Kai-shek and that he had been trained in the United States at Luke Field in Arizona. He had flown the P-47 and had fought against the Communists for a long time and had eventually deserted. He joined the Communists while staying with some relatives and had been with them ever since.

He was personable and probably the best interrogator that the Chinese had at the front. He seemed to be the one who was used initially to soften up the prisoners or to assess the approach that was to be used to gain the best results from each prisoner.

He asked if I was hurt or if I needed anything, then said that I did not have to worry about being killed. He stressed the lenient policy that was followed by the Chinese People's Liberation Army. He mentioned that if I co-operated there was a possibility that I could return home and asked if I remembered that at the beginning of hostilities some American prisoners had been released right after they had been captured.

He further stated that my crime was very serious, that I was guilty of violating the sacred territorial airspace of China and this fact I certainly could not deny. He stated that I was not to blame for these actions and that it was the aggressive United States policy and those people who formulated the policy, who were to blame. When I asked him what was expected of me and what was going to happen to me, he said that all depended upon my cooperation and then he asked me if I knew about the germ bombs that our forces had dropped on China and Korea. The preliminary sparring was over and the interrogation began in earnest.

Liu grilled me for 10 days. I was summoned to a room and saluted whom I assumed was their leader, but it was ignored and Liu told me to sit down. While they had been planning their approach, I had been planning my reaction to their interrogation. I adopted the attitude that I was uninformed, naive and rather surprised at the benevolence of my hosts. The latter was certainly true, for they were acting very differently from how I expected them to function. However there was nothing in my past that prepared me for what was to come.

I decided that I could tell them what I thought they already knew and to act dumb on things that were sensitive. This gave me a great deal of leeway to use my judgment. The questioning began with name, rank, serial number and organization. What was I doing in China? Did I know where I was? Who were the pilots with whom I flew? When I did not answer, they gave the answers. I originally began to tell them of the pilots who I had flown with in the 80th Fighter-Bomber Wing, giving them their names as pilots of the 51st. They let me go on, and then they told me the correct names of the pilots in the 51st. This took me aback and immediately gave me new insight into their intelligence system, and I hoped that ours was as effective.

Interspersed with military questions, there were personal questions and questions about my lifestyle. As time went on, I found that they queried answers that were truthful and accepted as fact, for the moment anyhow, answers that were fictitious.

The interrogation was interspersed with threats, veiled promises, friendliness, blackmail and psychological trickery. I fully expected physical violence to be unleashed upon me at any moment, despite the repeated statement that, "We do not harm our prisoners."

The questioning often ended on a very bad note, as it was intended to. I was ordered to write down the layout of our base, which I refused to do. I was also repeatedly ordered to list all the pilots in the organization.

A man who was evidently the political commissar lectured me at great length on the benefits to China that had resulted from the Communist revolution. It was interesting that even during the interrogations, I was subjected to political lectures.

Occasionally Liu would voice superficial concern about my welfare and treatment. It was freezing cold at night, and when I complained about the clothes that I had, he said that he would try to get me some warm winter clothes though emphasized that it was not easy to supply the prisoners with clothes. Food was another matter of concern, since there was very little Chinese food that satisfied my hunger pangs. The Chinese continually stated that the POW camps in Korea were ideal, that the troops there were given special food and ate better than their Chinese guards. I certainly could believe it, since I ate with the squad of soldiers whose food was adequate for the Chinese appetite but certainly not for a western man.

When asked what I wanted, the first things that came to mind were books. I indicated that I was interested in learning as much as possible about China, which I truly was. The first book that was given to me was "Yo Banfa", written by an Australian who had established a type of colony in China. It was interesting and though badly written, it did pass the time. When they realized my pleasure in reading and books they used them as a reward system. My fate was still a mystery and till the day that I left, I held the partial conviction that I would be sent to a Korean POW camp.

One day Liu informed me that there was going to be a treat for supper. My guards did their own cooking and one afternoon everyone came back early from their duties and made the equivalent of meat dumplings, which they called "jowtszas". Even though this was supposedly a delicacy, it held very little appeal for me. If I had known what the food situation would be like later in my incarceration, I would have eaten much more.

A visit to the latrine was a real experience. It was a community affair, in a long low building. Instead of stalls normally found in latrines, it was entirely open and the repository was a hole in the cement about 8x24 inches. It reminded me of the outhouses found on farms before inside toilets became common. Whenever I went to the latrine, which was a considerable distance away from the barracks where I was forced to stay, I often saw two soldiers in another barrack. When they saw me, one would stand on the lower level with the other above him and as a joke the one on the upper level held a rope tied around the neck of his friend below him, simulating a hanging. It spooked me and was bad for my morale.

Thoughts of escape were always on my mind and were particularly strong in the early stages of captivity and I constantly searched for an avenue of escape. In fact, the only reason I did not attempt it was that the end of the war might be imminent, and there was also the possibility of being sent to a Korean POW camp where at least I would be able to converse with my fellow Americans.

There is a vast line between thought and action in the average prisoner. Thoughts are always on escape and home and each new situation is carefully assessed according to its merits and in light of his feelings. Many times I thought that a person could take action if he only dared, and with audacity, could easily carry out his plans. It seems the intense urge to escape looms largest when a prisoner is initially captured and dwindles as he becomes accustomed to his surroundings.

A prisoner and a guard can never be friends unless there are some extremely unusual circumstances in the situation. Their desires and purposes are directly opposed, for the prisoner desires freedom and the guard's express task is to prevent his freedom.

I tried to find out from Liu what would happen to me but he usually professed ignorance. I asked him what the Communists had done with other U.S. prisoners who had accidentally crashed in China. I especially asked about Lieut Colonel Edwin Heller, a member of my outfit who had been shot down three months before I was. Peking Radio had made a big fuss about the fact that he had landed in Manchuria.

Liu knew all about Heller. He had broken his leg when he bailed out and almost bled to death before the Chinese picked him up. Liu would not tell me where they were holding him, but he let slip the fact that he saw him from time to time, so I presumed that he was nearby.

I learned later that a cannon shot had broken his arm and also severed the control stick disabling his ejection seat. He went into an uncontrollable dive from 40,000ft before managing to inch out of the cockpit and as he went out the horizontal stabilizer hit his leg. I heard that communist truce negotiators had seen his bailout from a nearby train. It must have been in utter amazement that they watched his descent.

I asked about Colonel John Arnold Jn and his B-29 crew that Peking Radio had claimed crashed in China, and Liu knew all about them too. He said that Col Arnold and his men denied crashing in China or of dropping germs and "that it would go very bad for them if they did not admit to it." I told Liu that we never dropped germs but he stubbornly insisted that leaflets found in Arnolds B-29 were 'germ infested'.

The morning of the 10th day arrived and I was told to gather up the few possessions that I had been given (a piece of Lux soap, toothbrush, toothpaste and a small towel) and was taken to a room crowded with about fifty other people. A Chinese official with an interpreter and two others in blue uniforms armed with movie cameras sat at the far end of the room. I had no idea what was about to happen. The situation looked favorable, since if this interview or interrogation was to be filmed, I felt that it would act as a record of sorts and someone might see it and know that I was alive. I did not believe that any word of my survival could have reached the outside world although I had told the Chinese that I had radioed before bailing out.

I was seated with a Chinese official on my right and the interpreter on the left. They again began to tell me what I had heard during the past interrogation sessions. The Chinese People's Liberation Army had a lenient policy toward prisoners and that I would go home when the war ended, for there was no reason to keep me. They reiterated that violating the Chinese territorial air space was a serious crime for which I was not held personally responsible as it was regarded as the "aggressive actions of the Wall Street warmongers." During this propaganda session the cameras ground away and the people watched and listened intently. I listened carefully since there is always a faint glimmer of hope that actions such as these might result in freedom by some miracle of great magnitude.

Immediately after the interview, four Chinese soldiers took me out to another of Uncle Sam's jeeps. I had not seen these guards before. I was placed in the back seat with two guards and a towel was wrapped around my head as a blindfold. There were two Chinese soldiers in the front seat. All of these soldiers wore red stars so they were not members of the Chinese People's Volunteer group; they were the People's Liberation Army troops. This should have given me an indication of where I was going but hope springs eternal in the human breast.

(Throughout the Korean War, China maintained the policy that all of its troops serving in North Korea were 'volunteers', and thus China as a nation was not directly involved with the conflict. Because of this, Chinese troops serving in Korea did not wear the insignia and unit patches of the People's Liberation Army)

The jeep traveled through a number of villages. Although I was blindfolded, I could peek out of the lower edge of the blindfold to the side of the vehicle and see a few peripheral things. Finally the jeep came to a grinding halt outside a railroad station and the blindfold was removed. I guessed we in Antung, the city close to the Yalu River. We waited here for a lengthy period of time.

Front page press report from the Swea City Herald Thursday April 9 1953.
CAPT H FISCHER IS MISSING Anyone who has received a telegram stating, "We regret to inform you.." knows the heartbreaking moments that follow.
Such a telegram was received yesterday by Mr. and Mrs. Harold Fischer who farm near Swea City. Their son, Capt Harold Fischer, Iowa's first jet ace of the Korean War, is missing in action.
That's all there is to the telegram. Nothing else other than a sentence stating a letter will follow. What thoughts must run through the minds of these parents?
Capt Harold Fischer, a cleancut Iowa youth is now missing. He achieved the enviable honor of being crowned a double jet ace, but now he is missing.
His ability as a jet pilot received national recognition with newspapers and radio stations carrying stories about him. In the March 26 issue, this newspaper reported that Capt Fischer had about 30 missions remaining before he completed his second tour of duty.
We know the hearts of everyone in the community, everyone who knows Mr. and Mrs. Fischer go out to them at this time.
May another telegram arrive saying their son is safe.

Press report Swea City Herald 16<u>th</u> April 1953

Last week's headlines, Capt Fischer Missing, was one of the most difficult things we've ever had to set up in type.

While we are not personally acquainted with him, we do feel we've gotten to know him through his parents and the releases sent to us by the air force.

Of course we feared the worst might have happened to him, like countless others did, and it was as if someone had suddenly lifted a huge load from our shoulders when we learned he was reported safe—even though a prisoner.

This is a time, we know, when God played His part in the safety of this young man!

Taken from a press report in the Des Moines Tribune March 23<u>rd</u> 1953

"I have never considered the possibility of not coming back", he said. Mental attitude plays a tremendous part in air battles, the captain believes. "The most important thing is really wanting to make contact with the enemy"

Perhaps the ripest compliment paid the captain came from Maj.JamesT Lyons of San Bernadino Ca, operations officer of this base.

"I have three daughters," he said. "I hope all of them marry men like Hal Fischer . "

CLASS OF SERVICE

This is a full-rate Telegram or Cablegram unless its deferred character is indicated by a suitable symbol above or preceding the address.

WESTERN UNION

W. P. MARSHALL. PRESIDENT

1204

SYMBOLS

DL = Day Letter
NL = Night Letter
LC = Deferred Cable
NLT = Cable Night Letter
Ship Radiogram

The filing time shown in the date line on telegrams and day letters is STANDARD TIME at point of origin. Time of receipt is STANDARD TIME at point of destination

Ck Pd FAX Washington D C 1150 a m Mar 8 1953

Mr & Mrs Harold E Fischer
Swea City Ia

It is with deep regret that I officially inform you that your
son Captain Harold E Fischer has been missing since
7 April 1953 as the result of participating in Korean operations.
A letter containing further details will be forwarded to you at
the earliest possible date. Please accept my sincere sympathy
during this time of anxiety.

Major General John H McCormick
Director of Military Personnel
Headquarters United States

N   1115 a m

THE COMPANY WILL APPRECIATE SUGGESTIONS FROM ITS PATRONS CONCERNING ITS SERVICE

CLASS OF SERVICE

This is a full-rate Telegram or Cablegram unless its deferred character is indicated by a suitable symbol above or preceding the address.

WESTERN UNION

W. P. MARSHALL. PRESIDENT

1204

SYMBOLS

DL = Day Letter
NL = Night Letter
LC = Deferred Cable
NLT = Cable Night Letter
Ship Radiogram

The filing time shown in the date line on telegrams and day letters is STANDARD TIME at point of origin. Time of receipt is STANDARD TIME at point of destination

ok Govt Pd FAX Washington D C 113 p m Mar 19 1953

Mr & Mrs Harold Fischer
Swea City Ia

We have received information enemy propoganda broadcast from Peking
China in which the name of your son Capt Harold E Fischer was mentioned
as prisoner of war. In the absence of authoritative information through
recognized official channels, we are continuing to list your son as
missing in action. However, we are airmailing you instructions for
addressing letters to him. You are assured that any new information
we may receive concerning him will be promptly forwarded to you. My
sympathy continues and I share your hope for the safe return of your
son.

Major General John H McCormick
Director of Military Personnel
Headquarters United States Air
Force

N 125 p m

THE COMPANY WILL APPRECIATE SUGGESTIONS FROM ITS PATRONS CONCERNING ITS SERVICE

Commanding Officer of Ace Writes of Hope to Parents

(Editor's note: The following letter was received by Mr. and Mrs. Harold Fischer, concerning their son, Capt. Harold Fischer, who was recently shot down while in combat over Korea.)

39TH FIGHTER INTERCEPTOR SQUADRON
51ST FIGHTER INTERCEPTOR GROUP
APO 970

11 April 1953

Mr. and Mrs. H. E. Fischer, RR 1,
Swea City, Iowa

Dear Mr. and Mrs. Fischer,

The need for writing you a letter of circumstance concerning the missing in action status of your son, Capt. Harold E. Fischer, fills me with the deepest regret and sympathy. Although the loss to our squadron is deeply felt by every member, we all realize that your shock and grief is even greater. Everyone in the squadron knew Hal well and we all wish to send you our most sincere condolances.

Although Harold has been officially listed as missing in action since the seventh of April, when he failed to return from his 70th mission, we have since had news which to us is a great relief. The Communists in their radio broadcasts have claimed taking him prisoner and have substantiated this claim with the serial number of the aircraft he was flying at the time and other data. This gives us the bright hope that we shall see Hal again, and perhaps soon, if the peace talks and the prisoner repatriation plans are successfully completed as everyone hopes and prays. In the meantime we feel confident that he is alive.

I know you are aware of the outstanding combat record your son has established. Even more outstanding though is the reputation he has gained among his friends here. None of us have ever met a man with a more pleasant and quietly charming personality, who at the same time could demonstrate an unbeatable flying skill and aggressiveness against the enemy. He literally lived flying, and his enthusiasm and pilot ability were of tremendous value in getting our new and younger pilots off to a good start in this combat theater. They all eagerly gave him their complete attention when he would tell his techniques of destroying enemy aircraft and I feel certain that he will be directly responsible for many of the Migs which will be shot down in the future by these youngsters. Harold always had a friendly smile and encouraging word for everyone. He was always willing to help others with their problems and was very highly respected by our officers and airmen alike.

On the afternoon of 7 April, Harold was scheduled for a mission along the Yalu River. The morning mission had encountered Migs and he was very eager to get to "Mig Alley." Shortly after arriving in the vicinity of the Sui Ho Reservoir, enemy aircraft were sighted and Hal led his flight to the attack. During the ensuing fight, several other Migs pounced on your son's flight and forced it to break up into individual aircraft. As soon as Hal's wingman called that they were separated, Hal told him to take it home, knowing the dangers of a single aircraft flying alone against several Migs. That was the last transmission from Harold. Search aircraft which were dispatched later in the day and the following day, could find no wreckage nor did they receive any signals from the ground. The next news was the Communist broadcast. We tend to believe their claim and I trust you may get as much hope from it as we do.

No one can ever take Harold's place, here in the squadron nor at home. Together we will hope for his safety and early return to his friends and loved ones. If there is anything I may do for you, I will consider it an honor if you will just let me know.

Sincerely,
GEORGE I. RUDDELL,
Lt. Colonel USAF Commanding

153

WESTERN UNION (05)

W. P. MARSHALL, PRESIDENT

1220

CLASS OF SERVICE

This is a full-rate Telegram or Cablegram unless its deferred character is indicated by a suitable symbol above or preceding the address.

SYMBOLS

DL=Day Letter
NL=Night Letter
LT=Int'l Letter Telegram
VLT=Int'l Victory Ltr.

The filing time shown in the date line on telegrams and day letters is STANDARD TIME at point of origin. Time of receipt is STANDARD TIME at point of destination.

MA004 SSB116 M.CEA044

(P.WB201-001) LONG XV GOVT PD REPORT DELIVERY= FAX WASHINGTON
DC 6 NFT=

MR AND MRS HAROLD E FISCHER=DELIVER IMMY AND REPORT DELIVERY=
SWEACITY IOWA ▬▬▬▬▬▬▬▬▬ FONE PER CAS INSTNS=

WE HAVE NOW BEEN ADVISED OF THE COMPLETION OF THE EXCHANGE OF
PRISONERS UNDER THE TERMS OF THE TRUCE WITH THE NORTH
KOREAN-CHINESE COMMUNISTS SIGNED 27 JULY 1953. I DEEPLY REGRET
THAT YOUR SON CAPTAIN HAROLD E FISCHER WAS NOT AMONG THOSE
REPATRIATED. YOU MAY BE SURE THE PERSONNEL RELEASED BY THE
COMMUNISTS ARE BEING QUESTIONED EXTENSIVELY IN AN EFFORT TO
SECURE ANY INFORMATION AVAILABLE CONCERNING YOUR LOVED ONE. ALL
DATA CONCERNING AIR FORCE PERSONNEL WHO WERE NOT REPATRIATED
WILL BE CAREFULLY EVALUATED BY THE DEPARTMENT OF THE AIR
FORCE IN ACCORDANCE WITH THE MISSING PERSONS ACT. PENDING
COMPLETION OF THIS REVIEW AND FINAL DETERMINATION OF HIS
STATUS, ALL PAY AND ALOWANCES WILL CONTINUE AS IN THE PAST.
YOU WILL BE KEPT INFORMED OF ANY NEW DEVELOPMENTS. MY SINCERE
SYMPATHY IS AGAIN EXTENDED TO YOU AT THIS TRYING TIME=
      MAJOR GENERAL JOHN H MCCORMICK DIRECTOR OF MILITARY
      PERSONNEL HEADQUARTERS UNITED STATES AIR FORCE=

(955 AM SEP 7 53)=

$ S E
TELEPHONE NO. *Long distance*
TELEPHONED TO *Post Missiles*
TIME *923 a*
BY_____ TO BE *mailed*
ATTEMPTS
TO DELIVER

THE COMPANY WILL APPRECIATE SUGGESTIONS FROM ITS PATRONS CONCERNING ITS SERVICE

CHAPTER 17

MUKDEN-CHINA

Where there is life there is hope.
I think he's done enough in the air now.
Being captured is a bad way to get grounded.
But it's better than the other.
Harold Fischer Sn

Finally I was taken to an empty American made Pullman railroad car. A man I later came to know as Chong drew the shades and took off my blindfold. He was very short and though only about 30 years old was beginning to bald. He had long sideburns, and for a Chinese had an unusually heavy beard. He was brusque and officious. I did not think that this train would be going to Korea because our air cover allowed nothing to move once it crossed the Yalu River and the bridge over the river was a nightly bombing target for the B-29s since they had stopped their day missions. Around 3pm the train moved south and gave me another twinge of hope but it was only to load at the station.

My heart sank when it finally started its trek northward. Where was I going? Was I going to disappear into the vast reaches of China never to be found or located or returned? Was I going to join the vast hordes of slave labor that the Communists were reputed to hold? All these questions raced through my mind. I had the guards with me and watched the train fill with people at each station. I was forced into a corner on the hard seat and crushed by the passengers squeezed in all around me and I felt like screaming in utter frustration. The heat and the pressure were stifling.

We traveled for 14 hours before reaching the outskirts of a large city that I took to be Mukden after deciphering a sign written in Russian and Chinese. It was about 100 miles from the border and under the Japanese had been a thriving industrial center.

Once all the passengers had disembarked my guards led me out to a Russian automobile. We passed a factory that I recognized from an article I had read in a post war issue of National Geographic magazine. It was an aircraft factory that produced biplane aircraft for the Japanese army and after the war, according to the article, the Communists had stripped all the machinery from the plant and taken it to Russia. There were still some motor mounts stacked in the yard. We stopped at the gate of what had once been a factory, a guard let us in and we drove into what was to be my home for the next two years, except for a very short period of time when I managed to escape.

The buildings looked as if they had been used for light industry and brick making. Around the main entrance, soldiers of the Peoples Liberation Army basked like lemmings in the early morning sun. I was taken through a dim, cold and damp hallway to a room that reminded me of a granary storage area. It had a high ceiling and at the far end two windows that were boarded over and about six feet from the floor. The room was bare, no bed or chair, and in the heavy door, an opening just large enough for a bowl of rice to be pushed through. This was my new home where I was held in complete solitary confinement.

I looked at the room, its size, coldness and I had never felt lonelier in my life. A blue steel cot and straw mattress was later brought to me and that was all the furniture that I was to have for a long time.

Cold was a major factor in my imprisonment and even when the weather was warm, the rooms were like meat lockers and it was almost impossible to get warm since any form of exercise was strictly forbidden, even within my cell.

The guard brought me a bowl that was to be used to relieve myself. All conversations were in Chinese so it was impossible to understand exactly what was expected of me. When I used the crockery bowl to relieve my stomach condition, I found that it was to be used only as a urinal and if I wanted to defecate I had to ask the guard. If another guard were available, I would be escorted down to the end of the hallway. The latrine was similar to the one that was used at the camp where I was held prior to coming to Mukden, except that it had stalls. Prisoners were not allowed the luxury of privacy and the guards held the door open to see if I actually did what I had asked to do. Initially it was impossible, no matter how bad my stomach cramps were, to relieve myself with a guard watching the operation. One guard was so avid in doing his duty that he would crouch down to see if I were successful. If a prisoner did not defecate as he had asked to do, he was told that he was "Poor how", which was the opposite of "Ding how", or very bad. This word was used more than any other that I can recall while in China. It was used with various emphasis of severity during almost every phase of the imprisonment.

The prisoners had to learn from bitter experience since rules were not initially stipulated and some were made up at the discretion of the guards who only spoke Chinese. Thus the prisoners rapidly picked up the language. However on my first day, Chong gave the directive that there would be no whistling, no singing, and no lying down except to sleep at night. I would under no circumstances talk to the guard in the passageway outside my cell. There were only three things I was allowed to do.

1. Walk around the cell very quietly.
2. Sit on the edge of my bed
3. Think.

When I was initially escorted to the latrine, a guard went ahead and closed the little sliding panels in the doors through which our food was served. This alerted me to the fact that there were other prisoners who they did not wish me to see, or for them to see me.

When the meals were brought, the guards went to great lengths to hide the fact that there was someone further down the hall or that there were stops prior to reaching my cell. With such pains being taken to conceal the fact that there were other prisoners it became very important for me to make contact with them, both for their safety and mine and also to ease the desperate loneliness. Escape was always on my mind and I thought it would be easier to plan and accomplish with a partner.

On about my sixth day, which I kept track of by scratching on the wall with a small stub of a pencil I found in my cell, I heard a string of oaths emanating from down the hall. I jumped up and put my ear to the door, but there were no further sounds. I had heard enough to know that there was another American in this prison very close to me, and that gave a spark of hope.

The opportunity came sooner than I had expected to find out who else was in the prison. A young guard who liked to talk and practice his language skills was on duty. He stopped at my door, peered through the peephole into the cell and asked if I would write my name on a piece of paper, which I gladly did and helped him pronounce it. I thought that he might be a good contact to supply me with information and could perhaps be bribed to do things for me. I asked in sign language and careful words in my very crude Chinese, to find out the name of the person in the next cell. When he hesitated, I offered him the only thing that I had of any value, and that was a pair of Marine Corp flying gloves, which I had managed to keep. He hesitated for a moment, glanced around nervously and I shoved my name on the scrap of paper at him and asked him to give it to the other American. He went to the next cell and I could hear bits of the conversation. The prisoner was reluctant to speak loudly and I could barely hear what he was saying but his name did come through and it gave me a great shock for it was someone I knew, and whom I thought was dead.

I heard the name "Mackenzie," the missing Canadian Squadron Leader. It was impossible to contain my excitement and I called out "Did you have a glass eye?" He responded with a resounding, "Yes. Is that you Hal?"" and it seemed like a miracle, for everyone thought that Andy was dead. The glass eye was a positive verification. He had picked it up from a friend of his when he was flying Spitfires from England during the big hassle. It had once belonged to a London lady of the night, who took it out at night when she pursued her business. A friend had given it to Andy who kept it as a good luck charm and when he was having a few at the bar, would often surreptitiously jam the eye into his socket and this protruding prosthesis caused much amusement and became his trademark. Everyone knew Andy and his glass eye trick.

When I called out to Andy the guard immediately panicked and ordered us to be quiet as he was doing us a favor. With a little persuasion I got the same guard to get a piece of paper to the other American prisoners to write their names down, and see mine. This was more or less mutual protection for there would be less of a possibility that one of us would be done away with if it were known by the authorities that we all knew who was incarcerated in the prison.

The other two prisoners were Lieut. Ronald Parks from my outfit and Lieut. Lyle Cameron from the 49th FBW. I got the impression from Chong that Parks, Cameron and myself were all in a 'special' category of POW's, fate unknown.

Ron had been with the 51st FIW and had gotten lost after he had been hit and had flown into China following what he thought was the coast of Korea. He had finally bailed out over Port Arthur, which the Russians held and where they had an airfield. Ron had transmitted a lot of radio chatter after he was hit and finally one of the pilots told him to shut up and die like a man, which was cruel in the extreme under the circumstances. However it might also have jolted him into making the right decisions.

So there were four of us in the cell block with someone occupying the fifth cell but with whom Andy was unable to make contact. It was difficult to make contact with Lyle and Ron since there was a partial divider in the hallway and the acoustics were such that it was virtually impossible to talk to them without shouting. However, when the guard was way down the hall, at the opposite side of the cell row, Andy and I could talk to each other with relative ease.

Contacts were necessarily clandestine and of short duration. Because of this, we decided that we should make contact some other way. Our cells were dirty and so we decided to ask the guards for a straw broom that they had in the hall. One of us asked for the broom, and having swept our cell concealed a message in the handle and returned it to the guard. We called the broom "Mabel." After a while Andy would ask for the broom to sweep his cell. In this way we kept in contact for a period of time and he told me how he had been captured, what the daily interrogations were about and how he had been treated.

Andy told me of his last mission where they had made an attack on some MiGs and were just pulling away when he was hit. His aircraft began an uncontrollable roll since evidently his hydraulic controls had been damaged. His only option was to bail out so he pulled the handles on the ejection seat and as he separated from the seat and pulled the ripcord, an F-86 went by him. He was convinced that an F-86 had shot him down and although he tried to view this objectively, he was never the less a little bitter about the incident, which he had every right to be. He drifted down and landed on the side of a hill about a mile and a half south of the Yalu River. North Korean soldiers had evidently been following his descent, for a truckload of them stopped a short distance away from him and began to pursue him. He ran to the top of the ridge and the soldiers began to fire on him. Soldiers were coming up the other side and he was trapped. His only option was to reluctantly surrender.

After his capture he was taken across the river into Manchuria, although he was blindfolded, he was well aware of the river crossing. There he met Liu the Chinese interrogator and after a short interrogation was taken back to Korea, where his serious interrogation began. He was very brusque and military at first giving only his name, rank and serial number and demanding to be shot if that was to be his fate. He kept this up for about two weeks and then the Chinese came through with information on his old squadron based in England and those in it, as well as information about the 51st FIW. This caused him to contemplate his fate and he decided that he would relent a bit in his answers and attitude. This evidently impressed the Chinese authorities and it was indicated that Andy would soon be returned to a North Korean POW camp. However, he made one mistake.

Where Andy was being kept there were other prisoners who had been shot down and included in this group was a B-29 tail gunner. One evening Andy was talking clandestinely with the gunner and he stated that he wanted to escape. They were planning the initial move when the interpreter who had been surreptitiously listening, walked up to the gunners window and asked him outright if Andy had been talking about escaping. The gunner in his frustration confirmed the talk of escape and within a few hours Andy was in a jeep and again taken across the Yalu River. He was driven all the way to Mukden, without his blindfold being taken off. Consequently he had no idea where he was and when I told him that he was being held in China, he could hardly believe it. His interrogator had continually told him that he was still in Korea yet he had been in this cell block in Mukden

Andy's main concern was about his wife and whether she was aware that he was still alive. She was a very beautiful woman and Andy wondered if she would re-marry if she thought he had died. It was a very disconcerting situation and in solitary confinement one is not always rational, which the Communists were well aware of.

After an initial settling down period a prisoner's existence for the first 30 days is a nightmare, before becoming accustomed to the prison routine. During this time a great deal of adjustment takes place, and in my case the fact that an early release would require a miracle. During the first few weeks at Mukden, when the time grew heavy, I actually counted the minutes and in order to make them go faster, I would see how long I could hold my breath. It is also during this time period that a prisoner under these circumstances believes that he will either be killed or soon released. There is no neutral belief of a possible long-term incarceration until a peace pact finally happens.

The Geneva Convention on the treatment of prisoners of war does not play a big part in the mindset of prisoners, for realistically speaking POW's are a lost cause for their own side and a liability to their captors. To a POW that fact is a glaring reality and will often wonder why he was spared when so many of his friends had been killed.

Another thought that dwells in ones mind is if the correct decision was made in bailing out and surrendering, and all the alternatives are weighed up a million times over. I debated in my mind over and over whether I should have stayed with the aircraft and risked ditching it in the mouth of the Yalu, or if my final decision and action was the only feasible alternative. Andy debated whether or not he could have rolled all the way to the off shore island or if his bail out decision was the correct one. At the time the action is taken, there is no doubt in ones mind, but given the time to think over and analyze the sequence of events, the situation certainly presents many doubts as to the pros and cons of that split second decision. With endless hours to contemplate matters, a prisoner in solitary confinement can exhibit paranoiac thinking patterns and our captors played on that fact.

Interrogations began in earnest when I arrived at Mukden. They could be classed as military, political and social interrogations and sometimes the sessions were interspersed with all three types. At times it was even difficult to determine whether it was an interrogation at all or whether it was merely a question and answer session. It became evident that our captors expected us to know everything about our military organization. They did not accept answers of "I do not know", and this led to giving them fabricated replies. Soon it became apparent that to get the Chinese to believe anything one had to tell the same lie three times, during three different interrogation sessions.

During the interrogations, we were cajoled and threatened with both direct and indirect threats and emotional blackmail. At the end of an interrogation marathon, we were required to write down various answers to the subject matter covered that day. The first subject that I was faced with were details of my relatives, what they did and their annual income. I recalled the words of the 80th FBS intelligence officer saying that we should always claim our entire family to be from a proletariat background. This was easy for me as that was indeed my background and from farming stock. Both Andy and I often wondered what would have happened to us if our relatives had been Wall Street families.

Chong was one of the Chinese interrogators who had picked me up at the camp near Antung, and it was only towards the end of our long train ride that I learned that he spoke English. I never expected to see him again but he was the first Chinese to enter the door of my cell as an official interrogator. He was short and sickly looking and his eyes were dilated which led me to initially believe that he was a dope addict. He swaggered into my cell with such an arrogant air about him that I almost felt like killing him and for a moment irrationality got the better of me. His abrasive and cruel attitude was such that his own people would have hated him. He remained with us for the full two years of our imprisonment.

At first the questions from Chong seemed aimless as though he had no real goal and purpose in mind. He took delight in trying to make me lie or contradict myself in cross-examination. Periodically he would bring up the subject of germ warfare, but each time I denied it as a ridiculous farce.

Gradually the days began to blend into one another and the words that characterized this time of imprisonment were:- lenient policy of the Chinese Peoples Liberation Army; violated the sacred territorial air of China and must be punished; war criminals; Chinese people desire that you should return home; your case is different; Wall Street war mongers; have faith in the Chinese people.

The meager food began to take its toll and my weight dropped dramatically. Looking at my legs one morning, I felt as if I was an atrocity case that I had seen pictures of during the end of the Third Reich. At first, sleep was impossible and I could never seem to get enough of it. The lights were always left on which took some getting used to. Sleep loss, tension and weight loss all played a part in the physical and mental deterioration that occurred during the initial phases of my internment.

In carefully measured doses we were fed clever propaganda of a theoretical nature, which fell upon susceptible minds in a weakened condition. This new concept of the world revolution for the proletariat was something that was foreign to all of us and exactly what we had been taught to hate and what we were all fighting against. In my conversations with Andy, I noticed that the information that had been given him and the talks that he had with the interpreter had influenced him. This was not a criticism of Andy or the rest of us for at this stage we were highly susceptible to brainwashing from our weakened physical and mental condition. Psychological manipulation is easier when a person is in a weakened and deprived state.

Along with Chong, another interpreter recently assigned to the unit was introduced to us. He was very young and wore a blue uniform, which signified that he was not a member of the army but rather a type of civil service worker. He was assigned the task of our political education officer and had long talks with us regarding our political beliefs. We had to be very careful of what we said. It developed into a game of guessing what he wanted us to believe in, outsmarting him in our answers and to keeping our true beliefs to ourselves. Sometimes these play actions were too much to cope with, which led to an outburst of true opinions which then led to "being guilty of reactionary thoughts" and ordered to write a "self criticism". The incongruity of the situation was the fact that the interpreter encouraged us to speak out, to say what was on our minds and thus trap us more easily. We were being conditioned.

The Chinese were shrewd and constantly manipulated our environment. After a while we were able to find out when an interrogation session was being scheduled for us because the food would improve significantly and small improvements in our daily living became noticeable. Sometimes we got extra food, tobacco or books or some little amenity that would give pleasure and raise our spirits. In this manner we were primed for the next session of questioning. On occasions we were all given the same bonus treatment, but given no indication of who would be selected for interrogation. By this time our grapevine was working well and we managed to pass to each other the type of questions they were asking, what the interrogators said and the atmosphere of each session.

Our contact around this time was often made by one of us distracting a guard with conversation or asking to be taken to the latrine. For this short period of time we spoke quickly; two would talk and one would listen.

It was interesting to analyze what the interrogators told each prisoner for they would tell one of us one thing and another just the opposite. It was a crazy complicated situation and one in which we had to try and keep our wits together.

Two entirely unrelated factors seemed to determine if the day was to be good or bad. The first factor was the weather; when the sun shone, my spirits were high but when the weather was dreary it was very difficult to remain in high spirits. The second factor was the attitude of the interpreter. If he hinted at an imminent release then my outlook was bright, and conversely when it was harshly stated that we were being considered as war criminals, my spirits hit rock bottom. There never seemed to be a normal day, in as much as we were either elated or dejected with no mid range of emotion. The mood swings could occur very rapidly.

Food, and fantasies of good meals, occupied our thoughts a lot. A meager diet of rice or unleavened bread, with occasional vegetables was hardly the proper diet for a man accustomed to a regular diet of meat, potatoes, bread, milk, coffee and desert. Consequently thoughts of good food were ever present. I remember walking around my cell one evening imagining that I was eating apple pie. The illusion was so real that I actually visualized it in my hand and I began snapping at it like a dog gulping down food. The guard peered in and told me to be quiet, for the gnashing of my teeth was disturbing him.

Five days a week we were served three meals a day and only two meals a day over the weekends. The midday meal left much to be desired and usually consisted of rice gruel or a little rice with preserved turnips to season it.

Occasionally on the holidays we were served relatively good food. I had always enjoyed good Chinese food so it was doubly appreciated when it was served to us but it was a rare occasion for our stomachs to be full and feel satisfied. To combat hunger pangs I would literally stuff myself with rice, of which we were allowed any amount, but thirty minutes later the hunger pangs returned.

Filling the spare time that was forced upon us was a serious problem. At first I spent a lot of time thinking and hoping for release, gradually the horizons narrowed to the confines of my cell and I began to look for amusement within the cell. I studied the shapes on the wall of the cell and with imagination pictured all sorts of shapes and memories triggered from them. I lived my life over time and time again, from my earliest memories and analyzed it all. I took a phase of my life and lived it over, dwelled on that particular period for literally days before passing on to another chapter of my experiences and memories. Under these conditions one also spends a degree of time feeling sorry for oneself and analyzing all the possible alternatives that could have been taken for the major decisions in ones life. Prisoners in solitary confinement undertake a great deal of self-analysis and I thought about my parents, girl friends, cars, farms, college, flying training in great detail. Sex is normally a tremendous motivator in a man's life, but became less and less of a factor in thought patterns and as time went on, only the memory stimulants remained. Poor food also contributed to the lessening of drive.

In solitary confinement I was not always rational and once gave vent to my rage against the injustice and frustration of being incarcerated. I shouted, ranted and raved at the guards, kicked the door of the cell and called the Chinese every name in the book with the majority of the choice names picked up from my short naval career. I made no attempt to control myself. This brought a rush of guards down the hall and I was hastily escorted to another cell where I continued to threaten everyone and everything in creation. Finally, rationality returned and I became peaceful and serene as if all my troubles had been washed away and a little sheepish at letting myself go like that.

I was taken before the camp commandant, a large Chinese man who always portrayed the air of being on the side of the prisoner. He always had a smile, which helped as I imagined it would be better to be shot by a smiling man, than one with a scowl and anger etched in his face, though the end result of death would be the same and make not one jot of difference to the outcome. "The Chief," as we called him, sentenced me to time in a small back room that I was to know later for another infringement. It had a solid, rough concrete floor, was totally bare with not even a bed or wooden board to sleep on, and the usual rules of no whistling, singing, scuffing feet or lying down to sleep except at night. I spent three days here, though it seemed longer and I also had to write a self-criticism for my actions and promise not to do it again. From a psychological standpoint this was a clever move as it put a prisoner on the defensive as he never knew exactly how many black marks or incidents of bad behavior could be placed against his name, thus putting him on the list of non-repatriates. This was always their most effective threat.

As prisoner's horizons narrow, ones attention and enjoyment has to come from small things in the confines of the cell. In my case there were spiders to study as they built their webs and caught flies. I had one particular spider that would weave a web in one corner of the cell and when I had fed him five flies, he would move and soon his web would appear in a new location. Five more flies and he would move again. It was little things like this that occupied my time.

In my youth I had built gliders from balsa wood. In China, this childhood hobby came forth again and the guards gave me empty matchboxes that I carefully took apart and was able to build small gliders that I flew around the cell. This was a source of amusement both to the guards and me. I was also given a deck of cards and I wore the cards to tatters playing solitaire. I had all but forgotten the rules so I made up my own rules and in time determined the probability of beating the game. Using the system that I devised I found that every fourteenth game I would win, and for a month, I played for at least eight hours a day. The cards were a welcome diversion in my life.

As an indication of the supposed lenient policy towards prisoners of the Chinese Peoples Liberation Army, I was given a set of paints and paper upon which to draw designs and pictures. Always having the desire but not the talent for the arts, this gave me an outlet, but little satisfaction with my meager attempts to emulate Van Gogh. Using rice paste, I had the entire cell ringed with pictures of flowers, landscapes and colorful designs. All of these things were outlets for frustration and helped to pass the time of day, for which I was grateful.

We were getting pale and asked for the chance to get some fresh air and exercise, which was eventually granted. We were allowed to go outside to a small courtyard adjacent to our cells where we enjoyed a little piece of blue sky and some sunshine if the hours were right and the sun overhead. It was also an opportunity to wash our clothes, which needed it very badly. By this time we were all wearing padded clothing which after two or three months without being washed could almost stand up of their own accord. But they were warm and when we were allowed outside, we were permitted to wash them.

July 1953 rolled around and the guards had been telling us that there was very little fighting, and finally that the warfare had stopped. This was what we were waiting for because our captors had said continually that once the war was over our status could be discussed. With the approaching end of hostilities, our treatment began to improve. The first indication of this was the fact that a recreation room was opened up for the prisoners. There were evidently a number of prisoners using this clubroom for we were only allowed about 15 to 20 minutes at a time. It was a small room and had an accordion, violin, Chinese checkers, some magazines, a ping-pong table and an old wind-up phonograph for our use. One of the treasures of this clubroom were some old V discs that had been cut during WW 11 and released to the troops. On the V discs were inscribed, "Company G, 2nd Battalion of the United States Marines stationed at Tsing Tao." Duke Ellington was featured on one side and I would close my eyes and be back listening to the greatest again. What a history those records might have told.

Excerpt from a press report in the Des Moines Tribune

'Go Home'
Knowland reported, "Our other two planes found something else. Hal and I prowled around looking for more MiGs. We sighted two more. One got lost in the haze, but Fischer went after the other one. He went into a maneuver and I lost him in the haze. I called to him on the radio, told him we were separated. He yelled back emphatically 'Get out, get out!' That meant for me to go home. Usually Hal is so calm and easy when giving orders, but not this time. He must have been in bad trouble. I didn't hear from him again.

Then I started getting chased myself. Some MiGs got on my tail, and I was damn lucky to get out. Flying with Hal was something like hanging onto the end of a rope in a game of crack-the-whip".

Tears
There were tears in the eyes of Fischer's friends. Said his squadron commander, Lt.Col.George Ruddel, "He was one of the quietest, nicest guys I ever knew. Unless he was talking combat, you'd never dream he was a tiger. He'd get so close to those MiGs he'd come back with pieces of MiGs stuck to his ship"

Paper Tiger.
Said his flight chief, Robert Hodges, Covington, Ky.,"I've been in the air force for 11 years but for my money Captain Fischer was about the best. Just about every day he'd come out and look at his plane. He'd say, "Isn't she a beauty." Paper Tiger he called her.

The day he got back from getting his tenth MiG, the nose of his ship was black. I figured that meant a MiG had exploded close to him. Then I saw him grinning, and he looked jubilant. He held up both hands——10 fingers, ten MiGs. Boy, I sure hope he gets out somehow."

Brown steer
Said Fischer's crew chief, Gerald Larkowski, Dannebrog, Neb., "He was so kind to me. The first time I met him he shook hands like we'd known each other a long time and said, 'Glad to know you, fella. We'll work together and I think I'll have more MiGs'. He never had a complaint."

A couple of weeks ago Bill Barnard of the Associated Press interviewed Fischer. He recalls, "Of all the pilots I've interviewed, Fischer was the nicest. His eyes really brightened when he talked about life on his Iowa farm. He was more anxious to talk about winning first place with a brown steer at the Kossuth county fair than destroying MiGs".

CHAPTER 18

COMRADESHIP

*It takes as much courage to have tried and failed
as it does to have tried and succeeded.*
Anne Morrow Lindberg

The interpreter finally told Lyle, Ron and me that the war was over, but they told Andy that hostilities were still going on, and this alarmed me. Why would they tell us one thing and lie to Andy? Just what the truth was and what psychological games they were playing was a mystery. It was a perplexing situation, so I told the interpreter that I did not believe him.

In my short experience with the Chinese, I found that they preferred for one never to have too much of anything, be it food, hope or despair. When I acted very dejected and stated my disbelief that the war had ended, a newspaper clipping was given to me to read which convinced me of its truth. The officials of both sides were meeting at Kaesong and signing the truce agreement. I convinced Andy as to the truth, but we were both unable to determine why he had been given false information and the reasons for the Chinese deception.

Everything had been going very smoothly. The guards had been given instructions to be friendly, though on occasions their orders were to be openly hostile toward us, a subtle method of programming to aid the next interrogation session. Our food improved, and was more plentiful and I was allowed to make a noise in my cell, but our political indoctrination continued. At one time, we were given more books to read, which was a miracle in itself, but looking back yet another method of softening us up. All this culminated in an event which all of us were waiting for, and were overjoyed with. It was a move that again strained our emotional pendulum to the upper limit and another ingenious psychological tactic.

I was taken to a room where I had often been interrogated and noticed that the guards were smiling. At the time I had no idea what was going to happen and entering the room was faced with a barrage and full entourage of Chinese. They said, "Your request has been granted, you may now live with other prisoners." With these words Lyle Cameron, a tall blonde pilot of about 25yrs old was ushered into the room. He was dressed as we all were, in blue padded clothing and after being introduced, we were told to sit down and Ronald Parks was brought in and introduced to me. Ron was short and wiry. He and Lyle had been together before. We were all smiles, happy to be together, and to see fellow Americans. This meeting was profound and highlighted our enforced incarceration at Mukden.

We were returned to Ron's old cell, which was large, and were given three beds and three writing desks. There was so much that we wanted to say that it was difficult to talk fast enough. There had been so much left unsaid during our short clandestine communications when the guard's attention was diverted that it was almost painful now with so much to relate. As a result only the most important subjects were initially discussed.

It turned out that all of us were from the mid-west: Lyle from Lincoln, Nebraska and Ron from Omaha, Nebraska. My own home, where my parents still lived was Swea City, Iowa. We were from an area within 300 miles of each other, thus we knew a little about the general areas of where we were all from. There was much to discuss and we had a lot in common.

With companions, the time now passed rapidly and there weren't enough hours in the day to talk. The guards knocked on the wall and door at night telling us to be quiet. It was interesting to find out how all of us had fallen victims of fate and ended up as POW's in China. On leaving our home shores we could not possibly, in our wildest dreams, have imagined what lay in store for us.

Lyle had been flying F-84's out of Taegu in South Korea. There was a lot of fog and early morning mist in the area of a mission and they let down from altitude over what they thought was their intended target and located a train which they dive bombed, scoring excellent hits. On his second bombing dive, he concentrated on the target and did not notice that he was too close to it and not far away from the lead aircraft.

The bomb from the aircraft ahead of him exploded and a fragment from it struck his aircraft in the right wing. It immediately started to burn and at low altitude he did not stand a chance. The fire curled around the wing and began to eat away at the main airfoil so he had no option but to bail out. The flight circled around him during his descent and then left. He landed close to the train, which had been used to haul wounded Chinese Volunteers from the front. He subsequently learned that the train he had attacked was in China and not in North Korea. There had been a gross miscalculation in the flights navigation.

The soldiers who were on the train immediately captured him and as he was being tied up one of the railroad workers approached him with a hammer used to tap the junction boxes of the railroad cars. It was sharp and if used as a weapon, would be deadly. The man raised the weapon and Lyle thought that his end had come. Fortunately the railroad worker was only threatening, and Lyle's life was spared. He was then forced to walk among the wounded soldiers who spat on him. A humiliating and degrading experience.

Ron had a somewhat different experience. In a fight near the Yalu River, he had damaged a MiG and then picked up a hit on his own aircraft. They had been below the overcast and when he climbed up, he was disorientated as his instruments had been damaged. He followed the coast of China, thinking it was the coast of Korea. When he ran out of gas, he glided down and beneath him was a cleverly camouflaged airfield. In fact, he saw aircraft landing and taking off from what appeared to be stacked corn stalks. Dusk was gathering so he bailed out.

He landed on the side of hill and moving down a narrow path he ran into an old Chinese man whom he threatened with a pistol and forced him, or so he thought, to take him to some food and shelter. The old man obeyed but with different intent to what Ron had anticipated. He was led to the center of the village where the old man started to screech like a plucked chicken warning all the villagers. Before Ron knew what was happening the local "mayor" had him hauled roughly onto a platform and proceeded to lecture the peasants in rapid Chinese. At this stage Ron thought that he was about to be hung. Soon the Russians arrived and took him into custody as the area was under their protectorate. While with the Russians he had been well treated and fed, but was turned over to the Chinese after a few days of interrogation.

Ron was shot down sometime in September of 1952 and was taken to a Chinese prison somewhere in Mukden, where Chinese Nationalists and Japanese prisoners were still being held from World War 11. He was there for about a month and a lonelier situation I could not imagine, until Lyle arrived in October.

Lyle and Ron were extremely fortunate to be placed together for their term of POW status in China. These two young unmarried Americans were being held in a prison in northeast China, placed with a race noted for their cruelty. The emotional shock of having to endure this existence must have been tremendous for both of them and they were fortunate to be in this predicament together, for to endure what they did alone would have been tough even for one with the strongest psychological disposition.

Their tales of living with the Chinese prisoners were both hilarious and sad. Both had suffered initially from severe cases of diarrhea but they were fortunate in having access to a private latrine. They spoke of prisoners in shackles and of some who had to sit facing the door all day and were not allowed to move without prior permission from the guards. One of the heavily shackled prisoners went out of his mind and screamed twenty-four hours a day. Only those of the finest mental stability could endure such deprivation and misery, although there was no evidence of physical punishment.

Ron and Lyle were together from October 1952 until April 1953 when they were separated and brought down to the prison where we finally met. They had been in solitary confinement from April until July, when the three of us were placed together. The primary concern now that we were together and had settled down was Andrew Mackenzie and his well-being.

What concerned us was the fact that Andy had not been told of the end of the war and that he was still in solitary confinement. What were they going to do with him now that we had lost contact with him? This concerned all of us especially me, since I had the closest contact with him through "Mabel", as we called our broom. One thing in particular that bothered me, was that he had unthinkingly told the Chinese that no one had seen him crash. Thus no one except the Chinese and we three knew he was alive, and the Chinese were unaware that we knew of his existence and might think he could be eliminated without trace.

We decided to do something about the situation so we told the Chinese what we knew of MacKenzie. This was not an easy decision for we realized that there were certain risks involved but if they wanted to eliminate him without trace they would have to eliminate all of us, something I believed they would not do. It was interesting to note the reaction that occurred.

When the interpreter came in the next day, (incidentally it happened to be a new one who had recently arrived), we told him about the prisoner down the hall. He flatly denied the existence of another prisoner and then asked us to write down what we knew of him. I wrote it down with an explanation of how we knew that he existed and what we knew about him. The repercussions occurred quickly. Later that day, I was taken from the cell and put before a panel of officers and interpreters.

The atmosphere when I walked in was grim, and I could see that it would not be easy for me. I was told that I was an activist and sentenced to be separated again from my compatriots. I was grabbed by the neck of my jacket and hustled off roughly to a tiny, dark, damp cell at the back of the building. I was thrown inside, the door slammed shut and I was once again in solitary confinement. Thinking that I might be in for a little longer period of time than before, I settled down to a waiting game that I thought would never end. There was no furniture in the room and no bed. The old rules were back in force: no noise, no singing, no whistling, and no scuffing of shoes. To make matters worse, one of my eyeeteeth, which had become infected prior to being shot down, began to ache. During the day the cell buzzed with a maddening high frequency whistle akin to the noise of a short wave radio

At the end of the week, I expected to be released, but instead a bed was brought in. At the end of the month, still in solitary, I received a desk. It was late September 1953 when the commanding officer of the prison told me that some prisoners were being repatriated and that after they had been exchanged we would in all probability be allowed to go home. He rather ominously remarked that our cases were 'different' but I still thought we would be home by Christmas. Little did we know how different our cases were to become.

The routine of eternal interrogations was stepped up in intensity, and the questions now concerned border violations and Chong seemed to have a definite purpose behind everything he did. I was grilled day and night, over and over, week in and week out. They wanted precise details on when crossings were made, at what altitude and how many aircraft. I had no way of knowing these details and they were well aware of this, but the pretense of credibility had to be made, so I lied for peace of mind. When I told the same lie three times, they believed it no matter how ridiculous it seemed. In the evening I went over and memorized the answers that I had given, for I knew that I would be asked about them again.

Of concern to all of us were the germ-bomb accusations. It seemed silly when we first heard the questions but the interrogators were insistent and actually gave a credible pretense of believing them. There was a great deal of semi-official literature supporting the controversy of biological warfare, which the common people might have believed when put out by their government. Chong wanted me to admit that I had dropped germ bombs on the Chinese and that I had been ordered to cross the Manchurian border. The charges were of course ridiculous as neither I, nor anyone else had ever participated in germ warfare and I had never been ordered to cross the Yalu. We had strict air force orders not to cross the border.

I was severely interrogated for this information, and in order to relieve the pressure put on me and the insistence of my knowledge, I made up a story so fantastic that it was a stress release just to invent it. Chong the interrogator knew that it was a fantastic lie but to save face, the farce proceeded. I made up the operation code name of *"Duress,"* which meant that this information was given under force and not necessarily a code name. Once I gave it the name and repeated it three times, it became official. Then I made up elaborate details such as creating a special oxygen system for the bacteria so that they would survive at high altitude. I stated further that there had to be elaborate precautions to heat the projectile that housed the "germs." It became a story that would have thrilled the heart of a science fiction writer. By making it so detailed and fantastic, the Chinese could not refute it. As far as I know nothing came of my story, nor was it ever mentioned again after the draft copy was submitted which was their usual operating procedure.

With the severity of the interrogations the Communists reduced us to putty. Looking back I believe that I was nearly driven out of my mind and that I had almost lost contact with reality. Never doubt for a moment that the Communists can break a man to that state of mind given the time and the right circumstances. They had years of experience with a multitude of human guinea pigs. There were times that I got very angry and prayed to God that He would help me get back at the Communists.

(Methods of subtle psychological manipulation and brainwashing techniques used by the communists were later discussed in a thesis for a MSc degree written in 1959. "An Analysis of Ideological Remolding" by Harold E Fischer.)

As the Christmas season drew near, I began to become very dejected and depressed for I was in my seventh month of solitary confinement, alone with my thoughts. After a lengthy period of time in solitary confinement it becomes virtually impossible to think of new subjects to debate with oneself. As Christmas approached I decided that if I was not home or at least on my way home by Christmas, that I would attempt to escape and this idea became an obsession. The more I thought about it, the more my mind fixated on it and I searched for a feasible way to escape and the various possibilities.

I set a few criteria, one of which was that I would not hurt any guard. My scheme started taking shape when I picked up a nail while out in the sun for a short exercise period. My cell was small with barely enough room for the bed and desk and adjacent to an outside wall. Four steps got me from one end to the other and often I spent hours pacing up and down the confines of the cell, like a caged animal.

I pushed the bed in a corner so that it would hide my excavation from the guards' view. I found that it was relatively easy to scrape away the cement when I soaked the area with hot water that was always given to us. It was January 2, 1954 when I began to remove the debris in earnest. I had to time my work under the bed to coincide with the guard being at the other end of the cell block.

During this time I was a model prisoner, smiling and being friendly to all the guards and thanking them for the water and food that they brought. Since I was so obliging they never bothered to come in and check my room. If they had done so and raised the blanket that I let hang to the floor, they would have found an increasingly large pile of debris that was accumulating from my constant chipping away at the wall of the cell. Some of the rubble I was able to dispose of under the eaves of the building through a small hole in the plaster ceiling. Many times the interpreter came in and sat on the edge of the bed. We talked and I smiled inwardly at my secret.

As the debris gradually accumulated under the bed, the tension mounted, for the danger of being found out grew with each particle of sand and brick. The walls of the prison were very cheaply constructed. There was a thin veneer of cement, then a tier of bricks, six inches of sand and a layer of bricks that formed the outside wall. By constantly dousing the wall with water, it loosened the small amount of cement and sand that bound the bricks in place. It was a simple matter but it took time and patience with my only tool being a rusty old nail.

After 10 days I had almost dug through the foot-and-a-half wall. Finally only the outside layer of bricks remained in place and I was very careful to loosen each brick just enough so that they would topple out with a gentle push. Once this was done, I waited for the right time to affect my escape and decided to wait until the weekend. The reasoning behind this was that the guards seemed to be just a little more relaxed over the weekends and my exit from prison might be easier.

According to the calculations that I kept on a rather crude calendar it was January 16, 1954. The weather was unseasonably warm and balmy for this time of the year and I decided that the time was right. Only two meals a day were served on the weekends and when the evening meal arrived I stuffed two small loaves of *mantou* (bread) in my Chinese winter style blue jacket as it was better to hide things on my person. Our cells were sometimes searched, though individuals rarely were. I also ripped off a piece of towel to wear like the typical Chinese face covering used against winter cold and also to disguise my Caucasian features.

Fortunately there was no search while I made a very quick trip to the latrine. One of the guards was in my cell, but I returned so fast that it was impossible for him to make a thorough search. He sheepishly walked out of the cell as I turned the corner with the chamber pot in my hand that I had emptied in the latrines. Waiting for the evening to lengthen and the lights to go out, I thought again about the feasibility of this escape and the plan that I would pursue once free.

Under the circumstances of the supposed end of the war, this was perhaps a foolish move, but I felt that if I was ever going to return home, drastic measures were necessary. There was also the distinct possibility of mental instability setting in as I began to hear a constant buzzing in my ears again. I thought that the Chinese had a radio station nearby and I could hear the hum of the equipment, but they emphatically denied having such equipment

I had decided to make my way directly to the airfield that was close to the prison and attempt to steal an airplane. This idea was born of desperation but one that was well worth trying, as it was quite a distance back to my base in South Korea. The second alternative was to try to board a train and travel either southeast to the Korean border or southwest to the port of Tientsin. Some form of transport was necessary because attempting to walk in the winter conditions of northern China would be inviting defeat in this unforgiving land.

I had to escape and the die was now cast, for giving up at this stage would have meant a great deal of my time and effort had been wasted. For a taste of freedom it was worth chancing my luck. I decided that after the 10pm guard change I would make the move. The new guard came on and by the sounds he was making I could tell that he would rather be somewhere else and not at his post guarding sleeping American prisoners. I piled some clothes in the bed to give the impression that I was sleeping. My desk was positioned next to the top of my bed so my head was not usually visible to the guards and they were used to this.

Slipping under the bed, I gingerly pushed out the remaining bricks in the outer wall. Pushing my heavy padded pants and jacket through the hole in the wall, I poked my head out of the building and breathed the fresh air of freedom. But I had misjudged the size of the opening, the hole was not big enough and panic briefly overcame me. Thinking rationally for a moment and sizing up the situation, I turned around and put my feet out first, and by hunching my shoulders, I was able with a little extra effort to extricate myself from incarceration and dropped to the ground.... a free man.

I stood still and listened for a moment and the realization that I was free was worth all the effort and every bit of anxiety that I had put into planning this escape.

CHAPTER 19

ESCAPE

***It is better to have a plan that might not be perfect,
might not even work, than no plan at all.***
HF

It felt good to be free. Since there was a possibility that this escape effort to ultimate freedom might fail, I had left a note in the cell stating that I had no intention of doing anyone bodily harm.

I moved to the side of the building and put on the heavily padded jacket and trousers and adjusting the face covering, walked away from the prison as fast as I could, across a cabbage field. I followed a drainage ditch I came across which led to a broad boulevard crowded with automobiles (including late American models), bicycles and a multitude of people out walking like any Saturday night crowd in any American town. I eased into the throng, walking with my legs apart and swaying slightly trying to emulate the Chinese gait, taking care never to be directly in front of anyone for too long. For maximum safety, I found the best position to be either slightly behind a group of Chinese or well ahead.

I proceeded directly to what I thought was the airfield and joined up with a large group of Chinese heading in the same direction. It was about 10:30pm and this was possibly a shift going to work at the airfield and my hopes rose thinking that by mingling with them, it might give me the chance to get on the airfield. As our group approached, all my hopes were dashed, as the Chinese had to pass through a checkpoint before being allowed onto the base.

Continuing south past the main hangars, I noted that the entire area and planes were behind high fences, patrolled by still more guards. I walked back and forth near the entrance to the field that was marked by a big red star with a spotlight beaming on it. I tried mingling again with the civilian workers in the middle of a shift change, but the plan to steal a plane seemed hopeless. Even if I did manage to enter, the difficulty would then lie in getting the airplane on the runway. It was a tough decision to make, but alas, the only choice I had was to abandon the somewhat idealistic plan and take up the second alternative.

I decided to try the other side of the field and started in that direction when suddenly out of the darkness loomed a guard from the airfield. He stood squarely in my path and I could not turn and run. To bluff my way through, I kept on walking and waved my arms wildly, indicating that I wanted to cross the runway, but the guard ordered me to turn around and go back. I staggered and gesticulated with my arms, pretending to be drunk, muttered a few words of Chinese and then turned around and walked away. He must have become suspicious for he kept shouting at me and although he was armed he evidently had no intention of using it. I would have kept right on going even if he had fired at me, for the elation of freedom was virulently strong within me. The guard was evidently shouting for the man in charge, since a jeep came racing by but I had already reached the road and hoped that I had mingled inconspicuously enough with the Chinese. My heart was pounding from the close call and the excitement of the escape had my adrenalin surging.

I became aware of many white vehicles with red crosses patrolling the main streets with their sirens blaring and they sent chills running up and down my spine. I chose to get away from the city as fast as possible, so I cut down a little alley running south on the very outskirts of Mukden. It led through a rather dank area where rotten garlic or garbage was dumped, for the stench was disgusting. The dogs from all these small fenced off houses set up a terrific din as I passed by. I bumped into a couple of Chinese lovers busy on a park bench, bowed in apology and got on my way.

Finally I found myself out in the country, and walked for about 6 hours, stopping to rest every half-hour. After the long imprisonment, I was in extremely poor physical condition and my normal weight of 165lbs had dropped to about 130lbs. I had very little strength or endurance. The weather was unseasonably warm and this should have alerted me for what was to follow. In fact my entire body was soaked with sweat from the physical and psychological exertion.

With my spirits up and confidence in my navigational abilities, I continued southeast on what I judged to be a heading of about 150 degrees. With the exception of the brief disappointment at the airfield, everything was going as planned and I felt good. Being confident that I knew where I was, the only remaining known obstacle was the river south of the city of Mukden where it was split to form a "Y". I knew it was somewhere ahead of me and expected no difficulty in crossing what I anticipated would be a completely frozen river in the height of winter.

Continuing southeast I began to hear the sound of the river in the distance. About 5a.m. a wide expanse of water loomed in front of me, as the Hun River cut its way through this flat area of Manchuria. I stood dumbfounded, knowing something had to be wrong. This was supposed to be frozen solid—a natural bridge waiting for me to cross at any point of my choosing. There was ice along the riverbanks but a wide expanse of dark, cold water ran between the icy banks. My heart sank as I stood on the bank wondering how in the world I was going to get across. Knowing I could not get across and keep my shoes and clothes dry, I headed south along the riverbank. My confidence and high spirits were starting to give way to encroaching despair.

I knew all the bridges would be guarded and well lit so I looked for a boat, a raft or a plain log, anything I could use to float across, but in the dark I found nothing. Finally my strength ran out and I collapsed on the bank and went to sleep. When I awoke shortly after dawn I was cold, covered in frost and hungry, so I ate a few of the crusts of bread I had stashed away in my jacket. I needed a drink of water, and looked around for a little clean snow but there was none. Survival training had taught me the necessity for water to stay hydrated, sharp and capable of endurance.

I saw peasants traveling along a road not far away. They were riding in, or walking beside small, grossly overloaded horse drawn carts. I fell in and for a while walked beside them in the bright morning sun, but realized this was dangerous exposure on an open road and my height and gait might be conspicuous. I returned to the riverbank and followed it until late in the afternoon. Finally I came upon a place where I could ford the river without immersing myself completely and thought it would be shallow enough to wade through. As soon as I got into the icy water I realized that I had made a big mistake, as my feet became numb. I had managed to cross it, but much later in the day than I had planned. My numb feet ached and no amount of rubbing and massage seemed to help.

I pushed on southwards over barren fields interspersed with small villages built of brown dirt bricks and skirted a village where the peasants were using the eons old method of threshing grain. These fields had been tilled by the Chinese for centuries, and seen much change, but the way of life here seemed little affected by progress. In recent years American and Japanese planes had occupied the skies above this serene setting and now Russian warplanes were flying over these fields daily to their base at Port Arthur.

The weather got colder and my feet more painful. Late in the afternoon I came upon a double track railroad and thinking this probably led south toward Antung, I followed it keeping off into the bushes. I thought I might be able to jump on a passing freight train. By now, hunger and cold were taking their toll on me and the lack of sleep was also beginning to affect me. By nightfall I could walk no further, physical exhaustion was close, and finally I had no alternative but to find a suitable spot to rest up. I found an old gun emplacement, probably built by the Japanese, crawled into it, took shelter and laid down to rest. It was now the second evening of my freedom and the weather was deteriorating.

Next morning my feet ached badly and it was obvious that they were frostbitten. I had no water and nothing to eat and there was nothing to be found in the fields. But I still had hope and walking south along the railroad, I discovered that each bridge had guards posted and this forced me to make a lengthy detour around each one. At one point I heard gunshots and saw a terrified peasant and his wife running away. I had no idea what this gunfire was about, but it gave me a little hope that there might be friendly Chinese in the area.

Approaching a village, I noticed a graveyard with the sign of the cross and in the distance a steeple indicating a Christian presence in the area. Walking down a path, I bumped into a white person and both of us were so startled that I rapidly moved on attempting to ignore my surprise. In my calculating state of mind it meant exposure and I didn't know his affiliations to the area.

The village seemed to be a railroad junction and a possible place to catch a train so I moved off into the bushes, watched for a while and tried to determine the best time to board a train. Some trains stopped briefly, others were large, carried heavy loads, and did not stop. It was interesting to note that much of the equipment had evidently been used in Korea, for it was riddled with bullet holes. It was almost nine months since the end of the war so the damage might well have been from guerilla activity.

As darkness fell, I emerged from my hiding place. It was cold and I had no water. My throat was parched and I was extremely thirsty. There was a little snow lying about but it was old and dirty with dust and weed stems mixed into it. I forced myself to eat some but it was hard to swallow and gave little relief to the thirst that now plagued me. My spirits were very low and my physical condition even lower. My feet no longer had any feeling in them at all. I was overcome with a desire for food and warmth so I took a calculated risk and roamed down the streets and saw people eating in local establishments. I went to the door of a little grocery store, and using the simple Chinese words I picked up in prison, asked for a drink of water. I was given water but no food and when I offered my wristwatch in exchange for some food, he declined. I wondered why he was not interested in such a bargain.

I did not press this issue to get food, and again went to the station where the Chinese were boarding trains. They were packed in like sardines in a can, and I briefly considered hitching a ride by getting on the roof of the train. I was getting colder, weaker, desperate and despondent. I again considered walking to the Korean border but deemed this idea hopeless, as I was weak and did not have much energy left. The cold was intense. I was hungry and feeling sick. The combination of these factors forced me to make a major decision. Winter is a bad season for escaping anyway and if you have no strength it is hopeless. I could either die a miserable death out here on the cold plains of China or I could go to the warm station and ask for food, shelter and warmth. As much as I valued and desired my freedom, at this stage there was little choice for me if I wanted to live.

Basically it was a question of survival. Be it in an airplane or on the ground, the human will to survive is by far greater that the prospect of impending death. My desire to live drove me once again to the railroad station, which offered warmth, food and shelter. There was no other place for me to go. The next ordeal was about to begin.....

I had no feeling of failure, only an overwhelming desire to get warm. If I could just get warm, I didn't care what happened to me. I walked into the office set apart from the passenger area, where a clerk, bedecked in a workers uniform sat, and said to him, *"Wade Migwa,"* which meant that I was an American, and asked for food. I certainly did not admit to being a prisoner. It was interesting, in a pathetic way to watch his reaction. At first he went about his business then did a double take, stared at me in amazement, brought me some food then got on the telephone, red-faced, gesticulating wildly, with a lot of incomprehensible yakking.

Shortly after his call, a group of Chinese soldiers arrived and descended upon me with a viciousness that was difficult to comprehend. Three of them jumped upon me and forcing my head to the floor they trussed me up and left me bound with my hands tied tightly behind my back. I certainly was not a threat to them in any way. One man held a gun on me, which irritated me for they were behaving as if I was a dangerous criminal. I was weak, tired, and in no way gave the impression of putting up a fight or being aggressive in any manner.

They forced me to lie down near a stove and suddenly a great weariness came upon me. The heat and the warmth gave me a feeling of security and comfort; yet strangely I still retained the feeling of being in control of the situation.

I was an avid believer in always having a plan to cover any emergency that might arise and constantly stressed this to all members of my flight. I emphasized that it was better to have a plan that might not be perfect, might not even work, than no plan at all. In this case I had planned an escape and when it failed, my next plan was to return and possibly save my life.

I enjoyed the heat and the warmth from the stove and in spite of what was in store upon my return to prison, I was at least alive. A northbound train stopped at the station and I was hustled head down out to the train, roughly installed in an empty Pullman coach and shoved into a corner away from the window. The guards grabbed my neck and shoved my head down. When the train began its journey north toward the city of Mukden, I was taken to a private closed compartment and my head roughly banged down onto a table. I was tightly bound and every move I made, no matter how slight, made the guards react with severe admonitions and threats. Arriving in Mukden I was hustled aggressively from the train to a waiting canvas topped jeep and taken to the headquarters of the railway authority. The wait inside the building was interminable. The prospect of a regular Chinese prison loomed large ahead of me.

Numerous Chinese authorities came in and many telephone calls with raised voices and harried manner were made, none of which I understood. Eventually two Chinese guards who had been with me prior to the escape arrived and led me to yet another jeep. I had visions of being taken to a prison with far more stringent security measures than the one I had been in before. I imagined that it might possibly be the prison where Ron, Andy and Lyle had originally been incarcerated.

I was surprised when it stopped at the prison gates from where I had so recently escaped and hoped that I would be returned to the same cell area close to Andy or Ron and Lyle. A delegation of highly agitated guards met me. From the debris under the bed in my cell it was obvious that I had been diligently working on the escape plot for a few weeks and this fact must have caused them great embarrassment when my empty cell was found. Their anger and rage towards me was intense, for my escape had indeed shown their laxity as prison guards.

The abuse began when the head guard came in with handcuffs. I was going to resist but there were too many guards, so I held out my hands in submission. He clamped the handcuffs on so tightly that pain shot up my arms and cut off the circulation. He did it with malice and smiled. I could have killed him for this. The metal contacted hard against my wrist bone, yet there was an additional click in the handcuff as it merged with my flesh in one of the last possible notches.

I was taken to a tiny dank cell in the middle of the building and thrown roughly into it. I remained handcuffed and the guards looked in the door with enjoyment.This was to remain my home for the next few months, and where a very difficult period of transition was encountered. There were no outside walls or windows; only a bed and mattress and a guard assigned to watch over me. I began to throw up because of the dirt and weed stems that I had ingested from the snow I had eaten in desperation for drinking water. My frostbitten feet throbbed and were itching and painful, though luckily no gangrene developed.

Chong's new instructions were that I would sit on the edge of the bed all day and not move, lying down was permitted only at night. The guards would not let me sleep without interruptions and when they saw me drop off to sleep they pounded on the door to wake me up. After two days I could stand this no longer and rebelled. I hit the door with all my might, disturbed the guards from their slumbers and they ranted and raved until I quietened down. I told them that I did not like their ancestors and with this remark my already tight handcuffs were clamped one extra notch, the last notch possible, and cut more deeply into my flesh.

The main guard would have been universally disliked, a typical sneaky, underhanded individual who got his kicks out of making life miserable for the prisoners. If the inmates had killed anyone it would have been this man. It was impossible to rest easily. I was sick, my feet hurt, I was retching and in a bad mental state. The handcuffs were a hindrance and made it almost impossible to sleep. They were clamped on so tightly that the pain was excruciating and the bands caused my wrists to swell so that there was little or no circulation in my hands, which caused them to throb and ache.

I believe that Chong was actually hurt that I had escaped and that he had been taken in so effectively. He did loosen the handcuffs a fraction so that a little blood circulation returned to my hands and for this I was grateful to him. I thought the handcuffs might be removed entirely but they were merely loosened and then began two weeks of difficult living, handcuffed the entire time. I had to think about every move, as my hands now had to be used as a pair. It was a frustrating situation. At night when I inadvertently jerked my hands, it would wake me up. The clothes that I had on could obviously not be removed, and it was almost impossible to wash with the meager facilities that were available. For a fortnight these difficult conditions remained for this must have been the time that they decreed I needed to be punished and to reflect upon my conduct.

My health, or what health I had left, gradually disintegrated under the strain of this treatment. I had violent nightmares, waking up two or three times a night soaked through with perspiration. Twice the left side of my face puffed out and became paralyzed, leading me to believe that maybe I had suffered a slight stroke or heart attack. After that Chong relaxed his iron fisted rules a fraction and let me get off the bed and walk around the cell for 10 mins a day. I was kept in this cell for three months.

Press report from Des Moines Register Friday August 20, 1954
Leased wire from N.Y.Times

Fliers Held Illegally by Reds

WASHINGTON, D.C.—The defence department Thursday accused the Chinese Communists of holding 15 United States airmen against their will as "political prisoners."

Their continued detention, the Pentagon said, is in direct violation of the Korean armistice agreement and of international law.

The airmen include one of America's leading jet aces—Capt Harold E. Fischer, Swea City, Ia.

With its formal accusation, the defense department renewed a demand that the Communists account for 526 missing Americans, a total that includes the 15 airmen.

Admitted by Reds

The fact that the fliers were alive and imprisoned was admitted by the Chinese Communist negotiators at the recent Geneva conference, the defense department said.

It charged the Peiping regime with "subterfuge" in classifying the Americans as "political prisoners" rather than prisoners of war.

By this device, the Pentagon statement said, the Communists evaded their obligations under the terms of the armistice to offer the airmen the opportunity of repatriation.

Twelve of the 15 were members of the crew of a B-29 bomber. Their capture had been reported by the Communists many months ago.

Shot down

The United States command said the bomber had been shot down in northwest Korea but the Communists contended that it had dropped in "neutral" Manchuria, north of the Yalu river frontier.

Airforce spokesmen said the remaining three Americans were flying single-seater planes when they were shot down or forced to land on Communist territory. Communist reports on the imprisonment of the 15 have been verified by repatriated prisoners of war. It added that these men had been told by their captors that the airmen would be used for bargaining purposes in connection with Peiping's campaign for admission to the United Nations.

CHAPTER 20

DEPORTATION

If you are remembered you are never gone.
HF

One morning the interpreter appeared in my cell and with a show of ceremony and a great flourish, produced a key and removed the handcuffs. It was little episodes like this that gave me hope. One of the stock Chinese phrases was, "You have a bright future." The days were monotonous but slowly little things began to change. I was given a lot of books and spent the days reading. It became a passion and also a lifesaver, for without it I believe insanity would have set in.

There was only one small 25watt light bulb in the cell. It was a wonder that my eyes held out reading in poor light, but when needed our physical weaknesses are overcome by our mental needs. So for hours I poured over books and when I could not get anything new to read, I reread many of them. This went on for months.

A new interpreter nicknamed "Happy Hank" often brought me the books and he and Chong periodically visited me to talk of the new political and social situation in China and the dawn of a new era. Slowly my living conditions improved, as did the food. The improvements seemed to parallel the skimpy news reports we got about the political situation.

It slowly dawned on me that our status as prisoners of war had been changed to political prisoners and this worried me. It was a difficult situation to be in, sandwiched between two nations each trying to gain superiority over the other. What compounded this difficulty for the prisoners was the fact that there were no diplomatic relations between China and America and no one would, or was, acting as the mediator between these two world giants.

In fact, the United States could use us as proof of the treachery of the Chinese Communists and the Chinese were using us as bargaining tools, holding us to ransom so to speak. We were now pawns in a political wrangle. I had never liked being the middleman, and suddenly found myself with the rest of the prisoners, in the center of a huge controversy of international implications. I was able to understand what our side was up against by reading and analyzing the news in the communist English newspaper, '*Hsin Hui.*' The fact that there was nowhere for the two sides to meet for negotiations was most discouraging to us. It became readily apparent that the Chinese were not deterred by threats of force that the United States exerted on them. However, it was also apparent that our continued detainment in China could act negatively for them apropos international public opinion and this was always a factor of utmost concern to the Chinese.

Spring came and with it a further extension of the 'lenient policy' of the Chinese Red Army regarding prisoners of war or political prisoners in detention.

On the morning of April 8th, 1954, Chong came into my cell early, shook me awake and ordered me to follow him to office of the commanding officer. There were four chairs in front of the CO's desk and I was told to sit down. A few minutes later Cameron and Parks were ushered into the room and after exchanging sidelong glances they also sat down. Then a thin, haggard and drawn man who vaguely reminded me of someone I once knew, shuffled into the room, looked at us, sat down and in a low voice, Andrew Mackenzie said, "God bless you chaps".

The C.O who we called "*The Honcho*", the GI's Japanese name for 'boss' or "chief" said, "You have all been asking for a long time that you be allowed to live together and we are going to make it possible. Your treatment will be more lenient."

Sure enough, everything was changed and we were allowed to sleep in a dormitory, Cameron's old cell. Park's room became our mess hall, my room the library and Andy's the clubroom. New furniture was moved into the cells. They even draped yellow and aqua crepe paper over the windows to hide the bars. They moved the phonograph, ping-pong table and accordion from the old 'clubroom' to our new one. They put four desks together in the 'library' and covered them all with a large blue cloth and finally decorated the resulting table with a Chinese vase. They gave us the daily 'newspaper' which was usually quotations from Peking Radio and I was given long withheld mail from my parents. We sat around in dazed disbelief over this change of attitude.

The reunion was joyful and we had a lot to talk about since our last contact and with Andy being new to our group, we questioned him a lot. It was easier to sleep at night with so much of our day's conversation to be analyzed before falling asleep. I found life easier having friends to discuss our mutual fate with. The idea of world domination by communism was discussed over and over again. We suspected that the place was "bugged" so our ideas were carefully phrased. When we disagreed with the accepted communist ideology, the doctrines of which we were now all well aware of, we did so in carefully modulated tones and in as isolated an area as possible.The old cellblock had changed substantially from the place we had entered so long ago.

The guards were no longer merely our jailers but there to assist us in our needs. Many of the guards who had been with us from the start, resented this change. The library now held over 200 volumes of the world's classics and if I was to be imprisoned again, (God forbid,) may it be in a library! We all appreciated the library and I systematically attempted to go through every book from Thorsten Veblens "Theory of the Leisure Class", to Tolstoy's "Anna Karennia". If I had to select any beneficial aspect to my life of this long imprisonment it would be the fact that I had the opportunity to read so many great works of literature which I would in all likelihood never have got around to doing.

I had always had an interest in music, and now it became a marvelous diversion. Lyle had at one time been an accordion teacher and the Chinese had given us a violin and an accordion. He taught me play "*Red River Valley*," "*Now*

Propaganda photo's taken by the Chinese while on an outing to a lake in Muken, to show how well the prisoners were treated.

While rowing on the lake we were being followed by a boatload of guards. It must have caused the photographer a headache in getting a clear photo without the guards getting into the picture

Left to right Cameron, Parks, Mackenzie and Fischer

is the hour" and *"Mood Indigo"*. He entertained us with the old favorites, like *'Body and Soul'* and *'Stardust,'* which was a reminder of home. We must have played a million games on the ping-pong table and devoted many hours to chess and bridge. We were given four tennis rackets, balls and a net, so we laid out a tennis court in our new outdoor recreation area as well as a basketball area and a set of parallel bars. So, all in all, the time was not entirely wasted as we applied ourselves to the various diversions made available to us.

We were now also allowed to write and receive mail from home through the Red Cross of China. Those first few letters were so carefully edited, and written with such a cautious selection of vocabulary that I considered them to be masterpieces. The Chinese intended for them to impress the public and friends we had back home as to the lenient and relaxed attitude of the Chinese people towards us. Since both our in coming and out going mail was heavily censored, we were not able to assess what our correspondents really felt or believed our situation to truly be. We had to be careful how we worded things for if we wrote truthfully of our feelings and conditions, or anything slightly derogatory about the Chinese or their government, the letters would not have been sent. Therefore, our letters were full of cheerfulness and hope with a little less than accurate indication of precisely what our living conditions were like.

There were ways to indicate that things were not as rosy as depicted and fairly easy to indicate that what we were writing in our letters was not exactly the way things were. For example, my father did not like chocolate malted milk and when I mentioned how I recalled his fondness for it, it became a clue that everything I was writing was not as it appeared.

One of our great pleasures was the fortnightly bath we were permitted. It was utter luxury to soak and luxuriate in hot water of the bathhouse. I still carry a scar on my butt from backing up against a radiator just prior to climbing into the concrete tub.

However good our living conditions, there were instances of personality conflicts within the group. One member of the four of us had a tendency to be selfish which was magnified under our circumstances. Another was unable to accept defeat in anything he attempted. I was an egotist and another was stubborn. The inevitable closeness and personality differences erupted in violence one evening and the guards arrived to break up the fight and prevent serious physical harm. No one in particular was to blame. It is impossible to change characteristics and lifetime habit patterns and the closeness and confines of prison life seriously accentuated these.

It was nearly two years since I had bailed out of the F-86. Naturally we wondered what momentous events had influenced the Chinese to change our environment so dramatically. We allowed ourselves to believe that the Chinese had plans to free us and they certainly encouraged this view.

Chong came in one day with the news of the Geneva conference, which had been called to supposedly settle the war in Indochina. He brought us numerous newspapers and encouraged us to read them. We wondered if our fate was directly linked to this conference and if the Chinese intended to use us as bargaining tools. If so, the good treatment became glaringly obvious.

Chong finally admitted that we might indeed be released as a result of the conference and might be traded for "Chinese students" who were being "detained in the U.S. against their wishes". We were given new leather shoes, which we termed our 'going home shoes' and the food became exceptionally good, which we reckoned was to fatten us up for propaganda purposes. Chong got us to pose in our recreation room for photos and we tried to indicate through finger signs that this was a lot of propaganda.

When the conference closed we were still in Mukden and the quality of our food deteriorated once again. However, around this time we were allowed to write letters home and were allowed to receive parcels from our parents.

I started writing a book about my experiences in Japan and Korea but with without condemning or praising the Chinese. I hoped to persuade them to let me take it home in its innocuous form where I would write the last chapter and really tell the true story. I worked for a few hours a day on it.

Sometime in September, Chong arrived in our room and announced with a grin from ear to ear that we were going to be taken on an outing to Peiling, a famous park in Mukden. We were duly taken on a tour of the mausoleum of the first emperor of the Manchu Dynasty, and were put in rowboats for a leisurely row around the lake. A photographer was with us furiously taking pictures so they could perpetuate the impression to the world that we were having a good time and taken on outings to entertain us. The photographer had a difficult task keeping the guards out of the photos especially the two boatloads full that followed us around the lake!

The number of American cars everywhere amazed me. We saw a new 1952 model, which could probably have told a very interesting story for there had been an embargo on goods to China ever since the new government had come to power and Chiang Kai-Check had evacuated to the islands of Hainan and Formosa.

About two months later, November 27th, 1954, Chong and "Honcho" came to us and without warning or explanation took Andy MacKenzie away. About five minutes later they took the rest of us to the library and I knew something was going on. Andy was obviously excited, caught my eye as I entered the room and gave me a 'thumbs up' signal. With us all seated, the Honcho got up and read from a small piece of paper something to the effect: "Squadron Leader MacKenzie, you have been with us for almost two years. Your case has been settled satisfactorily and you are a now a free man to return home."

We were stunned and at first I did not know whether to believe Honcho, as it had all the makings of being another show of trickery and deceit. However, after talking with Chong, who was due to escort Andy to Hong Kong, I believed Honchos' words were sincere.

Propaganda photo's taken by the Chinese give the impression of how happy we were and the "fine living conditions" that we had. These were taken in 1955 with our status being as political prisoners.

Playing tennis in the snow...?

Cameron and Fischer

Lyle Cameron, Ron Parks and Hal give the impression that this is a normal dinner

185

After Chong left, the radio mysteriously went dead and we were not given newspapers, so we became suspicious and not convinced that Andy had really been released until we got letters from home confirming the fact. Chong later told us that the reason for Mackenzies release and not ours, was that the British Commonwealth "had taken a more enlightened attitude" toward the "New China" than the U.S. and suggested that our "cases would be settled quickly" if the U.S. "would stop interfering in China's affairs."

With all sincerity, all of us had shared and enjoyed Andy's excitement and watched our friend and fellow prisoner go out of the door and our best wishes went with him. Our morale lowered when he left but sank even lower when not long afterwards we were told that Col Arnold and his B-29 crew had been sentenced as "spies" and were afraid the same charges would be leveled at us.

Another prisoner that we were aware of now came into focus. Many times, I had mentioned Ed Heller and wondered how he was. And many times during the stay, one interpreter or another had mentioned that Ed Heller was coming along well. They mentioned that he had been wounded and that it had taken him a long time to recover but this is all that we really knew about him. The three of us knew that books were being taken to another prisoner and we decided to place a message for Ed between the lines in one of the books telling him about us and where we were. When this book was returned a few days later, we eagerly paged through it looking for an answer to our message. Sure enough, these books had been going to Ed Heller. It was good to have contact with him and we all looked forward to seeing him.

Part of the Chinese ploy around this time was to keep our morale up and when we got downhearted they arrived with more amenities. We were given new sweaters and imitation leather photo albums for our propaganda pictures. When we needed a fourth for bridge, one of the interpreters sat in Andy's old spot. More parcels came from home and it was interesting to note that whenever we received food parcels, it would be after an exceptionally good meal, so that the delicacies would not have such a nostalgic impact on us.

Finally we were allowed to communicate openly with Ed Heller who we were told was still under medical care.

They tried to make Christmas of 1954 a special day for us and served a delicious meal. They took photographs of us eating a "typical POW meal". We were served a rare treat of meat dumplings called *"chiaotse"* and we got into a competition to see who could eat the most. I came in second having eaten 53, and for weeks after that we were lectured on the de-merits of over eating.

In early January our spirits soared for we learned that Dag Hammerskjold, Secretary General of the United Nations, had taken up our case and would come to China to negotiate our release. A Chinese doctor came to the prison and for the first time since coming to China we were given a complete physical examination.

I was still working on my book but getting to be afraid that Chong would confiscate it, so dreamed up a scheme to make him think that I had shelved the

A set up in the library to show the pleasures of prison life. Hal crosses his fingers and Parks uses a whammy sign to indicate to Americans who might see it that this scene is not real. The vases and flowers are part of the props.

Chess in the clubroom

Propaganda photo taken by the Chinese. When asked why he looked so happy, Hal replied, "The smile might be for the bath, haircut and news of possible release."

Learning to play the accordian in the prison clubroom.

project. I got two scraps of cloth and sewed them to the inside of my sweater to form a concealed lining and hid the manuscript in it. Then I wrote a note to Ed, knowing that Chong would intercept it, saying that I had got disgusted with the work, torn it up and thrown it out.

I found Chong sitting on my bed waiting for me one day. He asked where my book was. It was obvious that he had searched my space so I reached under the bed, extracted my sweater and gave all 160,000 words to him. I guess it is still in the official files and I wish I could get it back and finish it, especially the final chapter.

Toward the end of February we started to suspect that another American had been brought to our prison, and in early March saw strange footprints, larger than the average Chinese, in our exercise area. Our communications with Heller had ended abruptly without explanation about 3 weeks earlier and we wondered if he had been transferred from his place of recovery to our prison.

Soon after this discovery, Lyle was standing on a desk peering over the top of the shutters into the exercise area when he suddenly said, "It's him, a tall man with a bad limp". I jumped up and saw that it was indeed Ed, looking lonely and dejected. I felt sorry for him and wished that somehow we could get him with us. We began a concentrated effort to have him join us and our suggestions, as the Chinese encouraged us to make, were duly accepted.

One evening while I was sitting in the library writing to my family a wonderful thing happened. The gaunt figure of Ed Heller, trailed by Chong and the "Honcho," walked in. I was so glad to see him I almost cried, but looking up just said, "Hi Ed, it's been a long time." He was gray and walked with a noticeable limp. We were the first Americans he had spoken to in 26 months and he now took Andy's place in our quarters.

Prior to Ed joining us, both Ron and I had been through heavy interrogations about the border violations of the 51st FIW. The Chinese were building up a mass of evidence, false and partly true concerning Ed's case. It was finally agreed that he could join us. I had known him before and had admired him, for he was one of those rare men who dared to defy the ritual of the military, when he deemed it necessary. In other words, Ed Heller was a free thinker.

He was an ace from World War II and he would have been one in Korea had he not been shot down. He was a pilot who loved to fly, one of the old school where flying was everything. There was so much in the man to be admired.

I had received a huge pile of mail, as my mother had written every day and the mail had been held back. We would go into the library, read our letters privately and then share them by reading them aloud. We read that Andy had arrived home to a hero's welcome and true to his word he traveled from Canada down to Iowa and Nebraska and visited our parents. They were thrilled to get first hand news about their sons, but they also enjoyed the publicity surrounding Andy's visit.

Chong came in one day and asked us to pack our clothes and get ready to leave. We had been misled so many times by these men that it was hard to believe they might be planning our release. We ate what food remained in our packages, not wanting to leave a morsel for the guards.

We were escorted to the Mukden train station with an entourage in tow of Chong, "Honcho," a cook and a posse of miscellaneous Chinese. They would not tell us where we were going but judging from the direction and the terrain we guessed that we were going through Tientsin. We passed by many abandoned pillboxes that the Japanese had constructed along their main rail lines to protect their trains. We were happy, for any change in our situation was now exciting, with the anticipation of freedom a real possibility.

We arrived in Peking and were hurried onto a Russian bus and driven to our new quarters, a home with gardens, patios and many rooms. It was a paradise after our prison cells. A wealthy Chinese had evidently owned it for there were three buildings. One for the head of the family, one for the children when they married, and one for the servants. The servant's quarters included the kitchen and the latrine that was used by all. As customary with this type of home, a high wall surrounded it.

Food parcels began arriving in earnest and mail from all over the United States flooded in as the publicity grew surrounding our imprisonment. The good food we were now getting altered our outlook for when we had very little to eat, our thoughts excluded the female sex, but now with good food from home and the stimulation of the letters, our thoughts again returned to past times, and sports all healthy men engage in with the opposite sex.

We were taken on an outing to the Dowager Empress's summer home, one of the great tourist spots of the world before the arrival of the communist menace. She reigned in the late 1800's and was notorious for signing death warrants. Near her summer home was a large lake where she reviewed the Chinese navy, which, according to our interpreter, had to be transported inland for her viewing. Close to her summer home was a large marble replica of a paddle wheel boat, which had once so impressed her that she had one built. She had seven homes constructed in the area, one of which contained her personal shrine and housed an enormous Buddha.

The sights in Peking were more impressive than our first outing to the park and lake in Mukden, but did not have the same emotional impact as that first taste of freedom. The first outing we had photographs taken, which we sent home but in Peking, there was no photographer so we theorized that there was not enough time to get them developed before being sent home.

The usually dour Chong now became quite cheery and kept telling us that we would soon be going home and lecturing us on the Bandung conference. Our skepticism waned a little and we finally began to believe that our freedom was imminent. However, interrogations continued into every aspect of military life and we were now interrogated as a group about our countries military and government affairs.

Chong called us together and with a grave face said that international affairs change very rapidly but did not elaborate. Our spirits sank and the guards and cooks seemed to be settling in for a long haul and so did we. The communist 'news' was heavily censored so we got no indication that Chou En-Lai had been castigated by his own fellow Asians at the conference and had lost face. We assumed the change in attitude blocking our release was because of the crash of the *Kashmir Princess* aircraft carrying Communist officials, which Chinese propaganda blamed on "American-Chiang secret agents."

Chong arrived one evening around May 23rd with a new group of officials who told us that we were going to be tried in a court of law, but that we were also to remember the leniency of the Chinese policy. We were not told the charges but told that we would be given legal counsel and hints that our sentence had already been decided but that there was nothing to worry about.

It was alarming but we felt that it was a formality that would have to be endured. An active imagination does not rest easy under these circumstances. We met our duly appointed counsels from the university. All were supposedly instructors at the University of Peoples Law. I met mine and we talked for a few minutes and he asked me how I would plead to violating the sacred territorial air of China. This was not the time to refute my violation since I had indeed landed in China, so I pleaded guilty and placed myself at the mercy of the court. This was to be the stand we all took.

The day of the trial dawned. We were taken to the main municipal court building in Peking, the Supreme Court of China, and marched into a courtroom before a packed audience of Chinese civilians, officials, and three judges in military uniforms. Our charges were read, first in Chinese and then in English and we each stood up and pleaded guilty. The entire proceeding was a play-act and from time to time the audience snickered as if this was a comedy act.

Finally we were asked to stand up again and with Ed on my left, Ron and Lyle on my right, we received our sentence with a great deal of relief. A court official read the decision that had obviously been printed up before the proceedings, and they were the greatest words I ever heard. We were to be deported from the Peoples Republic of China without delay, and if we ever sullied the soil of China again, we would be duly punished.

From the courthouse, we were escorted to a train and traveled down to the south of China, across the Yellow river by ferry, as there was no railroad across this huge river, then south to Canton where we were delayed to complete the final deportation processing. We stayed in an old abandoned army camp and were again taken on an outing to an impressive park and the graves of the Seven Martyrs.

We were taken through the foreign settlement where the ambassadors and foreign dignitaries once lived in fine western homes. The area had been off limits to all Chinese and been surrounded by a moat that kept the 'unwanted' away. Now it was a symbol of the new regime and the homes had been turned into workers apartments.

We noticed that around the city, there were more armed Chinese soldiers than we had seen anywhere else. Canton was close to the coastal waters and to our destination of Hong Kong, to where we were being expelled to freedom.

The final day arrived; a normal day for millions of people around the world, but for the four of us, it was freedom day. A day that we had dreamed of and never known if it would arrive. We had another train journey to the outer environs of Hong Kong, and then yet another delay, where we ate in a small diner surrounded by "hate America" posters pasted on the walls.

At last a walk over a short strip of border area and after being examined by custom agents, the gates dropped down and shut behind us. For a moment we were in no mans land and the first man who greeted us was a Jesuit priest, who said, "Welcome to a free land again".

CHAPTER 21

RETURN TO FREEDOM

"Perhaps an attitude towards life starts out when you are small and pick up a nickname, derogatory or complimentary. Mine has been kept unknown since the fifties. Somehow I was associated with Tarzan of the Apes and as a boy became known as Tarz. The nickname symbolized for me freedom and independence. It represented a free and independent spirit, a non-conformist and opposed to authority."
From a speech given on July 25th 1988 by Hal Fischer

In putting together Hal's story I had so many questions after his release. He ended his Korean story as he walked across the Hong Kong border to freedom and through press cuttings, letters dragged up from dusty depths of cupboards and gentle questions, I have put the final saga together with smiles and chuckles from Hal. He tends to underplay his experiences and has a total aversion to talking about himself. I had no idea what sort of reports and official support families get from the military when their loved ones become missing in action. I hope this will put some light on what families go through.

After crossing the border to freedom their first destination was the Jockey Club in Hong Kong. Then a long hot bath with a scotch and soda and a good shave. "It was paradise", Hal said, "We were then ready for Hawaii where close relatives awaited our arrival. We were debriefed at length, had press conferences, extensive physical examinations, an immense amount of dental work, and time alone with our families. The reunion with my parents was emotional and I was proud of how they coped with the ordeal and the uncertainty of the situation".

"On 7th April 1953 my parents were notified at 3:30 p.m. that I was missing in action.

On 8th April, on the eight o'clock morning news, Beijing radio reported they had captured me.

On 1st May 1953 my parents got the following from the Department of the Air Force about the exchange of prisoners".

Taken at a media conference in Hawaii after release from China in 1955. When asked about the grave expression, Hal replied, "Too much stimulation, too little free time, and too little rest!"

193

Dear Mr and Mrs. Fischer:

"It is with deep regret I must advise you that in the recent exchange of prisoners, no definite information was obtained concerning the welfare of your son, Captain Harold E. Fischer. In an effort to obtain as much information as possible about the fate of our personnel who have been or may still be held by the enemy, the released prisoners are being questioned. All details regarding individuals with whom they came in personal contact while being held by the Communists as well as information they may have received by word of mouth is being officially recorded. In this manner and with the constant pressure on the Communists by our peace negotiators, we hope to secure positive facts and the earliest possible release of all prisoners. You will of course be notified immediately of any additional information that becomes known concerning your son.
Major General John H McCormick

The Commander of the 39TH Squadron replied as follows to a letter my parents had written.

39TH FIGHTER INTERCEPTOR SQUADRON
51ST FIGHTER INTERCEPTOR GROUP APO 970
9 May 1953

"Dear Mr. Fischer,

I received your letter and I am happy to answer the questions with which you are concerned.

First, with respect to Harold's personal effects, they have been packed and crated. You can be certain they are being properly safeguarded until such time as they can be returned to the United States. By regulation, the effects of a soldier listed as missing in action must be retained within his organization for thirty days. Then from Korea they go to the Personal Effects Officer of the Far East Air Force Headquarters in Tokyo Japan, where they are held for a period of four months. From there they are sent to the Army Effects Bureau in Kansas City, Missouri, which then sends them to the next of kin as quickly as possible. I know this sounds like a long, drawn-out procedure but experience has shown it necessary to take this period of time to protect the missing soldier's interests as well as interests of the government, by assuring the effects are sent to the proper person. In your case, Mr. Fischer, we have recommended that your son's belongings go to you and your wife, due to the recent divorce of Mrs. Fischer from Harold. However, the final decision on this matter will be made by the Army Effects Bureau in Kansas City, where our recommendation will be given full consideration.

You asked about injuries incurred during a bail-out from an aircraft. Normally the pilot will get bruised up a bit and be stiff for several days, but unless he lands on a rough piece of ground and breaks an ankle or leg, that is usually the extent of his difficulty. Of course we have no way of knowing Harold's condition, but evidently he landed in a populated area since he was apparently picked up shortly afterwards according to the Communist radio broadcasts. That should assure him any medical attention he may have required in the event he did have a rough landing. Yes, the prisoner exchange certainly presents a hope that Harold may soon be back in friendly hands. Everyone here is praying with you."

On 29 May 1953 the Air Force sent a letter to my parents as follows:

"Since I last communicated with you, a report has been received from the overseas commander concerning the known events leading to your son's missing status, I know that you are anxious to learn as much as possible of what happened to your son, Captain Harold E, Fischer. Our report states that Captain Fischer was flying lead position in a flight of F-86 type aircraft which departed Suwon Air Base, Korea, 7 April 1953 on a combat mission over the Yalu River in North Korea. Upon entering the area, Captain Fischer's flight encountered enemy aircraft and during the ensuing action, the flight became separated. At this time, in maneuvering to evade the enemy planes, the wingman lost sight of your son. Captain Fischer immediately contacted the wingman and advised him to leave the area. This was the last transmission received from your son. When he failed to return from the mission, an aerial search was conducted, however, efforts to locate him or the missing plane met with negative results. He was apparently captured at that time for, as you know, his name was mentioned as a prisoner of war in an enemy propaganda broadcast dated 9 April 1953. One of the repatriated prisoners later reported seeing him and that he was in good health on 20 April 1953. Even though we cannot guarantee delivery of mail, may I again suggest that you write to him as often as you desire, adhering to the procedures as outlined in my letter of 14 April. Should you succeed in establishing communication with Captain Fischer, please notify this headquarters as requested, since this information may assist us in establishing his actual status. "

Another letter from the Air Force elaborates on the prisoner report.

"This is in reply to your letter of 5 May 1953 concerning your son, Captain Harold Fischer.
I would like to explain why we cannot furnish you the name of the repatriate referred to in our letter of 29 May 1953. Following the exchange of sick and wounded prisoners of war in April 1953 (Operation "Little Switch"), we received a report from the Far East Air Forces which

indicated that an Army corporal had mentioned seeing Captain Fischer in Prisoner of War Camp 2. The former prisoner was hospitalized at the Army Medical Center, Washington, D. C., but his physical and mental condition precluded further questioning. However, a member of this headquarters was permitted to interview him at the hospital. The repatriate had suffered a complete breakdown and was still unable to remember clearly most of the period when he was a prisoner. He could not identify a picture of your son, nor could he recall having seen Captain Fischer in a prisoner of war camp. Shortly after this interview, the repatriate was transferred to a Veterans Administration hospital and, in view of his condition, it has not been considered advisable to subject him to further questioning."

On the 13th of June 1953, my parents received a call from the Post Office in Des Moines, Iowa, regarding a strange message.

UNITED STATES POSTOFFICE
Des Moines 18, Iowa
June 13, 1953.

My dear Mr. and Mrs. Fischer;

Am herewith enclosing a letter received from the Postmaster of Paramaribo enclosing a letter with reference to your son which was written and forwarded to him from Shanghai.

This is the correspondence I telephoned you about this evening. As the name was incorrectly given, and the address also incorrect, it only was when you verified the serial number that it was certain that it belonged to you. It being Saturday afternoon, I could not obtain verification of the serial number from the air force offices.

On June 13th, 1953, the letter was received from the Postmaster in Des Moines, Iowa. It had been sent to: Post Office, Des Moines, Iowa State, USA. The following is the virtually unintelligible message that remains a bizarre mystery that has never been figured out.

Forward to Holy family of Aviator Fesgher, Harold Edward, A-2204126, Duies City, Ceral Route No. 1, Iowa State, U. S. A. from Paramaribo, Suirinam, in South America which came from Shanghai, China.

Dear Sir

I am regret to write this letter to your good. What I had learned and from China; i.e. nowadays, A Holy Spirits aviator Mr. Fesgher Harold Edward had jumped on Korea's district field safely from fighter which message shall be transfer to his family. Please through yours hands. I am holy, wish you are holy. God bless your Holiner.

Aviator Mr. Fesgher Harold Edward had descended down within Vaon City North East forty miles distance Saue-doan city suburb, Manchurian, China. 7th, 15:4 PM, April 1953 whose series number A-2204126, 5th Aeroadeum corps, 51st division, 39th regiment c squadron, Captain F-86, one of fourth had been shooting down. Pilot (Aviator) safety.

1st May 1953
95, Lana 913 Yean Rd (cf)
Shanghai, China

Dear Messers,
Glory to God in heaven! and on earth Peace to the men be favors brother Fesgher Harold shall be transferred into the reason of the light, to be under the son of God.
Chinese Engineering Engineer
Machinist
Blessed are you when people abuse you and persecute you and falsely say everything of you, on my account. Be glad and exalt over it for you will be richly rewarded heaven, for that is the way they persecuted the prophets who came before you! From New Testament.

The Department of the Air Force responded to a letter from my mother on Oct 19, 1953.

Dear Mrs. Fischer:

"This is in reply to your letter of 11 October, concerning your son, Captain Harold. E. Fischer, Jr

I regret that we have no further news pertaining to Captain Fischer. However, you may be assured, that the United States Government is bringing constant pressure to bear on the Communists for the release of all our missing personnel believed to be in their custody, and an accounting for those not returned. In the meantime, we are utilizing every available source, including repatriates' statements, in an effort to clarify their status. Reports from repatriates are being reviewed and evaluated, as they are received in this headquarters and it is hoped that they may furnish information about your son. In the meantime Captain Fischer will continue to be recorded in a missing in action status.

You are again assured, that you will be promptly notified if any new developments occur concerning your son.

After receiving the strange letter from Shanghai, via Surinam, my parents sent it to the Pentagon for clarification that I was still alive.

After the prisoner exchange at the end of the Korean War, when I was not among those released, my parents started writing to President Eisenhower, the United Nations, Congressmen and anyone else they believed might help in effecting my release. When President Eisenhower visited Des Moines in 1954, an interview was arranged with my parents and they asked him personally for his assistence.

From Hawaii, Hal, Parks, Cameron and their families were flown to San Francisco in a Lockheed Constellation and transferred to a C-47 for the final flight back home. Parks and Cameron were dropped off in Nebraska and Hal's destination was Fort Dodge, Iowa. Hal said, "I recall coming back from California in a C-47 and the countryside got richer and greener as we approached Iowa. It was beautiful. It was almost like a re-birth."

The day before his return the town had been preparing for his arrival home and was a hive of activity with crews putting up red, white and blue banners and bunting while others painted, mowed lawns and even graveled a street.

The following is from a press report dated June 9, 1955:-

> It was a humble but appreciative young airforce man and his family who were honored at festivities here on Wednesday afternoon. Capt Fischer, a mild mannered youth full of personality, spoke to the crowd estimated by two daily newspapers at between 7000 and 7500 people. With a voice choked with emotion, Fischer said, "It's been a long time. I think everyone has a point in his life which is his biggest moment....a crest. I think I have reached that crest today. This is the most marvelous

thing that has ever happened to me. Great writers express pleasures in many words and they are very nice to read. But none could put down what I feel today. I can only repeat an old word. It's terrific."

He said that the tribute given to him was not for him alone, but for all the wonderful Americans who had similar experiences. Fischer went on to remind the people there are still others in prison. Others who were not as lucky as he to be freed. He asked that people do all they can for those still being interned. He said," I hope that you will continue to work as I am going to work, so that others may be free as I am today. Prison is not a nice place and I want all those other Americans back".

Fischer's open car was flanked by honor guards and followed a parade of 36 different units including the Governor Leo Hoegh, various generals and Iowa National Guard members. A flight of eight jets made three passes over Fischer as a tribute to a national hero. Newsmen, radio and TV cameras were set up in batteries and five of the six trunk lines were leased for the day by radio stations. The sixth line remained open for emergencies.

Fischer beamed through the welcoming ceremonies and appeared relaxed as he joked good naturedly with the crowd. He laughingly said, "While in Hawaii I had a lot of dental work done in a big hurry. Now I have come to Iowa to recuperate."

I asked Hal what he had to say in looking back and on his time in Korea and his life. He spent a day reflecting upon it and this is his answer: -

LOOKING BACK August 2001

There is a time in life and not just when one is classified as older, when one says, "I wish I had done this or that differently." Rarely does one find a person, who says, "I would not change a thing." They usually refer to major events in their lives.

In my world as I exist, I was taught that from a psychological standpoint, one would make the same choices over again since all the emotional and environmental factors would remain the same. As the French say, "The more the world changes, the more it remains the same."

There are things I may regret but I would not change. In essence the German question remains, "Why do I grow old so early and smart so late."

Somehow my world had one direction, in order to be an Ace, one had to be healthy, one had to be a fighter pilot, one had to have a war, one had to have an enemy flying airplanes and the timing had to be right. All this came together.

Hal gave me the following poem, stating that it summed up his feelings in words that he could not better.

"Combat Pilot"   *by G. Wiedenheft*

The story is now over, the chapter's closed and yet...
Written in my memory is a place I can't forget.

Where all my boyhood dreams met the light of day
And long forgotten values refused to fade away.

This place of men and heroes, the finest I would meet.
Whose actions spoke of virtue and whose courage stood concrete.

Where love took on new meaning, where friendship did too.
While the serious side of life shouted 'ATTENTION' at you.

A time for nerves of steel, when shakin' to the core,
Knowing all my limits, I learned to push for more.
'cause beneath my trembling hand that mighty bird could shine.
But it was living not power that was always on my mind.

Every call a close one, any time of day.
And every flight out was another time to pray.
Another mission over and I'd be worn to the bone
Adding hope to weary hope that I might just make it home.

I never dreamed back then standing face to face with fears
Someday they'd be behind me; all those war-torn years.
And the medals still remind me every birthday is a friend
'cause I lived to read that story from its beginning to its end.

The Korea War, known as "The Forgotten War", claimed the lives of more than 50,000 Americans, uncountable Chinese and more than a million Koreans. It was the proving ground for the first jet aerial warfare. The Sabres and MiG's, originating from the same basic design, pitted their skills against each other over the now famous MiG Alley and produced the first jet aces. There remain over 8,100 American men missing in action. The following is a fitting tribute to those who gave their loyalty, and their lives to their leaders.

It is not the critic who counts, nor the man who points out how the strong man stumbles or where the doer of deeds could have done better. The credit belongs to the man who is actually in the arena, whose face is marred by dust and sweat and blood; who knows great enthusiasm, great devotion and the triumph of achievement and who, at the worst, if he fails, at least fails while doing greatly—so that his place shall never be with those cold and timid souls who know.neither victory nor defeat...
From "Close to the Wind" by Pete Goss

And finally some words of wisdom, a beautiful poem that says it all about the fine warriors who serve their country. As true today as it was when it was penned around 1897. For that matter, true throughout the course of human history.

To The Valiant

Clifton Chapel

THIS is the Chapel: here, my son,
Your father thought the thoughts of youth,
And heard the words that one by one
    The touch of Life has turn'd to truth.
    Here in a day that is not far,
You too may speak with noble ghosts
Of manhood and the vows of war
You made before the Lord of Hosts.

To set the cause above renown,
To love the game beyond the prize,
To honour, while you strike him down,
The foe that comes with fearless eyes;
    To count the life of battle good,
And dear the land that gave you birth,
And dearer yet the brotherhood
That binds the brave of all the earth. —

My son, the oath is yours: the end
Is His, Who built the world of strife,
Who gave His children Pain for friend,
    And Death for surest hope of life.
To-day and here the fight's begun,
Of the great fellowship you're free;
Henceforth the School and you are one,
And what You are, the race shall be.

God send you fortune: yet be sure,
Among the lights that gleam and pass,
You'll live to follow none more pure
Than that which glows on yonder brass:
'Qui procul hinc,' the legend's writ, —
    The frontier-grave is far away —
        'Qui ante diem perlit:
        Sed miles, sed pro patria.'

Sir Henry Newbolt 1862-1938

A letter received from Col Yermakov in 1992
Translated from Russian

Dear Harold E. Fisher!

I'm infinitely happy to have received a letter from you and, most importantly, that you are alive and well.

When I received a letter from Don Roberts and realized that he was collecting autographs of distinguished aviators, I though that if he found me, then he must know his own fliers. Therefore, I sent salutations to you through him; although, I had little hope that my greeting would reach you. But they did, and you, dear Harold, responded.

On 7 April 1953, after completing its mission, my regiment started on final approach to Dapu airfield, was cleared and started on landing approach. I was located to the right of the landing approach and observed as the regiment's fliers landed. At that time the command post transmitted the signal that no enemy aircraft were present. I had not believed in such reports since the Second World War, because that was when the enemy usually appeared. That is what happened on 7 April 1953. After the signal from the ground that there were no enemy aircraft, I looked at the aircraft that were landing and in the distance from behind and from the left, I saw a pair of aircraft that did not inspire trust. Just then Chinese fliers approached and started to edge their way into our landing approach formation.

I did not rush to land, even though I was low on fuel. After escorting one group that was landing, while I was at the end of the airfield and had started a left-hand turn at an altitude of 600 meters, I heard from one of our pilots that he was being fired upon. It became clear to me that the "raider" would start to make a left-hand turn at the middle of the airfield (prior to this there had been an incident where a taxing aircraft had been fired upon, I saw this from the ground) and I immediately saw your aircraft. In a left-hand climbing turn you appeared to stall, your air speed was low, and there was nothing left for me to do except to fire a short burst from a distance of 400 meters. I saw smoke and fire gush from your engine.

While turning away I saw you catapult out, then I started to look for the second aircraft. Convinced that it was gone, I landed. Once on the ground, I found out that you had fired on two aircraft on landing approach, first a Chinese aircraft - it had 11 bullet holes, and then one of ours - 7 bullet holes. Both aircraft landed safely.

I sent two officers to where you landed (the regimental counter intelligence officer and the assistant political officer) to protect you from the willfulness of the Chinese authorities. You saw them. The counterintelligence officer cut some documents and other things out of your pocket, and the political officer tried to have a conversation with you in languages you did not understand. When I arrived, they reported that the Chinese inhabitants and authorities had done nothing violent.

So that is how we became acquainted. In August of 1991, I received a letter from George Dalton in Australia. He sent five separate autographs with photographs. I recognized four of the individuals in the photographs, but not the fifth one and I didn't pay any attention to the signature on the fifth. After receiving your letter, I accidently noticed the identical signature and carefully examined your autograph. When I saw your photograph on your identification, it was a lot lighter.

In Korea I had to shoot at F-86F's 12 times, two fell on the mainland, four had good hits, they surely withdrew to the bay, so they could not make a second attack before reaching the coast.

After you, my squadron commander shot down your second ace. He parachuted into the bay and was rescued. They mentioned his name, but I've already forgotten it.

I didn't discover any special air combat tactics to use against your fliers, I learned everything I know in World War II against German fliers. The fliers of the 54th Squadron of Koenigsberg Aces were especially brave. They managed to shoot me down twice.

I consider the MIG-15 and F-86f to be identical, except the MIG-15 had twice the fuel capacity. Your fliers were much better trained than ours. I had to take command of the regiment 42 days before we departed for China. Prior to that I had been an air army inspector. I knew very well that our common training was weak. The regiment had just been retrained from piston aircraft and our fliers had only three to five hours of flight time on the new aircraft. In essence, they only knew how to take off and land, and couldn't do that correctly.

They had no combat experience at all. In China we managed to do some training between combat sorties, and I told the fliers that the rest the Americans would teach them, like the German fliers taught me in World War II.

The organization of your combat operations was at the proper level. Your command saw the entire air situation in the combat operations area and skillfully employed its aviation without limitations. They quickly managed to develop an aviation that "exceeded us by three to four times."

We were forbidden to cross the line Pyongyang - Wonsan and the coastline. We had no guidance what so ever. I simply do not want to write about our command's lack of talent, everything I knew I farmed out to the fliers.

Due to these and other questions, I always had arguments with my higher command until the end of my service in the Air Force; therefore, I was always in disfavor. I had especially big disagreements with the Communist Party apparatus, and it gave me a lot of trouble.

I never pursued political goals in war. Sporting accomplishments in air combat were what interested me. After the armistice in Korea, I served in the Far East where I commanded the same regiment. In 1955 I started training the regiment to be interceptors, and by the end of 1957 the fliers had become first class interceptors. Only then was the regiment truly ready to conduct combat operations. However, this training cost me dearly. Disagreements on aviation combat training, combat application, guidance, aviation control in modern warfare and on other questions kept me in continual disfavor with the leadership, and in order to be rid of me they simply demobilized me.

In 1958 after demobilization, I returned home to live on a pension for length of service which doesn't especially let you go on a spending spree. I suffered a hearing loss after a contusion in 1943. Medicine recommended systematic bee stings, so I moved from the town of Kuvshinovo to the country and took up bee keeping. That was perhaps the only business that was neither persecuted nor taxed in any way. That's how the opportunity arose for me to live with more freedom and independence. I still associate with the aviation community. I often meet with those with whom I served. Fliers from all eras visit me. I feel good in spite of my 72 years. I have no limitations.

Harold E. Fisher! I would like to hear about your fate, about how it developed after our meeting. I heard that you were exchanged for someone, but that's where the rumors stopped. Fate, however, has brought us together once more, and I'm very happy.

I'm sending a photograph from 1990.
Respectfully yours,

Dmitri Vasilevich Yermakov

Colonel Dmitri Vasilevich Yermakov
Hero of the Soviet Union
16 victories in WW2 and 3 victories in Korea.

VIETNAM

VIETNAM

CHAPTER 1: The Beginning

"The human race will probably nuke itself.
What difference does it make?
Some new species will come along.
They may be wiser".
Admiral H. G. Rickover

I had passed through Travis Air Force base in California in March of 1951 as a newly graduated fighter pilot off to fly in the Korean War. Twenty years on, September 1971 and I was off to the Far East again, this time to Vietnam. Someone once said that each generation has a war to fight or experience; this was my third war. I thought that one war was enough and casually dismissed the notion.

It had taken me a long time to be assigned to Vietnam. I had volunteered in 1968 during the buildup phase of the war when supposedly another 50,000 Americans would lead to winning the war. That figure grew to over 500,000. The reason for not receiving orders to go to Vietnam was that "policy" did not permit former prisoners of war to go. Having been a POW of the Chinese during the latter part of the Korean War, I was therefore ineligible.

I had heard that a fighter ace of the Korean War had been shot down while flying in Vietnam. The publicity attatched to him being an ace and having returned to Vietnam spurred me to query the USAF Headquarters of a possible policy change. However his assignment had been an oversight on their part and the policy had not changed.

At that time I was assigned to the Pentagon and constantly stopped in on personnel to volunteer. After repeated harassment, I was finally told of a policy change that would allow me to volunteer. I was thus able to escape from a four-year assignment in the Pentagon after a mere year and a half. My peer group in the "Puzzle Palace" said, "Fischer you're just damn lucky"

The assignment was as an Air Force advisor to the 3rd Air Division of the Vietnamese Air Force. My major duty was to advise them on the utilization of helicopters, so I was duly assigned to the rotary wing school at Fort Rucker, Alabama, to learn the intricacies of the machine. Helicopters flew like conventional aircraft when they reached forward flying speed, but I soon learned that hovering was like balancing on a basketball while playing a trombone. After a few hours in a helicopter, it all came together and I was able to keep it in one place, a few feet above the ground, in spite of the vagaries of the machine and pervasive winds.

The majority of the trainees were army warrant officer fixed wing pilots, transitioning to rotary wing aircraft. Many had been to Vietnam four or five times.

My instructor, on one of his tours in Vietnam was just transitioning to forward flying speed after take off, when a fixed wing aircraft flew into him from behind. He survived, but the injuries to his head affected his speech and he was inclined to slur. He was extremely lucky to have survived and my admiration for Army Warrant Officers increased enormously.

Futher training was necessary, so I was packed off to Counter Insurgency Training at Hurlburt Field in Florida. We were instucted on the type of war we were fighting where there were no battle lines and well nigh impossible to differentiate the friendly from the enemy, since there was no distinctive clothing or physiological characteristics. One of our lecturers was a fellow POW from Korea, who spoke of what we might expect to go through if captured.

Survival training was mandatory and I spent a miserable early January in Washington State. When I arrived, the airman in charge of the program said, "What are you, a Colonel, doing here? All Colonel's go through when the weather is warmer." We had to spend a period of time living in the mountains and surviving off the land. Living in the snow was a miserable experience. We had to become adept at orientation minus a compass and be able to get ourselves to a predetermined point. I had always prided myself on an intrinsic sense of direction but became hopelessly lost and began to wonder where North was. It was a blow to my pride and ego.

Due to my rank, I was placed in charge of the student contingent going through survival camp. Another phase of the survival school was a mock prison camp run by a Russian defector, an expert in Communist techniques of prisoner control and indoctrination. At this time, information was coming out through clandestine sources about the treatment of the American POW's held in North Vietnam and the camp taught us in what to expect if captured. This phase of our training started when we had to infiltrate, at night, an area adjacent to the camp. We lay in the snow until we were sure the patrolling guards were oblivious to our presence and slowly moved forward to a point near the camp. Upon reaching that point undetected, we were allowed to stand up and walk into the camp with no severe harassment from our "enemy captors". I crept forward in the snow, cold and wet and almost made it to the safe area, when a gruff foreign voice challenged me. I had been captured.

Two guards took me in with the other prisoners, stripped and frisked me, as no food was allowed during this three-day period. I was forced into a box about 2.5 feet high and just wide enough for my shoulders. I did not fit well and had to be forced in. Squatting with my head on my knees, my arms filled the rest of the available space. It made a sardine can seem spacious. After 30 minutes, I was cramped, claustrophobic, cold, wet and miserable and the process was only just beginning. One prisoner broke down while in the box and was removed from the program.

In the compound we were formed into ranks and being the ranking officer, was placed in charge of the prisoners. The rules were many and diverse and it was inevitable that all would be violated at some point. The penalty for a rule violation was to be caged in the freezing cold for a period of time. We were not allowed to use the sleeping quarters on site and the food was meagre portions of rice and water. After two days I was dismissed as leader of the prison camp due to my natural development into being a resistance leader. This was part of the plan as the Communists removed anyone they considered to be authority figures and providing a focus on resistance. At the end of the prison camp training, we were confused, uncertain and had a good idea of what to expect if captured. At that stage death seemed preferable to incarceration. When the camp ended, I walked back to the base rather than wait for the bus. I ate and then slept a full 24 hours. It was the second POW camp that I had been exposed to and I did not like it.

Thousands of dollars had been spent in preparing me for my job assignment and I was now eager to get to Vietnam. I tried to understand the protests of the 1960s, personally knew a few of the protesters, and had attended an anti-war rally in Washington DC. It seemed to be a small hard core of genuine protesters, with a large following of young people who were into the drug scene; a vocal minority who thrived on publicity. I had met and attended a lecture by Daniel Ellsburg, when the Rand Corporation briefed a group of us, which was largely an Air Force "think tank". Ellsburg worked for the Rand Corporation and used his office to steal classified information. His briefing was that we should not be in Vietnam, a conviction that seemed inappropriate to be voiced to the Air Force officers at that time.

I mentioned to George Lovell, a friend of mine and a fighter pilot ace who was in charge of our group, that Ellsburg should be working elsewhere if he supported such radical views and that the Pentagon should be made aware of his attitude. My feelings about the war were ambivalent; we were not winning either on the battlefield or at home and, like the French, were bogged down. To honestly evaluate our role in Vietnam, I felt that I should see it personally. I also missed the thrill of combat.

Before reporting to Air Force Advisory Team HQ in Saigon for briefings, I flew to Clark Air Force Base in the Philipines for jungle survival school. This made a lot more sense than going through survival school in Washington State in winter.

We were immediately taught what to expect in the jungle, what was edible, and how to survive in an environment completely foreign to the majority of Americans. It emphasized the doubts that many of us had on just what we were doing in an environment and a country so alien and hostile to us.

The second day we were shown the booby traps, the pungee sticks, which were sharpened sticks impregnated with faeces and placed on trails. Part of the course included the utilization of poisonous snakes fastened in place on trails, trip wires that detonated artillery shells and release branches with spikes on them. The lectures and demonstrations were supplemented with photos of wounds caused by these devices. The instructors had all done time "in country," as an assignment to Vietnam was called, and all had first hand knowledge of the booby traps and the stories that accompanied them.

They emphasized that Americans were not safe anywhere in this very foreign enviroment and that we were to remain vigilant at all times. On the third day we were taken out into the jungle to put all this learned theory into practice with native tribesmen as our guides and teachers. We ate the food of the jungle and drank the water heavily laced with chlorine. We were shown the poisonous snakes and I can recall a small bamboo viper clinging to a vine a few feet away from me, being practically invisible until it was pointed out to me.

On the final day we were taught the art of concealment and when our backs were turned the native tribesmen simply disappeared like magic, a mere few feet away from us. They melted into the surrounding undergrowth. Our final exercise was to utilize the art of concealment. We were given two hours to melt into the jungle before the native tribesmen were set to find us. When we were found, we were to give them a piece of cloth that they could redeem for money or food.

Thirty of us were released to find a hiding place. I planned to put as much distance as possible between me and the tribesmen for one hour and 50 minutes and then to use the last ten minutes to find suitable concealment. I climbed up the side of a mountain as far as I could go, found some vines to conceal myself and settled down to wait. I could hear the natives in the valley finding my companions. After three hours we were told to reveal ourselves. Out of the thirty trainees, only two of us went undetected.

On the way back to the base, the driver told us of caves that still held the bones and weapons of Japanese who had not surrendered. He said that the Japanese government had sent recovery teams to find them, but had not been able to enter some of the caves because of the inaccessability and danger from poisonous snakes. We passed many of the caves used by the Japanese during the final days of WW11.

Finally all the training was behind me, and the Vietnam experience lay ahead.

CHAPTER 2

BIEN HOA

If you want to know about an organization or an area,
ask a senior enlisted man.
HF

I flew back to Saigon, to Ton Son Nhut, the combination military, civilian Vietnamese airport with the military terminal adjacent to the civilian terminal. There were revetments for both the Vietnamese gun ships and United States Air Force transports. Vietnam had recently increased the size of their airlines from two engined DC-3s to the four-engined DC-4s.

The temperature in this area of South Central Vietnam seldom varied through the two seasons, a dry and a wet season. During the latter, huge afternoon thunderstorms developed with torrents of rain bucketing down. During some stages of the war, fighting slowed down during the monsoon season and began in earnest once the dry season arrived and maneuvering was easy. There was a great deal of activity at Ton Son Nhut and it was hectic when our forces in Vietnam hovered around 500,000 men for this was the main entrance and departure airfield for the troops. When I arrived our forces were less than one-half of that figure as we were drawing down every month and turning the fighting over to the Vietnamese.

Gathering up what little baggage I had, I found my assigned quarters on the airfield where the Air Force Advisory team was located and then headed for the officers club and to the bar. The bar at happy hour was not much different from those during the Korean War and WW11 days, except that now there were more flight suits in evidence. The bar was filled with pilots just back from flying their day's mission; men waiting to be flown to their units; commanders back for briefings at the HQ of the Military Advisory Command Vietnam, or MACV as it was known.

The following day, I went to the Air Force Advisory team HQ for briefings and to meet the commander, to whom I would directly report. General Watkins was a two star General, whom I liked immediately. He was direct, believed in his mission and the Vietnamese he advised. His counter part, General Tinh, was the Vietnamese Air Force Commander. I was then given the standard briefings for newly assigned Vietamese Air Division Advisors, which involved intelligence, operations, personnel and support.

There were five Vietnamese Air Division Advisors. The one stationed at Danang near the northern border advised the First Air Division on helicopter operations and supply. The Second Air Division advisory commander was located at Nha Trang on the east coast, and was responsible for advising the Vietnamese Technical Training Center on the training of their Air Force pilots and crews. It was modeled on the USAF Technical Training Centers in Denver, Colorado, Biloxi,

Mississippi and Rantoul, Illinois. A large aircraft repair base was also established here. They flew the small twin engine Cessna jets, which were also used in training Air Force pilots.

The Fourth Air Division was located south of Saigon in the Delta at Can Toa where the Air Force Advisory team helped with Huey helicopter operations and supply. The Capital Air Division was based in Saigon and the Air Force Advisory Team assisted them with cargo operations and supply. They were equipped with C-119 cargo airplanes.

The Air Force Advisor at Vietnamese Logistics Center based at Bien Hoa was Colonel Cline, a man with an extensive background in logistics. He was the only non-rated Colonel assigned as an advisor.

I was assigned to the 3rd Air Division to advise the commander, Colonel Tinh. It was the largest in Vietnam and stationed at Bien Hoa, thirty miles north of Saigon. There were two squadrons of helicopters; a squadron comprised 18 aircraft. One squadron of six medium lift helicopters, the Ch-47 or Chinook; one squadron of twelve Cessna O-1 aircraft; a squadron of twelve Douglas Skyraiders; and a squadron of twelve Northrop F-5 aircraft.

As the commander of the 3rd Air Division Advisory team I had under me 12 officers and 32 enlisted men, each hand picked for their assignment based on expertise and ability to work with the Vietnamese. Nine of the officers were pilots and assisted the Vietnamese in helicopter operations, fighter attack, ground attack, observation and flew missions along with the Vietnamese. Two of the advisors were army helicopter pilots who flew, trained Vietnamese pilots and provided liaison with the Army. They were the most valuable men in the team. The other three officers were non-rated, that is they were not pilots, but had expertise in personnel, supply and civil engineering. The enlisted men were assigned to work with their counterparts in the Vietnamese Airforce, in maintainece, supply, personnel, the hospital and civil engineering.

The day finally arrived for me to report to my new assignment and Sergeant Knowles arrived outside HQ in a Jeep to collect me. The jeep was right out of WW11, with a canvas roof cover and no sides to it. I threw in my meager belongings, my helmet and parachute. Both the helmet and parachute had been carried from the States as they were in short supply and each pilot was required to carry his own. We drove through Saigon with its many mopeds cramming the streets. We passed over a railroad track and Sgt Knowles told me that it was the national railway system and ran for about thirty miles over tracks that were safe.Any further and the communists either stopped it and demanded tribute or derailed it. A grenade had recently been thrown into a passenger compartment, killing and injuring a lot of the passengers including women and children.

Sgt Knowles told me which roads to Bien Hoa were safe to use and which not to use at night or even during the day unless armed and traveling with someone. One route passed through a market that the Viet Cong supposedly used for supplies

As I listened to him, it confirmed my opinion that if you wanted to know about an organization or an area ask a senior enlisted man. As we traveled north, I noticed an impressive facility spread over about five acres. There were a number of high cylindrical structures that towered over 100 feet in the air. Sgt Knowles gestured to it and said that it was the sewage disposal facility for Saigon. It was built at a cost of millions of dollars under the aid program and was deserted. When it was finished it was discovered that the sewage system installed by the French was not compatible with the existing infrastructure. The high towers were to provide water pressure to evacuate the system. When they turned on the system, it did not operate and so it stood unused.

We crossed a bridge over the Dong Nha River which circles Saigon and I saw cargo vessels lined up by the piers being unloaded with supplies for the war effort. I was told that a large amount of cargo was lost on the dock through stealing. A Chinese had control of the dock workers and they paid tribute, bribe money to him for the privilege of working on the piers. He acted as the fence for the items and almost everything that one got in the Post Exchange could also be found in the market place, including items supposedly in short supply. There was no gasoline sold for commercial vehicles, yet mopeds were running in abundance and roadside vendors sold jugs of gasoline. All this came from theft and pilfering on the dock side of military supplies and also from our bases.

We passed a series of buildings that Sgt Knowles pointed out as an orphanage that the Air Force Advisory Team was helping to support with donated clothes and other items they collected. The Vietnamese government did not support orphanages, so they relied heavily on outside help for food and clothing.

Reaching our destination we were stopped at the gate by American military police. There was an identical checkpoint manned by Vietnamese military police for the Vietnamese airmen, soldiers and civilians.

We went directly to the Advisory Team Headquarters near the flight line and the revetments for the F-5's and 0-1 aircraft. Major Ferree, the executive officer welcomed me to Bien Hoa and I was shown into my office and introduced to the two Vietnamese typists. There were numerous small offices in the building and at the back was a meeting room where all the officers were assembled awaiting my arrival. Each officer was introduced to me and briefly stated his duties in the organization. After I met them, I said that I was pleased to be on this assignment and knew that they were a very select group of men.

Major Ferree suggested a tour of the base so we drove down the flight line past the revetments where Cessna attack aircraft were preparing for a mission and bombs and napalm were being attached to the underside of the wings. The base was under the control of Colonel Griese, a slim and dynamic academy graduate.

It was pointed out to me that there were two organizations occupying Bien Hoa, each with their seperate areas, the Vietnamese and the Americans. The Americans were instructed not to go on the Vietnamese side of the base. The runways were essentially the only part shared by the two forces. The Air Force Advisory

Team had a compound in the Vietnamese area where we had officers and enlisted quarters, clubs, a dining hall, and movie theatre. The dining hall got its food from "scrounging" and trading with the Army units. A volley ball court was an integral part of the social unit and a means to exercise after work.

The headquarters of the Vietnamese Third Air Division was the former French Army Officers Club. It was an impressive building and in front of it was a Grumman F-8 Hellcat. The Grumman was an aircraft that the United States gave to the French who used them to equip the first fighter units of the Vietnamese Air Force after WW11. The architecture of the Vietnamese side of the base was traditional French colonial of the 1800's.

Driving around the perimeter of the airfield, we saw where the Viet Cong had breached the perimeter of the base during the Tet offensive of 1968. Major Ferree said that one of the US Air Force officers had lost his life here while leading a team to repel sappers. There were still scars on some of the buildings from the Viet Cong shells and rifle bullets.Around the perimeter were ammunition storage areas, where bombs, rockets and machine gun ammunition were cached in domed revetments surrounded by dirt embankments.

During the tour of the base, we went by my quarters. I had a choice of being on the American or the Vietnamese side. I chose the Vietnamese side, close to the 3rd Air Division HQ. The windows were boardered up because of rocket attacks, which made it dark inside. It had one bedroom with a large shower and commode area and equipped with ceiling fans. The only concession to the 1900's was electricity and air conditioning.

I scheduled a meeting with Colonel Tinh, the 3rd Air Division Commander and my counterpart in this war. The American whom I was replacing had left a few days before so I did not have the benefit of having him hand over to me and advising me of current happenings.Colonel Tinh was tall and thin, and would have been considered striking in any society. We exchanged greetings and he invited me to have coffee or tea with him as we sat in an informal meeting area in his spacious office and exchanged pleasantries. I told him that I was glad to be there and was looking forward to working with him. He invited me to a welcoming party to meet his staff, which I graciously accepted.

The welcoming party was attended by the offficers of the advisory team and their counterparts. Cocktails were served followed by Vietnamese cuisine of light soup, spring rolls and shrimp taken from the Don Nai River, all washed down with the local beer. Colonel Tinh gave an after dinner welcoming speech, which I responded to with toasts to liberty, equality and fraternity. This was followed by a floorshow, culminating with a strip tease act and thus the pattern was set for many future parties hosted by the Vietnamese.

A good advisor should have a knowledge of the language which I attempted to learn while still in Washington DC with the aid of language records and books. I wanted to have the basics for communicating with my counterpart but it transpired that he had an excellent command of English and French. Since I had been stationed in France and spoke somewhat inadequate French, I could communicate with some of the other Vietnamese officers whose command of English was not as good as Colonel Tinh's. The entire senior ranking officers had been educated in French schools during the period Vietnam was a French Colony, so they were fluent in the language.

I soon found out that there was little to advise a senior officer who had been fighting the war for twenty years. He should have been advising us on how to fight this war in his own country. Colonel Tinh had been fighting the war ever since he had received his commission in the French Air Force. He was the son of a rich plantation owner in the Delta, which was now controlled by the Viet Cong. He was also a French citizen, which was a privilege given to few Vietnamese in the French Colony.

The role of a good advisor, in the eyes of the Vietnamese was how much material and supplies could be procured through the advisor for the utilization of the Vietnamese. The standard operating procedure soon evolved: I would receive information from members of the Advisory Team on how to solve problems, which I would then present to Colonel Tinh. Some of these were very good but not feasible under the circumstances. Those that were both practical and feasible, I would diplomatically present to Colonel Tinh. Some of the ideas could be implemented by the Advisory Team and some I forwarded to our HQ in Saigon. A common theme ran through the requests from Colonel Tinh; along the lines of, "Give us more equipment, supplies and training. We like your advice and accept you but our needs are great."

I soon realized that all of the Advisory Teams had common problems and it would be of benefit to hold a meeting sponsored by HQ to talk about them. I wanted to know how the other Advisory Team commanders operated. I realized that our individual advisory roles due to circumstances were different, but that basically our techniques were similiar. I also wanted to know what the criteria for being a successful advisor was. As a preliminary step, I decided to use the autovon system, the telephone system set up throughout Vietnam to contact the other advisors on a rountine basis. Sharing our common problems provided the basis for a series of meetings first held at HQ in Saigon, then hosted in turn by each of us at our respective bases. They were held when there was a lull in activity that was infrequent, for fighting was always going on somewhere in Vietnam, which involved the Advisory Teams.

One of the advisors to the Vietnamese Capital Division, mentioned Father Forrest, a professor at Saigon University, who frequently lectured on Vietnamese customs and traditions. I arranged for him to speak to our advisory team and also invited the base commander, Colonel Grice, to attend. I felt strongly that to advise the Vietnamese, an understanding of their culture was essential and thus made it mandatory for all members of the advisory team to attend. Father Forrest had lived in Vietnam for most of his life and had a deep affection for the Vietnamese people. He gave us a history of the Vietnamese war and the affect of Catholicism on the conduct of the war. He said that when a peace was negotiated between the North and South, and a boundary line established, the majority of Catholics moved south as they were opposed to communism. The North Vietnamese encouraged the Catholics to move south because they presented a united front and would not assimilate into their form of government. That is why there are so many Catholic villages in the south, each with its own church and they represent a strong bulwark against communism. He gave a short narrative on the Buddhist religion and the aspect of ancestor worship and the family tomb. We, as advisors, were told be aware of the extremely strong family ties that are an integral part of the local culture. Even in families divided in their allegiance to either the Viet Cong or the South Vietnamese government, they are still bound together by family ties. The Vietnamese have a different concept of time than do the Americans. Their concept of time is circular, in that if they do not achieve a harmonious existence in this life, they will come back again and whatever form of government exists, if it is onerous to them, they will just wait, and in time it will change for the better. Consequently the ruling power is something to be patiently endured but not supported. For the peasant, the government is always there, sometimes good and sometimes bad. The peasant must always pay his taxes and the form of government is not important. Only when the peasant sees that the government is doing something for him or his village, will he support it.

The concept of time for the Americans is linear; goals must be accomplish in a certain time frame. The Americans are in Vietnam for a year and want to see some progress. The Americans are impatient. In 1966 Westmoreland said, "The war has reached a turning point, the Viet Cong can no longer sustain his casulties. We are finally winning the war." The majority of Americans are not aware of the difference in the concept of time. The French were not aware of it either. The peasant has seen the French, the Americans, the South Vietnamese and the Viet Cong, and cannot see much difference between any of them. He will till his fields the same as he has always done and the authorities will eventually go away, and a new government take its place. He has no more fear of the Viet Cong than he did the French. The Americans wonder about the Vietnamese and regard them as apathetic. They should be fighting just as hard for their freedom as the Americans are fighting for it. Father Forrest said, "This causes a great deal of problems for you as advisors, for you too have these same feelings."

I had tried to determine what to pay Father Forrest. He had initially refused payment of any kind. On the advice of Major Erway, one of the Army helicopter pilot advisors who was fluent in Vietnamese, I purchased two bottles of Courvosier and presented them to Father Forrest with my heartfelt thanks. It was the first time that an advisory team had received a lecture on Vietnamese culture and thought patterns and I considered it to be a significant event. It may not have had an affect on the way we operated but it certainly gave us an insight to the people with whom we were working. I often wonder if Father Forrest remained in Vietnam and what sort of reception he received from the North Vietnamese when they took over the government in 1975.

As commander of the Air Force Advisory team a routine soon developed; report to the office, look at the schedule, take care of paperwork, respond to any deadlines that were levied by higher headquarters and then visit the advisory team members on the base. Sometimes I had breakfast with them and always made a point to visit with each Sergeant, often at his place of work to see if he had any problems. From this I learned a great deal about the effectiveness of our efforts. We were highly successful in establishing rapport, but our impact as advisors on the overall war effort was minimal. It was the time of Vietnamization and we were turning the war effort over to the Vietnamese. The United States Air Force, Army, Marines and Navy were still fighting, but the political emphasis was to train and equip the Vietnamese to fight their own war and our overall effort was to minimize our presence and return to the status of purely advisors. This was the way it began in 1962 and this was the way it was envisioned to end.

My routine also involved flying, particularly the helicopters, for our major emphasis was on helicopter operations. I checked out again in the Huey with refresher training from Major Erway and a final combat check by a Vietnamese instructor. My biggest problem was getting in and out of a three-sided revetment, which was not much bigger than the size of the helicopter. Sand bags extended up to five feet on three sides of the helicopter and when the wind was blowing, it was quite a feat to get it into the revetment. It required hovering six inches off the ground, and then moving sideways which necessitated the utmost in skill and a lot of luck. Often when the wind was blowing, the helicopter was landed just beside the revetment and skidded into place.

After my checkout, I routinely scheduled flying three to five times a week and sometimes more when operations were going on. Unlike the Army, which was responsible for flying their own helicopters, the Vietnamese Air Force had the helicopters assigned to them. This had been a political decision at the highest levels in the Department of Defence and involved the Air Force and Army. At the combat level in the U. S. Army it was still felt that the helicopters should be assigned to the Vietnamese Army. It was the old "roles and missions" battle fought in 1947, when the Army Air Corp evolved from the Army and carried on anew during the period of Vietnamization.

Whenever Colonel Tinh was scheduled to fly, I requested that I fly with him. On helicopter operations we would go up in a command and control helicopter and observe the operation. Often times I would be the only American on these operations. When he attended a staff conference, we would fly in a four place Cessna. He had his own personal pilot and the Cessna was his personal airplane. He also had a command helicopter assigned to him and befitting a commander, it was kept in immaculate condition. It was rumoured that he was on the list for General and was later promoted just before the war came to a close in 1975. It reminded me of General Paulus at Stalingrad, just before he surrendered he was promoted to Field Marshal.

VIETNAM

CHAPTER 3: Operations

"You have never lived until you have almost died.
For those who have fought for it,
life has a special flavor that the protected will never know."
Special Operations Association

The French prior to WW11 had built the Air Base. The Japanese used it when they conquered this part of Asia during the early stages of the war and occupied it for the duration. There was an uneasy peace between the French and the Japanese after Hitler had defeated France. The French troops were largely confined to their barracks and training area and although they were supportive of the Vichi government, friendly to Germany and Japan, the Japanese did not trust the French. During the closing days of WW11 the Japanese, anticipating defeat, attacked and disarmed the French and massacred their officers. This was the same airbase from which the Japanese had sent their Betty bombers off to attack our naval forces.

My quarters were the ones used by the French and just outside was the reported site of the execution of French Officers and civilians late in 1945. The interior was dimly lit as the windows were shuttered closed due to rocket attacks. I always had a strange feeling of uneasiness in these dim quarters and frequently during the night heard loud thuds and upon investigation there was never any ascertainable reason for the strange noises. General Kye, the leader of the Vietnamese Air Force, had lived in these quarters when he was a Captain of infantry in the French Foreign Legion and he said that he too was bothered by strange noises at night and on investigation had sometimes seen the floor covered with blood. He did not remain in those quarters for long. I was soon granted permission to live in a trailer on the American side of the base and although they were not nearly as secure from rocket attacks as the French quarters, they did allow me to get a decent nights sleep with no interuptions from unexplained "noises in the night".

Rocket attacks on the base were a frequent occurrence, and although the damage in terms of casualties and destruction of materials was minimal, it was psychologically damaging knowing that we were never entirely secure from these random attacks. The Viet Cong managed to infiltrate close enough to the base to set up crude bamboo shafts to use as rocket launchers, aimed in our general direction. During the night there were free fire zones and artillery was fired to discourage such infiltration.

The Vietnamese had set up a command post where Colonel Tinh, Colonel Cline and other senior advisers would go to monitor an attack on the base when it was in progress and take whatever actions were necessary to ensure its security. The Vietnamese were responsible for all the security measures and the American forces were merely considerd tenants. During my first experience of a rocket attack, I dived under the bed, waited there until it was over then proceeded with Colonel Cline to the command post. Only two rockets had landed on the Vietnamese side of the base injuring two people. With an indication of an impending attack, the sirens sounded and everyone took cover. More often than not, there would be no warning, and we would hear the rockets going off followed by the sound of the siren. After the first few attacks, Colonel Cline and I would go to the command post to review the situation, and after the all clear sounded we went to inspect the damage.

During one attack, the enemy's rocket struck the F-5 revetments, destroying two aircraft and damaging others; one ignited and burned in the revetment. When the rockets were fired, the army radar picked up the trajectory and would pin point the area from where they were fired. The artillery returned fire in the general direction but rarely would there be any evidence the next day of where the attack had originated. The attacks were mainly directed at the American side, and often at base operations where cargo airplanes were unloading. Once a C-130 received a direct hit and burned. Our Air Force Advisory Team HQ also received damage but during my year in Vietnam we were lucky and never had any casualties from these attacks. Coincidently they often happened when I was at another base and it occured frequently enough for remarks to be made that the base was usually safer when I was around!

Directly across from our headquarters was a large hangar used to repair the Vietnamese helicopters. One night when I was away, it was destroyed and a marine was killed. Walking to my quarters one night, I saw an incoming rocket which struck about 1500 feet away and it made me realize our vulnerability. On another occasion a round struck close enough to the trailer compound to rip the paneling from the inside of the trailer. The trailer was like a tin can and the inside reverbrated like someone beating on a drum.

After sappers were killed trying to infiltrate the base to attack the ammunition storage area, we took the precaution and initiated dusk patrols by helicopters around the perimeter of the base. I occasionally flew these patrols which we did at about 50ft, searching for trails and evidence of rocket launching activity. We did once see primitive rocket launching tubes and sent a patrol out to investigate.

The Viet Cong brought up the rockets and launchers at night, concealed them and set them up and returned the following night to fire them. Intelligence reports from the villages sometimes provided information of impending attacks and we would put the base on condition red alert, meaning that an attack was likely. Often attacks were made during bad weather, when surveillance was difficult and we became well aware that during the day we had a little control over the villages, but at night, they belonged entirely to the Viet Cong.

There was a leper colony not far from the base, which the Advisory Team helicopter delivered medical supplies to. Generally, there was radio contact with the colony, and we called before we arrived. One morning I flew out with the Army pilot to deliver the supplies and when we were about 75ft above the ground, transitioning to hovering flight to the landing pad, the pilot suddenly applied power and we left. He was ashen faced and said that he had seen a long stick with two antennas which was a booby trap commonly used for helicopters. The rotors would strike the antennas, which detonated a satchel charge, destroying the helicopter. We flew back to the base, and alerted a team to investigate. They reported back that the night before the Viet Cong had entered the leper colony in search of medical supplies, had destroyed the radio and set the booby trap. One of the nurses had tried in vain to warn us about the booby trap before we landed.

This helicopter pilot had been on two tours to Vietnam and before he drove a jeep that had been parked outside the base he checked it over thoroughly, both inside, underneath and the hood. One of his friends had been killed when the jeep he was driving was booby trapped while parked in a village. The price for vigilance is a longer life.

Routine operations, and not only combat situations, took their toll of lives as well. A Cessna attack aircraft had bombs on board that failed to jettison. The pilot made a standard pattern and turned too tight on final, spun, crashed and burned right at the threshold of the runway. The pilot of an A-1 lost control on take-off and his bombs exploded. A Jolly Green Giant, a huge six rotored helicopter used in air and sea rescue missions crashed in the Dong Nhi river after loosing power. The same river claimed a pilot on a test flight of a Cobra gun ship when the controls became inoperative and his last transmission was "I am going into the Dong Nhi River at 280 knots."

The crayfish taken from the Dong Nhi River were huge and fat. It was rumoured that they fed on the corpses of the dead.

When I arrived at Bien Hoa, I made it a standard practice to fly with the Vietnamese on combat missions. There were no problems with the fighter pilots and army pilots but the Air Force helicopter pilots felt that their job was to advise and not fly and fight. I had to monitor their operations, and insist that they fly combat. Their timidity became aparent when we were going to "Parrots Beak," an area northwest of Bien Hoa where there was a forward air strip and landing pads for helicopters, from which the Vietnamese Air Force picked up their army troops for helicopter assault missions.

On the way to the pick up point, the Air Force helicopter pilot flew over the main road, instead of taking a direct route to the pick up area. I asked him why he was not taking the direct route and he said, "The direct route might be controlled by the Viet Cong. This way is safer." I flew the direct course to Bien Hoa on our return flight and noticed his intense discomfort. He had never been in a situation where risk of combat was involved and had devoted his career to saving lives and thus had difficulty transitioning. The other two Air Force helicopter pilots were of a like mind and required constant surveilance.

I made it mandatory that they fly one combat operation mission a week and to brief me on the operation afterwards. The other pilots were exemplary, flying as many missions as the Vietnamese would permit, in conjunction with their duties as advisors. Every time we took off it was logged as combat time since we were subject to ground fire anywhere from within ten miles of the base. The only pilot exempt from flying combat, was the Air Force flying safety officer and his job was risky enough as he was called upon to go into hostile areas to recover and ascertain the cause of a crash. He was often accompanied by the Vietnamese army for protection and many times was required to remain overnight at the crash site

A Major assigned as an Air Advisor to the squadron had a narrow escape flying the Douglas A-1, commonly called the Skyraider. It was like a tank and could carry its own weight in armament and was a favourite of the pilots who flew them. I had flown a close support mission with him near what was called the "iron triangle." We picked up a Vietnamese FAC flying an O-1 observation aircraft. He vectored us in on a tree line where Viet Cong had fired on a patrol and marked the target with a phosphous rocket, where upon we set up a pattern by first dropping napalm and as the black oily smoke billowed skyward we emptied our ammunition by strafing the area. It typified the majority of targets in this war, where pilots could not see the targets they were supposed to hit but were told to strike an area in general.

We began to receive reports of the Viet Cong receiving hand launched, heat seeking rockets in the 3rd military region. A Navy A-4 had been shot down and other navy pilots reported that rockets had been shot them at. The Navy solution was to release flares as they pulled off their firing runs to divert the rockets. I was flying a helicopter north of Bien Hoa observing a combat assault operation, when a radio call indicated that a pilot had been hit by a rocket and had bailed out. The coordinates were given and we proceeded to the area to see if we could pick up the pilot. An Army chopper had already picked him up and identified him as the Major assigned to the Air Force Advisory Team.

We followed the army chopper and when he landed for refueling, we picked up the Major who was unhurt except for a burn on his neck from the parachute shroud lines when it opened. He excitedly told us, "I was pulling off after my last run and looking back saw a rocket. It hit me in the engine and it started to burn so I turned toward home and bailed out. I landed in a field with tall grass and got on the radio. I could hear shouting close by so I hid until I saw a chopper and then I ran and jumped aboard." Landing at Bien Hoa, we took him to the hospital and then to intelligence for debriefing. The end result of being fired at by the rockets was that the pilots were briefed to pull off much higher from their attacks, and this considerably decreased their effectiveness.

Although I routinely flew the helicopters, I also flew with the F-5 and O-1 squadron. Based at Danang the F-5 squadron had a detachment of aircraft operating in an air defense role to counter the threat of enemy bombers flying south to attack cities. I flew with them on a routine patrol to observe their operations. The main complaint the Vietnamese had, was that the Americans in the tower would not give their aircraft their due priority in the landing pattern; a fact that I observed on our let down upon our return to base. We were placed in a holding pattern until all the American aircraft returning from a combat mission had landed. At that stage we were low on fuel and it was apparent that the Vietnamese were not considered as being part of the A-team.

The F-5 aircraft also had a ground support role but had a limited range in both the interceptor and ground support role of about 150nm. On a ground support mission northwest of Bien Hoa we circled at 10,000ft over the target waiting for the FAC in an O-1 to mark the target. We watched it wheel and dart just above the trees until finally it rolled level and a rocket streaked from the aircraft. The white phosphorous rose from the ground and sparkled in the sun. The leader called to arm the switches and then descended in a dive and released one of his bombs, which hit close to the rocket strike. We dove and released one bomb and looking back, saw it detonate. Each of the four aircraft made four diving attacks and after the last pilot called that he was off the target, we joined up and circled while the forward air controller flew close to the target area to assess the damage and provide a strike report. We were getting low on fuel when the FAC called, "Tiger flight, it looks like you got ten bicycles." The strike report summarized to me the war effort that we were engaged in; a war of technology on one side, applied essentially on a rural and urban guerilla war.

While at Danang, I visited and met the staff of the Red Cross hospital ship docked in the harbor, a huge white ship with large red crosses painted on it. Its purpose was to go to any international disaster or war area and render aid. It was staffed by an international medical team with neutral affiliations, who treated anyone who was injured or ill; soldiers, women and children.

I flew an observation mission deep into Cambodia in the Cessna 0-1 with Major Craig, our resident Advisory Team member. We flew over the plantations of rubber trees and saw where the B-52s had pattern bombed these magnificent plantations. It was like flying over water; so desolate and remote. We were out of radio range, but within range of the Kyhmer Rouge, as the counterparts to the Viet Cong were called in Cambodia. On our return we refueled at a base at Loc Ninh, about 100 miles northwest of Saigon and the center of a huge rubber plantation. The airstrip had been built by the French plantation owners and was the base for an army reconnaissance unit. Close by was a large rubber refinery that had been closed down. In this beautiful setting the French had built fine two story homes, with large shuttered windows, high ceilings, red tile roofs and light beige stucco walls for the administrators of the rubber plantations. The homes were now empty except for a caretaker.

French army units had once been stationed at Loc Ninh and barracks had been built within the compound, along with a magnificent civilian and officers club. Stepping into the club was like stepping into the past where the colonials lived like Royalty. What we saw were the remnants of a colonial empire.

Major Craig and I borrowed a jeep and drove into the village surrounding the rubber refinery, where we found a large church and a nunnery, with a school run by Vietnamese nuns. We talked in French with the nuns, and were invited to have refreshments with them. Major Craig and I asked if they needed any supplies for their school, to which the mother superior replied that they would be grateful for any amount of paper and writing materials. We promised to return with as much as we could fit into our small airplane. This seemed to me to be a positive form of assistance that we could give and something that would directly benefit the Vietnamese village school. Before we could return, the war came to Loc Ninh and destroyed it. I often wonder what happened to the nuns and if they survived the attack. It was also near Loc Ninh that a hand launched missile struck the A-1 and took down our Advisory Team member.

As we took off from Loc Ninh, a Dornier airplane with civilian markings came in to land. It was flown by Frenchmen in the employ of the plantation owners and although the plantations were no longer in operation due to the war, it was reported that the owners paid tribute to the Viet Cong to prevent them from being destroyed. The plantations around Loc Ninh produced the finest rubber used in racing tires and Michelen had large interests both in Vietnam and in Cambodia.

When I was not flying with Col Kye, I would fly with his executive officer, Colonel Tuong; an effervescent fighter pilot with a checkered carreer and connections in high places. He had personally rescued General Tinh from being captured by the North Vietnamese, when they were flying with the French. At that time they were both Lieutenants. At one time he had been assigned to fly with the newly formed Vietnamese airline but had rejoined the Vietnamese Air Force where he flew all the airplanes and helicopters of the 3rd Air Division.

He had many influencial friends, civilian, Army, Air Force and especially with the paratroopers so flying with him opened many avenues normally not available to Americans. I flew a mission with him in the CH-47 when the Vietnamese invaded Cambodia in early 1972. At this time no Americans were allowed to set foot on Cambodian soil, so the operational plan was for the Vietnamese army, supported by the Vietnamese Air Force, to go into Cambodia and destroy the supply bases that the Viet Cong had in Cambodia. The US forces were to assist them with supplies and support but only within Vietnam. The operation began with every chance of success as intelligence had located the supply areas; the attack was during the dry season and the plans were well coordinated between the participants. This was strictly a Vietnamese operation and at a planning conference between the Vietnamese Army and Air Force, all American advisors were excluded. I flew with Colonel Tinh to the conference but remained outside. I felt that this was an important step in the Vietnamization process.

When the operation began, I flew with Colonel Tuong resupplying the army alongside the invasion highway leading into Cambodia. The US Army established a refueling and resupply area close to the Cambodian border where huge transportable fuel bladders were placed in large dirt revetments and tons of supplies for the invasion were brought in by truck and helicopters. As the forward units entered Cambodia, we airlifted supplies, food and ammunition to the army units along preselected areas of the invasion route.

Accompanying us were Cobra helicopter gunships to attack the enemy soldiers if they fired on us. The CH-47 because of its size and slow speed was like a sitting duck and invited fire. The gunships appeared infrequently, much to the consternation of the Vietnamese flying the CH-47s and they felt that they were not getting adequate support from the US Army. My duty as an advisor was to forward these complaints to the Army when we arrived back at the main base. I talked to the Army officer responsible for the air support and he said curtly, "I will forward your concern. You know that the Cobras must keep up their air speed in order to be effective." I told him, "We could not even contact them in the air, so they must have been some distance away." The situation did not improve but we continued to fly into Cambodia. One of our resupply points was at Krek, in Cambodia. I assisted with the unloading of supplies there as we were extremely vulnerable on the ground and thus there was at least one American who did, in fact set foot on Cambodian soil.

For the first few days the operation was a success with caches of all kinds of weapons being found and destroyed, as well as food and medical supplies. An entire underground hospital was also found. Representative weapons were sent back and displayed at command HQ. Then disaster struck, the columns of men, vehicles and tanks encountered resistance and were forced to pull back and abandoned their equipment. What started out as a significant campaign, entirely planned and executed by the Vietnamese, turned into a defeat. At this stage of the war, it was important for the Vietnamese to succeed for psychological reasons and prove themselves to the Americans. It resulted in a "loss of face" to the Vietnamese, for they are a proud people and dashed the hopes of the Americans that Vietnamization would work.

Tension increased on both sides, the Vietnamese felt that the Americans did not give them enough support and the Americans felt that the Vietnamese did not have the national will to fight to save their own nation from being dominated by the Viet Cong.

The second time that I went into Cambodia was with Colonel Tinh when we flew to the capitol, Phom Phen, to coordinate planned air operations with the now somewhat friendly government. The Vietnamese had a contingent from the Air Force stationed there. The Russians had been asked to leave and the evidence of their support to the Cambodian government was apparent as soon as we touched down on the runway, as there were destroyed and damaged MiGs and other Russian aircraft on the ground. Driving into town we saw many Russian military vehicles on the streets. All of us wore civilian clothes since we did not want to advertise our presence.

I flew in without prior clearance and without a passport. After the conference, we had some free time and I walked around the market and the gift shops filled with antiques for tourists who were not in evidence, and not visiting Cambodia at that stage. It was like being in a time warp, viewing the remnants of a colonial empire. No results were forthcoming from the planning conference and I believe the plan for joint operations was finally dropped.

The Vietnamese Air Force had trouble enough meeting their own requirements without indulging in foreign commitments. The Secretary of the Air Force, Seamans, visited Vietnam to ascertain the effectiveness of Vietnamization. He stopped for briefings in Saigon, and then visited the Air Force Advisory Team where Colonel Tinh briefed him on the 3rd Air Division and I briefed him on the Air Force Advisory Team.

An introductory flight was arranged in the helicopter assigned to the Advisory Team and we flew to Vung Tau, a resort area on the coast, close to Saigon. Accompanying us were two extra helicopters in case our helicopter went down. We had lunch at Vung Tau and then circled Saigon so he could see the city, with its network of rivers surrounding it and the dock area, where supplies were unloaded. This time, we flew over the main roads, instead of going direct, since endangering a political figure, is neither discreet nor wise. We flew with the doors open so that he could see the countryside and the view was certainly striking as we also went south of Saigon so that he could see the delta; the rice bowl of Vietnam. In times of peace Vietnam exported rice but with much of the delta area under the control of the Viet Cong, South Vietnam had to import rice. What the Viet Cong did not control, they taxed. We flew over the "Parrots Beak", the area just west of Saigon, which had never been conquered. The US and South Vietnamese Army had tried to penetrate and control the area but it was interlaced with caves and tunnels and the terrain made it so difficult that all attempts to neutralize it were abandoned and was thus acknowledged as Viet Cong territory.

We flew west of Bien Hoa and pointed out a village that specialized in making ceramic elephants, which many Americans brought back as souveniers. One had to drive or fly in during the day, because the Viet Cong controlled the roads at night. We subsequently gave that same tour to other dignitaries visiting Vietnam and I came to realize that the most important part of my job was its political connotations.

One of the American innovations of the Vietnamese war was the utilization of a helicopter repair ship, which was anchored off Vung Tau. It was a medium sized freighter that had been converted to a complete machine shop where all helicopter parts could be manufactured or repaired. Landing pads were on the forward and rear deck of the ship and landing on them was quite an adventure. The area was small, and the touch down had to coincide with the rocking of the deck. I had to make several attempts before I reduced power and shut down the engine. It was reported that Viet Cong frogmen had attempted to blow up the ship and a constant look out was stationed to prevent these sneak attacks. The ship itself was a complete factory for helicopter maintaince and repair for both the US Army and Vietnamese Air Force. The concept of a repair ship was used by China Air Transport, when the Communists took over China and Chiang Kai-Scheck established his government on Taiwan. The Chinese airline based itself in Taiwan and the repair and fabrication of parts was done on repair ships docked close to the airport.

The Choi Hoi program was part of our assistance to the Vietnamese and aimed at encouraging the Viet Cong to rally to the side of the South Vietnamese. The bulk of the men in the Choi Hoi program were prisoners, and special camps were set up where these ex-Viet Cong were fed and trained to take a place in society. We had an advisor with expertise in psychological warfare who helped to rehabilitate these former enemies of the state. Literally millions of pamphlets were dropped over suspected Viet Cong positions encouraging them to desert and assuring that they would be well treated, fed, and trained in basic skills such as auto mechanics and carpentry, which would enable them to secure jobs. The concept was basically sound, but there were too few schools to cope with the influx of people and the basic economy could only support a certain number of mechanics and tradesmen and most houses where built by families, so carpenters were not needed.

Consequently the Choi Hoi camps were filled with people who sat idle.

VIETNAM

CHAPTER 4: The Monument

In war, what one man builds,
another destroys in the name of freedom.
HF

At Lai Khe I came across a pyramid shaped monument erected in memory of the French Divisions who had been stationed there. The inscription in French, read:

To the memory of the officers, senior enlisted men and privates of the Fourth Division who gave their lives for the defense of freedom in Cambodia and Vietnam.
1947-1954.

On the opposite side the inscription read:

To the memory of the officers and men of the Third Division in Vietnam and Cambodia
1947-1954.

This monument made a tremendous impression on me for it was a symbol of the men who had fought similar battles, in much the same way we were doing and it had made little difference. Both the French and the Americans had fought for the same length of time. They were involved from 1947 until 1954, and the USA had been involved from 1963 until 1971, both a total of eight years. It gave me an eerie feeling reading that inscription and I wondered if there would be a monument erected to the Americans who were also giving their lives for freedom.

Tay Ninh, north west of Bien Hoa, and close to the Cambodian border was frequently used for helicopter support operations for both the US and the Vietnamese Army. A degree of animosity had arisen between the two armies. I usually accompanied the Vietnamese Air Force either flying with them or piloting a helicopter to Tay Ninh and from there flying off to observe the helicopter assault operations. They carried troops to an area, deplaned the soldiers in the landing zone, and returned to base. Depending on the mission the aircraft would return the same day if the troops were only to enter and search a village or a few days later if they intended to sweep the area for suspected Viet Cong. Sometimes it would be a joint operation with the US Army and the troops and helicopters of both "teams" would converge on Tay Ninh. There were two airfields, Tay Ninh north was used for helicpoter operations and controlled by the Vietnamese. Tay

Ninh west, controlled by the US Army, had a runway and was used by both helicopter and fixed winged aircraft. Air America also regularly used this base.

There was a great deal of tension between the US Army and the Vietnamese soldiers and incidents had been reported of the Vietnamese firing on US Army helicopters when they flew over the bases. At Tay Ninh north I observed US Army troops throwing rocks at the Vietnamese soldiers waiting to be loaded onto helicopters. The frustration of fighting an almost invisible foe, with no discernable front lines and feeling perpetually unsafe resulted in hostility directed toward the allies who physically looked like the enemy. When the US Army troops observed me walking toward them, they broke off their rock throwing efforts. I reported the incident to their commanding officer and apologized to the Vietnamese.

On joint operations the US Army loaded their troops first, due to having more experience and more rigid time schedules. I bore the brunt of the contempt that the US Army had for the Vietnamese troops though these feelings were not universal and I met men who had a genuine understanding and respect for the Vietnamese people.

The medium lift CH-47 Chinook helicopters were flown by both the US Army and the Vietnamese Air Force. On combined operations from Tay Ninh to support the army units in the field, further tension was created as the US Army flew double the number of missions because, unlike the Americans, the Vietnamese always took lunch breaks.

The US Army had a great deal of experience in helicopter operations compared to the mere two years that the Vietnamese had. On these joint helicopter cargo lift missions, the Americans observed that the Vietnamese were not doing their share and disregarded the cultural difference and lack of experience. Hence the Americans reacted in an attempt to improve the situation by verbalizing their criticism and scorn to me, the advisor to the Vietnamese. I was the scapegoat for both sides, and the hostility and frustrations were funneled through me to act as mediator. I had a feeling of empathy for both sides and tried to smoothe matters over.

There was also seperation at the Command and Control post where operations were done not as equals, but at superiors and subordinates. The Americans had taken over the conduct of this war in 1966 and in 1971-1972 had still not relinquished it to the Vietnamese, although the Vietnamization program had been in progress for 2 years.

My role as mediator was highlighted when I accompanied Colonel Tinh on a visit to the resort area, Dai Lat, in central Vietnam. He had been invited to visit the Vietnamese military academy, (equivalent to West Point) to watch an anniversary celebration of the founding of the academy. We had flown there dressed in civilian clothes and set down on a landing pad to immediately be confronted by a US officer saying that the Vietnamese had to use the other side of the field. Being in civilian clothes, I identified myself and said, "We will remain here and if there is not enough room, then the Army can go over to the Vietnamese side."

We departed and drove into the city of Dai Lat. As I was walking with my Vietnamese friends, two American military police came up to me and said that I was to accompany them to their compound. I explained the situation to the military police officer and asked him why I had been arrested, whereupon he stated that I had "created a disturbance on the airfield and interferred with the operations of the United States Army." I replied, "I directed the landing of the helicopter and the pad was unmarked. There was no sign that said for Americans only. This is Vietnam and we are guests here. Either charge me or let me go."

I was duly ushered out of his office by a military policeman who said that I was free to go and gave me a ride back to Dai Lat to join my Vietnamese friends. From that moment the Vietnamese accepted me, since I had experienced the discrimination that they dealt with daily. With that acceptance I became one of them and was included in their military and social life. This marked a turning point in my tour of duty.

Close to Tay Ninh, was a mountain called Nui Ba Dinh, which translates as Black Virgin Mountain. The Americans and the Vietnamese controlled the summit and base of the mountain. There was a radar facility on the summit that was supplied by helicopter and occasionally attacked by the Viet Cong. The center of the mountain contained a network of caves and a labyrinth of passageways, which had not been cleared of Viet Cong. Friendly forces surrounded the base. The Black Virgin Mountain could be seen from a great distance and was used as a landmark for identifying the landing area. Although we controlled the area and conducted operations daily from Tay Ninh, we did not entirely control it; at best we had cordoned off parts of the countryside.

Within the town itself there was a beautiful temple with rather bright garish colors, used as the center for the Cao Dai religion. Surrounding the Church were large gardens and pathways stretching for about two miles. The Cao Dai religion was a combination of all the major religions; Christianity, Buddhism, Islam and Taoist. It was founded in early 1900 and one of the saints was Vicor Hugo. On entering the church grounds, monks asked for our weapons and stored them, for arms were not allowed on the grounds. We were given a pamphlet on the history of the religious sect and a monk, speaking acceptible English acted as a tour guide and explained the religion. At one time the Cao Dai had a large army under a warlord who controlled the area around Tay Ninh and conducted his own campaign against the Viet Cong. When the French departed, and Diem became the premier and president of Vietnam, he reportedly used the millions given to him in US aid, to simply buy off the war lords for their allegiance to the central government. Instead of going to war against the warlords, he paid them off. The warlord of Tay Ninh then disbanded his Cao Dai army and many became members of the Vietnamese army. He reportedly took the millions given to him from US aid and retired in France. There is a large Vietnamese population in France from emigrees after WW11 and in 1971 it was still the custom for the rich to send their children to France to attend French schools.

When there was a lull in activity at Tay Ninh, we would fly out to an Army fire base close to the Black Virgin Mountain and resupply them with luxury items such as coca-cola. It was occupied by an army detachment and was situated in a cleared area about a mile in diameter. Around the cleared area were barbed wire fences and mine fields. The soldiers largely lived underground and went out on patrols in the nearby countryside. We would establish radio contact and if it was clear, we landed and hastily unloaded our cargo.

The deprivations of the Army men in these outposts were enormous. They would literally live underground for months on end and the only breaks in their monotonous life were the infrequent operations they were called upon to undertake. They were under frequent mortar and rocket attack by the Viet Cong and had to face ambushes and booby traps. Their only break from Tay Ninh in their 12 month tour was to go on recreation and recuperation leave after six months duty or be evacuated by helicopter if they were wounded. The "grunts" of the Vietnamese are the real heroes and casulties of Vietnam. They received no homecoming. Their only reward upon their return was that they had survived.

Within the Vietnamese army, the select unit was the paratroopers. As in our army, these individuals were volunteers and had a reputation for being aggressive. Just outside of Saigon was a practice jump area where the units kept in shape and new recruits were trained. Often when I was flying from Saigon to Bien Hoa I watched a C-119 dropping their human cargo. At a New Years Party with the Vietnamese paratroopers, which I attended with Colonel Tuong, the 3rd Air Division Vice-commander, we both volunteered to jump with the troops. I already had four parachute jumps, three practice and one real and a fifth would qualify me for the US Army paratrooper wings.

At the party the notion of jumping seemed like a smart idea. Reality occured a when I was seated on the floor of the helicopter, with a seasoned Vietnamese jumpmaster behind me. When I was tapped on the arm to signal that we were over the jump area, I do not remember leaving the helicopter. I do remember the opening of the parachute and the landing. What looked like nice soft dirt turned out to be hard soil, compacted by many landings of troops and pick-up vehicles. A young Vietnamese of about 14years old helped pick up my parachute and at the same time relieved me of my wallet from my Army flying fatigues.

Major Erway, having pilot and paratrooper wings also made the jump with me. Later, at a ceremony with the paratroopers, Colonel Tuong, Major Erway and me were formally presented with our Vietnamese Paratrooper wings. I had been assured that receiving my Vietnamese paratrooper wings would guarantee that I receive my US Army wings. However, when I applied for the wings at the Military Advisory Command Vietnam HQ, I got a very cool reception. I was told that if I had been in the Army and made a jump without training, and had been hurt, that I would have been court-martialed. So I never did receive my US Army jump wings.

In early 1972, Major General Hollingsworth took over the Army units in the 3rd military regions. He was a "blood and guts" General along the lines of Patton who he had reportedly fought with in WW11. He was a gruff commander with the ability of uniting his staff and troops into a cohesive and dedicated fighting unit. He was able to develop a rapport with his officers and enlisted men, which is rare in any military service. When the Army units were sent on operations, General Hollingsworth, often accompanied by his staff, would drop in with his command helicopter and if he did not like the way the fighting was being conducted would address the battle commander in stringent terms.

His helicopter showed battle damage from his close proximity to the front line action. He was a great political-military officer for he was equally as good a military commander as he was an able political commander, uniting the US Army, Vietnamese Army and the civilian aid program into an effective fighting unit against the Viet Cong.

One of his first acts as the commander was to initiate daily staff meetings at his HQ near Bien Hoa, which I attended and gave briefings on the daily activities of the 3rd Air Division. General Hollingsworth also toured Bien Hoa and was briefed on the Air Force Advisory Team and met with Colonel Tinh and Colonel Grice, the base commander. At my briefing, I mentioned that there were problems between the Vietnamese Army and Air Force and the US Army. He asked that any future problems in this regard be brought to his immediate attention. This seemed to alleviate the overt aggression on both sides since this information was passed down through both US Army and Vietnamese channels.

The Easter invasion of 1972 began in April and lasting 88 days affected the 3rd Military Region northwest of Saigon. The North Vietnamese 5th, 7th and 9th divisions moved eastward out of Cambodia and captured the border town of An Loc after driving back the 5th Division of the South Vietnamese Army, and surrounding it at An Loc. It was under intense artillery and rocket bombardment and was totally dependent upon aircraft for supplies. The seige lasted 80 days. Battered and outnumbered, the South Vietnamese troops fought on until the better parts of two North Vietnamese divisions were shattered by American air power. The South Vietnamese tenacity gave the Air Force the opportunity to strike. An Loc held because the province chief rallied the defenders. He pulled together the regional, popular forces, police, and self-defence militia and blunted the North Vietnamese offensive.

B-52's flew 250 missions, tactical fighters flew 3,500 sorties and C-130's flew 600 airlift sorties delivering food and supplies. The South Vietnamese Army and Air Force fought well and were given high marks. General Clay, commander of the Pacific Air Forces, called the Vietnamese Air Force performance, "tremendous, the brightest spot of the whole Vietnamization program." The Vietnamese Army defenders at An Loc were cited by Major General Hollingsworth, who said he had "seen nothing in his thirty-four years as a soldier to surpass the determination of the South Vietnamese soldiers at An Loc."

When the Viet-Cong began the spring offensive and aimed it at An Loc and the Lai Kai area, for the first time in the 3rd military region, tanks were sighted and used, as well as the hand launched anti-aircraft rockets and radar controlled anti-aircraft guns. The build up was reported by intelligence but not when or where an attack would occur. It coincided with the beginning of the monsoon season and this time, the weather became a factor in the offensive because it prevented the Air Force from rendering maximum assistance. At the beginning, our forces at Lai Khe, where the rubber refinery was located, were attacked. The Vietnamese army units were overun and the small US Army unit was completly surrounded. General Hollingsworth ordered a chemical agent to be used and when it was dropped, it rendered all in the vicinity physically ill and unable to fight. A few survivors were brought out by helicopter.

The Viet-Cong, accompanied by regular North Vietnamese army units continued toward Bien Hoa and surrounded our forces at An Loc. In this offensive, tanks were sighted during the day and this was the beginning of a new phase of the battle. When tanks were sighted the Vietnamese army would often disburse. The tanks were able to maneuver during the day, when the weather conditions precluded effective air operations. With An Loc surrounded, there was no way to resupply our units except through cargo drops. As the defense perimeter became smaller, the air drops often landed among the enemy. The use of radar controlled anti-aircraft artillery caused many of the cargo aircraft, Vietnamese and US Air Force aircraft to be shot down.

The Vietnamese pilots were accused of cowardice and we had conferences at MACV headquarters on how to resupply the encircled base. New techniques of dropping supplies were used. Flying low level was ruled out so flying at altitude and dropping the pallets with radar controlled fuses for the parachute opening was attempted. Our success rate in resupplying was not good and the radio men on the ground often reported the cargo landing outside their perimeter. The resupply was often done at night and in bad weather. With the supply situation becoming critical, the weather broke for a short period of time allowing the fighter planes to suppress the anti-aircraft fire and permit the cargo airplanes to drop their loads. One radar anti-aircraft mobile unit was reported destroyed five times before a 500-pound bomb eventually hit it.

The B-52's were used for the first time in this region during the offensive. We could hear the rumble and the earth would shake from a strike 30 miles away from us and then we would see a huge cloud of dust arise from where the bombs impacted. When a strike was planned, we would be warned to stay away from the area. After one of these strikes, I flew a helicopter over the area to see what damage had been done. As we started to descend over the area for a closer look, the Army advisor on board shouted that we were taking fire. Although I could not see anything, he said that he could hear the rounds going by, a noise that I was unfamilar with. Looking down, I saw the muzzle flashes and in an ugent voice he said, "Let's get out of here." From all reports, the B-52 strikes decimated everything in a given area. but evidently the Viet-Cong burrowed in and after the bombings emerged like angry hornets.

Another myth of air power effectiveness fell by the wayside. The supposedly secret raids of the B-52's were not so secret, as Russian trawlers stationed off Okinawa where the B-52's were based, radioed the take-off time and flight direction to the Viet-Cong. They monitored their flight path and alerted the Viet-Cong on the ground of an impending attack, so if there was time they could move or take to shelter.

During these operations we would fly to the forward area and frequently Major Erway made radio contact with the Peoples Forces in the villages. They were similar to the National Guard in the United States; they worked during the day and stood guard against the Viet-Cong at night. They were issued weapons and radios and if they were attacked they would call for help from the regular army units. As the result of one such call, we found out that the village was surrounded and that they desperately needed supplies after being under siege for 30days. The Vietnamese Army units were all committed and the village needed ammunition and medical supplies. We air dropped supplies to them in special containers which minimized the impact damage. A few days later we tried to contact them and they did not respond. Major Erway commented, "It is those little guys who are defending their villages who are the real hero's of this war."

When the weather cleared, a relief column was able to drive up the road and resupply the beleagured garrison. Soon afterwards Colonel Tuong and I flew up and entered the perimeter. We were the first Air Force officers to enter the city. A Vietnamese army jeep picked us up at the helicopter landing area where the day before three officers from General Hollingsworth's staff had been killed by an artillery shell.

The area looked as if a low-grade atomic weapon had hit it. Rubble was everywhere and there was not a building left standing. We entered the heavy sand bagged command post and met the commander. He had been there throughout the seige and said, "I had the only operating jeep in the area, and it was heavily sandbagged. One of the pallets of supplies did not open and fell right on top of it." He took me on a tour of the area and said, "If a mortar comes in, watch me and hit the ground when I do. I can recognize one that will be coming close. There is a Charley around here in the rubble who calls in rounds when he sees troops out in the open and we have not been able to find him."

He showed me a radar controlled 40-millimeter anti-aircraft gun mounted on a tank. It had been destroyed by a direct hit and listed in the hole that the 500-pound bomb had made. He said, "The reason that it was hard to destroy this weapon was that it was constantly moved around." Occasionally a mortar shell flew over and twice we hit the ground and the shell landed nearby. He was used to this, but to me it was a new and unnerving experience. As we drove back to the helicopter landing area, we looked at the rubber trees. The commander commented that these trees had provided some of the finest racing tires in the world but it would be a long time before they produced again.

During the battle of An Loc, I monitored the radio transmissions and got first hand reports from the advisors flying missions in the area. The Major who was shot down by a hand-held missile told me of the destruction of the French buildings and the city and said that he got a direct hit on a large building in the compound. When he described it to me, I recognised it as the civilian and military officers club that I had seen when we had stopped at An Loc. He said, "The church is no longer there and all the buildings in the town as well as the rubber refinery is destroyed." In war, what one man builds, another destroys in the name of freedom.

At the end of the battle for An Loc, we had gained a victory but a new phase had begun. The Viet-Cong were getting stronger and with the strength, they were getting bolder. Both sides retired to rest and replenish the supplies used and lost. Infrequent rocket attacks were the only reminder of the war.

A new aerial weapon was turned over to the Vietnamese for use against ground troops. It was a gas which when dropped, would spread over an area of about 2,000 square feet and then a delayed action fuse would detonate it. The resulting pressure would kill any living thing within that area. It would cause a massive hemorrhage without apparent outward bodily damage. Only two were given to each military region for the use of the Vietnamese and approval had to be requested from the U.S. Commander in chief for its use. It had to be dropped a few feet above the ground at a certain airspeed. A training film was shown to the Vietnamese about how to use it and the results of its use. Goats were tethered in the drop area and the results vividly depicted in the training film. Both weapons were used by the Vietnamese during the battle of An Loc.

The Vietnamese Air Force was also given the mission of dropping listening probes along infiltration lines in Laos and Cambodia, along what was known as the Hoa Chinh Minh trail. This was the Viet Cong supply route in Cambodia and Laos, which was used to bring troops, tanks and supplies from North Vietnam. The trail was heavily forested and was a complete network of roads and supply bases. The probes or listening devices had their own batteries and were designed to look like forest vegetation. When released they would stike the ground in a vertical position and transmit any sounds along the trails to receivers. Since they were effective for about six months, the trails had to be reseeded and this mission was given to the Vietnamese. The main base for the reception of the signals and the analysis of the data was at Project Alpha in Thailand.

To enable us to better advise the Vietnamese, I went to Thailand with the advisor to the F-5 squadron that was given the mission to implant the probes, and visited Project Alpha. It was the result of what was known at one time as the Macnamara "electric fence." The idea was that the probes would send signals about troop and supply movement, and knowing approximately where the probes were located, attacks could be made to stop or impede the flow of men and material to the south. In theory the idea was excellent, but impractical to carry out.

Firstly the precise position of the probes were not known, just an approximation and secondly bombing through a jungle canopy was extremely difficult, for napalm would not work, bombs would detonate before striking the floor of the jungle, and when delayed fuses were used, the jungle absorbed much of the force of the explosion.

Project Alpha was a huge underground emplacement, manned twenty-four hours a day. I listened as a tiger passed a probe, tanks passed and troops could be heard talking. Each probe's positon was marked on a huge map and the progress of people passing could be chartered. We had remarkable access to the enemy and knew what they were doing. The problem was that we had not perfected the means to stop them.

Sitting in my office one day, I received a call that the Colonel, my counterpart in the 4th military region had been hit while on a helicopter assault operation. I immediately flew down to the Saigon hospital to visit him. He was heavily drugged, but conscious and in good spirits. His left arm was swollen to three times its size and in a brace that held his arm at a 45-degree angle upward and away from his body. He said that he had been flying left seat with the commander of the 4th Air Division on a helicopter assault operation. Just as they were flaring he took an AK-47 round through the bottom of his seat. The round went upward and exited through his shoulder.

He was air evacuated out the next day and a new Colonel replaced him. He was not as lucky, for while trying to airlift a L-19 observation aircraft with the Huey helicopter, he crashed. The cables snapped as they were about 100 feet in the air and became entangled in the rotor. The Vietnamese commander of the 4th Air Divison was flying with him and both were killed.

Shortly afterwards General Watkins, the commander of the Avisory Group, also had a close call. While flying an F-5 on a close support mission, he was hit by enemy fire but managed to land safely. I had had several close encounters, both alone and while flying with the Vietnamese. As a result of these and the injury and death of the two advisors to the 4th Air Division, General Kye, the commander of the Vietnamese Air Force, restricted General Watkins and I from flying combat. Colonel Tinh was then made personally responsible for our safety.

The battle for An Loc began on the 7 April 1972 and ended around the 20th September. My tour of duty was completed in September, but I elected to stay another month.

VIETNAM

CHAPTER 5: Afterthoughts.

There has never been a good war or a bad peace.
Benjamin Franklin 1706-1790

"In the past four years, American or Vietnamese units have fallen into traps at precisely the same places French units did in 1954; traps often laid by the same Communist units, which succeed far more often than they should."
Bernard Fall

I had occasion on the flight back to the United States to reflect on the Vietnam Odyssey, what we had accomplished and how we failed to achieve what we had started out to do. It was the beginning of a long agonizing reappraisal

The cost in American lives was 1.8% of its force each year, which is a 1 in 55 chance of being killed. There were 56,000 deaths as a result of the Vietnam conflict which does not take into account the suffering of the wounded and maimed as a result of the war. This compares with 5% killed during the Korean War. The Vietnamese forces lost 2.5% of their forces each year, yielding a 1 in 40 chance of being killed, higher than the odds for the American forces. These percentages were well below those suffered by the French and their allied forces of 5%, equivalent to our loses in Korea. The French lost 96,000 men, killed during the similar eight-year period.

The monetary expenditure lavished on the Vietnamese conflict was staggering. During the 1969 fiscal year an estimated $21.5 billion was spent on the Vietnam War effort. U.S. military activities used more than 80% of this total and South Vietnamese activities accounted for the rest. This equates to $60 million a day being spent on the war. The tremendous U.S. expenditures in the war, not only unbalanced the South Vietnamese economy, but eventually helped lead to unprecedented inflation in the United States, thereby adding another kind of cost that can be attributed to the war.

First, it was a clash of cultures. The Americans were mainly a product of modern religion. We were taught that to be good, one must strive to be a success, the Protestant Ethic. We were unable to understand, in the main, the concept of time, of family and of daily life that existed in Vietnam. We were aware of the graft, known to us as corruption and bribery, which is regarded with a high degree of disgust in our society. In Vietnam graft was not openly talked about but there was a term for it, it was the cost of doing business, as ingrained in their way of life as paying sales tax in America is to us. The head of a village was not elected, but was appointed, for which he paid a fee either in money or grain, and then he could control and collect from the villagers. Being appointed therefore went to the person who had the money to buy a position. If he did not have money then he was put in a position where he could collect from the villagers. This "cost of doing business" was passed on to the sector chief and then to the province chief, who in turn would pay to the central government. As long as the payment was sufficient, each was left alone at their specific level, to get on with their business.

If it was an important position, it might cost millions of Vietnamese dollars. This filtered through the entire government infrastructure including the Army, Navy and Air Force. Promotions and schools and even being assigned to a relatively quiet sector or at headquarters could be purchased. It was rumored that the base Colonel did not make General because he did not have the money or the capability to make a lot of money in his position. The Colonel of the 35th Air Division reportedly also received money from the Vietnamese vendors on the base, who set up small restaurants and shops for the men under his command. He also reportedly received money from the funds given him to feed the enlisted men. This was accepted as normal. Another example was of the Vietnamese base engineer requisitioning air conditioners, and when they arrived, reportedly sold them on the black market.

The "cost of doing business" infiltrated every level of their society. If a father had enough money he could purchase draft deferments for his sons. Consequently, young men were seen on the street or attending the university in Saigon. There was a regular show of rounding up young men who had not served in the military, but it was only a show, a farce and a sham. There were many marriages between Americans and the Vietnamese. To get a marriage permit required a background investigation and a license; those Americans who did not cough up a bribe to the administrator often waited months for a marriage licence. If they paid up the required bribe fee to the right person or had a degree of influence, the procedures were completed within a few days.

The "cost of doing business" was a fact of life in their culture and the Americans viewed it with contempt and tried to control it. But it was impossible to eradicate for we had neither the time, the energy nor the right to change it. Enrichment and monetary endowments is an integral part of the appointments to power in the eastern cultures. There is however, an unwritten rule in countries that sanction "corruption" as a regular and normal practice of government that requires for it to be kept within sensible boundaries. What rankles in graft-tolerating systems is either the flat denial of corruption or its monopolization by a small and unchanging group.

Since positions in the Vietnamese Army, cabinet, and civil service were frequently filled by new appointees, there existed a shadow army, cabinet and a shadow civil service. These were people who were no longer in favor, yet possibly were better people than those who were appointed to the positions. We did not find an effective way to deal with the corruption or graft, which affected the leadership of both the Army and the civil service. We understood far better what needed to be done, rather than how to do it.

There were contradictions in military culture between the Vietnamese and the Americans. There is a Chinese novel of the 14th century, "The Romance of the Three Kingdoms" which is widely read by the Vietnamese and is part of their culture. Each successful General in the book demonstrates that he has clear political objectives in mind when he embarks upon a military campaign, and uses armed force to strengthen his political moves. The Generals were politicians who had military skill, and would forgo the use of armed forces if an objective could be won by other means. It is the ethic taught by Sun Tzu and equally so by Mao Tse-tung.

This ethic is alien to an American military man, who is conditioned throughout his military service to civilians making the political decisions, which the military then put into affect. An American military man might understand Clausewitz's idea that war is the final instrument of politics or Machiavelli's teaching about the use of force for political ends. However American ethics perceive political and military operations as separate entities.

The battle ground of Vietnam saw the confrontation of these two significantly different viewpoints and cultural backgrounds and beliefs. The Vietnamese Generals saw their armed forces as instruments primarily to gain political goals. The American Generals saw their forces primarily as instruments to defeat enemy military forces. One side fought battles to influence opinion in Vietnam, the other fought battles to finish the enemy, keeping tabs by body count.

The French had at this time, about the same amount of experience in fighting in Vietnam as the Americans, about eight years. In terms of their casualties, about 5% a year, the French fought a long tough war in Indochina with considerable drive, although with much fewer material assets and combat support than the Americans and South Vietnamese.

There are striking similarities in some of the basic patterns of the French and American experience in Vietnam. The annual cycles of combat in both wars appear similar, with both influenced by the weather, which led to heavy fighting during the first half of the year after the rains had stopped. The locations of major combat were also similar. The areas that caused the most problems for the French in South Vietnam were also the worst trouble spots for the United States and South Vietnamese troops twenty years later.

There were other similarities, both the U.S. and France had trouble at home, as early support for the war declined and thus began to affect the efforts in Vietnam. Both had to start withdrawing troops from Vietnam before accomplishing their objectives, and long before all of their forces were finally taken out of combat. Neither began large-scale efforts to build up the indigenous forces until domestic pressures placed a ceiling on the availability of French and American troops. Both forces were unable to send units into combat anywhere near their full personnel strength. Both had terrible problems finding an elusive foe and in inflicting a long lasting defeat when they did find him. Both had identical problems with the

Communists who turned their dud artillery shells into deadly mines.

The French experience in Indochina was almost totally written off and disregarded by the Americans. The lessons that the French learned in the course of the prolonged conflict should have offered something more than simple historical data. The French were never asked if they would be willing to help the United States by sharing the details of their experience and lessons learned. Had they been asked to do so, there were indications that they would have assisted. Their military attache in Saigon, in 1964, was selected by the French Government because of his exceptional knowledge of the English language and his distinguished record in Indochina and Algeria. He was told to help the Americans in whatever way he could. During the first eighteen months of his assignment, the only American who visited him to ask about the war was an American defense contractor of French origin.

The US were condemned to make the same mistakes, since we had not even attempted to learn from the French experience, and trained the Vietnamese army to be a counterpart of ours. It was trained to be a field force ready to face its North Vietnamese rivals in the kind of set-piece battle that they had refused to do for the French for eight long years. The mobile groups were merged into light divisions, and then into field divisions under the command of a Corp.

After WW11 we sized, equipped and trained our general purpose forces primarily to compete with the Soviets on the plains of central Europe. Instead of adapting to the unique Vietnamese situation, we fought the enemy our way at horrendous costs, and with some tragic side effects because we lacked the capability to do otherwise. We imported the American style of war to Vietnam and under the pretext that it worked in two world wars, we utilized the same strategy in Vietnam.

We took similar actions with the Air Force. Strategic bombing was developed to be used against the Soviets and we designed and equipped the Air Force to conduct such campaigns. Consequently, when air power was required in Vietnam because there were not enough ground troops, or the mission called for air support, air power did what it was trained and equipped to do. When the propeller driven aircraft were more effective in close support in Vietnam than jets, they were incorporated into the inventory, since jets were more effective in what they had been designed for; fighting on the plains of Europe and aerial warfare, not guerilla insurgency and jungle warfare.

Trying to mold the Vietnamese forces into the mirror image of the U.S. forces was the only way we knew how. We organized, equipped, and trained the Vietnamese to fight American style, with American weapons and ammunition. The Vietnamese army and air force, were miniature copies of U.S. forces. When it was pointed out that this was not quite the answer, the U.S. could not comprehend intellectually that their methods were utterly unacceptable to an organization (the Vietnamese forces) which was unable to accept our methods operationally. Just as the French did not understand that this was not the answer to fighting a revolutionary war.

Khe Sanh could be a symbol of how the U.S. fought the Vietnamese war. We used our infantry, the marines, as bait and used technology to kill the North Vietnamese soldiers. It was a battle of attrition. The battle began when 5,000 U.S.Marines defended a small plateau in western I Corps against 20,000 North Vietnamese. The North Vietnamese stood their ground, exposed their position and laid siege to the Marine outpost thinking that another Dien Bien Phu would be achieved. The battle became of great psychological importance to the United States related solely to the Dien Bien Phu syndrome. We used infrared sensor communications and radio finding techniques, permitting us to pinpoint every company and battalion of the two North Vietnamese divisions that were in operation. The results were fed to a command center where we recorded where every bomb went, where every unstruck target remained and where every anti-aircraft gun was located. The devastation that took place around the small garrison at Khe Sanh was appalling by any standards. The beginning strength of the two North Vietnamese divisions that participated in the siege was estimated at 20,000 men. Before the two-month siege ended, they had lost an estimated 12,000 men, while the Marines lost 200.

For the first and last time, we relied on the French experience. Eight French Generals were brought into Vietnam by the Air Force to advise on the siege of Khe Sanh, many were survivors of Dien Bien Phu, and they assisted with excellent strategic and tactical advice. Using sand tables, they spelled out in detail what was wrong.

The battle of Dien Bien Phu also lasted about two months and resulted in a resounding victory for the North Vietnamese over the French. The French defeat at Dien Bien Phu, in May 1954, marked the end of an era. It was more than the death knell of French colonialism in Asia; it showed that a revolutionary warfare force could defeat on the open field of battle a far better equipped conventional force. The North Vietnamese were trying to emulate the battle of 1954, when they chose to fight at Khe Sanh.

There were steps taken to adapt to the Vietnamese situation. Special schools graduated men trained in long-range patrolling to find the enemy in the jungle and call down artillery and air strikes, including the need for the use of larger contingents for this purpose. Old C-47 propeller-driven transport planes from WW11 became a weapons platform capable of using flares to turn the night into day and by striking the enemy with 6,000 rounds a minute from each of three "mini guns". It was called "Spooky" or "Puff the Magic Dragon." In Road Runner operations, armored vehicles reconnoitered likely ambush sites with pre-emptive fire. Scout and sentry dogs sniffed out the enemy, with enemy defectors as guides. Electronic sensors reported on enemy movements. A Riverine Force, not unlike those employed on American rivers during the Civil War, patrolled the inland-waterways. Five-man teams lived with and trained South Vietnamese paramilitary forces. U.S. and South Vietnamese naval patrols sealed the long coastline against enemy supply trawlers. The success of these and other programs were the basis for optimistic speeches about the progress of the war in South East Asia, as different approaches were attempted to influence the ebb and flow of the war.

There was no unified conflict management to pull the disparate aspects of a complex political-military conflict together. This led to an over-militarization of the conflict by facilitating military predominance, just because the military were more effective in deploying resources to the Vietnamese. The lack of unified conflict management had an adverse impact in Vietnam. It led to a proliferation of overlapping programs, and competition for scarce resources. Counter insurgency was neglected, because there was no vested interest and no department charged with this vital function. This, more than any other single factor, led to the failure to carry out any kind of a pacification program on any scale commensurate with the need, for so long.

The lack of any combined command over the Vietnamese, as we learned in WW1 and practiced in WW11, led to the Americans and the Vietnamese fighting largely separate wars. It deprived the Americans of any institutional framework for getting better performance from the Vietnamese. The four military regions dividing the country segregated the Vietnamese forces, and separate battles were fought within these regions, and rarely would one military region join forces with another. This permeated and affected the U.S.Army. The division commanders within a military region were given a great deal of freedom and latitude to conduct operations within their region as they saw fit.

The end result of our involvement in the Indochina war, was that for a time we brought freedom to about twenty-one million people out of thirty-eight million, and for about 223,000 square miles of land out of 285,000. And this is perhaps as good an epitaph as any, for the men who had to hold down the joyless and hopeless road that was the Vietnam War.

<u>Inspecting a Chinese MiG while on a visit to Beijing in 1998</u>

Here is what happened when I climbed out of the MiG and the reason for the smile. The MiG was at the back of the museum in Beijing and a museum attendee tried to open the canopy using the latch on the right. It would not budge so I climbed up on the MiG, and using my Swiss army knife we worked together and managed to get the canopy open. Television cameras and lights had the scene lit up like a lighthouse.

I climbed into the cockpit and assessed the instrumentation. I also checked to see the controls for the air brakes, which all reports had claimed that if you could taxi it, you could fly it.

The smile was for finding myself in a situation of climbing out of a museum piece MiG-15 in China, with national and international television cameras rolling. It amused me. When I stepped down, a microphone was pushed at me and I was asked which aircraft I preferred, the F-86 or the MiG-15. My reply was a preference for the MiG-15, since it could go higher and had better armament. It was a politically correct statement and also quite true.